The Principal Nav Voyages, Traffiq Discoveries of the English Nation — Volume 07 England's Naval Exploits Against Spain

Richard Hakluyt

Alpha Editions

This edition published in 2024

ISBN 9789362516893

Design and Setting By
Alpha Editions

www.alphaedis.com
Email - info@alphaedis.com

Contents

VOL. VII

ENGLAND'S NAVAL EXPLOITS AGAINST SPAIN.

ENGLAND'S NAVAL EXPLOITS AGAINST SPAIN

A voyage to the Azores with two pinases, the one called the Serpent, and the other the Mary Sparke of Plimouth, both of them belonging to Sir Walter Raleigh, written by John Euesham Gentleman, wherein were taken the gouernour, of the Isle of Sainct Michael, and Pedro Sarmiento gouernour of the Straits of Magalanes, in the yeere 1586.

[Sidenote: The gouernour of S. Michael taken prisoner.] The 10. of June 1586. we departed from Plimouth with two Pinases, the one named the Serpent, of the burden of 35. Tunnes and the other the Mary Sparke of Plimouth of the burthen of 50. Tuns, both of them belonging to sir Walter Raleigh knight; and directing our course towards the coast of Spaine, and from thence towards the Isles of the Azores, we tooke a small barke laden with Sumacke and other commodities, wherein was the gouernour of S. Michaels Island, being a Portugal, having other Portugals and Spaniards with him. And from thence we sailed to the Island of Graciosa, to the Westward of the Island of Tercera, where we discried a saile, and bearing with her wee found her to be a Spaniard: But at the first not greatly respecting whom we tooke, so that we might haue enriched ourselves, which was the cause of this our trauaile, and for that we would not bee knowen of what nation we were, wee displayed a white silke ensigne in our maine toppe, which they seeing, made accompt that we had bene some of the king of Spaines Armadas, lying in wait for English men of war: but when we came within shot of her, we tooke downe our white flagge, and spread abroad the Crosse of S. George, which when they saw, it made them to flie as fast as they might, but all their haste was in vaine, for our shippes were swifter of saile then they, which they fearing, did presently cast their ordinance and small shot with many letters, and the draft of the Straights of Magelan into the Sea, [Sidenote: Pedro Sarmiento the governour of the Straights of Magellan taken prisoner.] and thereupon immediately we tooke her, wherein wee also tooke a gentleman of Spaine, named Pedro Sarmiento, gouernour of the Straights of Magelan, which said Pedro we brought into England with us, and presented him to our soueraigne Lady the Queene.

[Sidenote: A ship laden with fish taken and released againe.] After this, lying off and about the Islands, wee descried another saile, and bearing after her, we spent the maine maste of our Admirall, but yet in the night our Viceadmirall tooke her, being laden with fish from Cape Blanke, the which shippe wee let goe againe for want of men to bring her home. The next day we descried two other sailes, the one a shippe and the other a Carauel, to whom we gaue chase, which they seeing, with all speede made in vnder the Isle of Graciosa, to a certaine Fort there for their succour, where they came to an anker, and hauing the winde of vs, we could not hurt them with our ships, but we hauing a small boate which we called a light horseman, wherein my selfe was, being a Musqueter, and foure more with Caliuers, and foure that rowed, came neere vnto the shore against the winde, which when they saw vs come towards them they carried a great part of their marchandize on land, whither also the men of both vessels went and landed, [Sidenote: One of the ships taken and sent away with 2. persons.] and as soon as we came within Musquet shot, they began to shoote at vs with great ordinance and small shot, and we likewise at them, and in the ende we boorded one wherein was no man left, so we cut her cables, hoysed her sailes, and sent her away with two of our men, [Sidenote: The Caravel is taken.] and the other 7. of vs passed more neere vnto the shoare, and boorded the Carauel, which did ride within a stones cast from the shoare, and so neere the land that the people did cast stones at vs, but yet in despight of them all we tooke her, and one onely Negro therein: and cutting her cables in the hawse, we hoysed her sailes and being becalmed vnder the land we were constrained to rowe her out with our boate, the Fort still shooting at vs, and the people on land with Musquets and caliuers, to the number of 150. or thereabout: and we answered them with the small force wee had; in the time of which our shooting, the shot of my Musquet being a crossebarre-shot happened to strike the gunner of the fort to death, euen as he was giuing leuell to one of his great pieces, and thus we parted from them without any losse or hurt on our side. [Sidenote: The prises sent home.] And now, hauing taken these fiue sailes of shippes, we did as before, turne away the shippe with the fish, without hurting them, and from one of the other shippes we tooke her maine Maste to serue our Admirals turne, and so sent her away putting into her all the Spaniards and Portugals (sauing that gentleman Pedro Sarmiento, with three other of the principal men and two Negroes) leauing them all within sight of land, with bread and water sufficient for 10. dayes if neede were.

Thus setting our course for England, being off the Islands in the height of 41 degrees, or there about, one of our men being in the toppe discried a saile, then 10. saile, then 15. whereupon it was concluded to sende home those prizes we had, and so left in both our Pinasses not aboue 60. men. [Sidenote: Two Carracks, 10. Gallions, 12. small ships.] Thus wee returned againe to the Fleete we had discried, where wee found 24. saile of shippes, whereof two of them were Caracks, the one of 1200. and the other of a 1000. tunnes, and 10. Gallions, the rest were small shippes and Carauels all laden with Treasure, spices, and sugars with which 24. shippes we with two small Pinasses did fight, and kept company the space of 32. houres, continually fighting with them and they with vs, but the two Caracks kept still betwixt the Fleete and vs, that wee could not take any one of them, so wanting powder, wee were forced to giue them ouer against our willes, for that wee were all wholly bent to the gaining of some of them, but necessitie compelling vs, and that onely for want of powder, without losse of any of our men, (which was a thing to be wondered at considering the inequalitie of number) at length we gaue them ouer. [Sidenote: The 2. pinasses returne for England.] Thus we againe set our course for England, and so came to Plimouth within 6. houres after our prizes, which we sent away 40. houres before vs, where wee were receiued with triumphant ioy, not onely with great Ordinance then shot off, but with the willing hearts of all the people of the Towne, and of the Countrey thereabout; and we not sparing our Ordinance (with the powder wee had left) to requite and answere them againe. And from thence wee brought our prizes to Southampton, where sir Walter Ralegh being our owner, rewarded vs with our shares.

Our prizes were laden with sugars, Elephants teeth, waxe, hides, rice, brasill, and Cuser, as by the testimonie of Iohn Euesham himselfe, Captaine Whiddon, Thomas Rainford, Beniamin Wood, William Cooper Master, William Cornish Master, Thomas Drake Corporall, Iohn Ladd gunner, William Warefield gunner, Richard Moone, Iohn Drew, Richard Cooper of Harwich, William Beares of Ratcliffe, Iohn Row of Saltash, and many others, may appeare.

* * * * *

A briefe relation of the notable seruice performed by Sir Francis Drake vpon the Spanish Fleete prepared in the Road of Cadiz: and of his destroying of 100. saile of barks; Passing from thence all along the coast to Cape Sacre, where also hee tooke certaine Forts: and so to the mouth of the Riuer of Lisbon, and thence crossing ouer to the Isle of Sant Michael, supprized a mighty Carack called the Sant Philip comming out of the East India, which was the first of that kinde that euer was seene in England: Performed in the yeere 1587.

Her Maiestie being informed of a mightie preparation by Sea begunne in Spaine for the inuasion of England, by good aduise of her graue and prudent Counsell thought it expedient to preuent the same. Whereupon she caused a Fleete of some 30. sailes to be rigged and furnished with all things necessary. Ouer that Fleete she appointed Generall sir Francis Drake (of whose manifold former good seruices she had sufficient proofe) to whom she caused 4. ships of her Nauie royall to be deliuered, to wit, The Bonauenture wherein himselfe went as Generall; the Lion vnder the conduct of Master William Borough Controller of the Nauie; the Dreadnought vnder the command of M. Thomas Venner; and the Rainebow, captaine whereof was M. Henry Bellingham: vnto which 4 ships two of her pinasses were appointed as hand-maids. There were also added vnto this Fleet certaine tall ships of the Citie of London, of whose especiall good seruice the General made particular mention in his priuate Letters directed to her Maiestie. This Fleete set saile from the sound of Plimouth in the moneth of April towards the coast of Spaine.

The 16. of the said moneth we mette in the latitude of 40. degrees with two ships of Middleborough, which came from Cadiz; by which we vnderstood that there was great store of warlike prouision at Cadiz and thereabout ready to come for Lisbon. Vpon this information our Generall with al speed possible, bending himselfe thither to cut off their said forces and prouisions, vpon the 19. of April entered with his Fleet into the Harbor of Cadiz: where at our first entring we were assailed ouer against the Towne by sixe Gallies, which notwithstanding in short time retired vnder their fortresse.

There were in the Road 60. ships and diuers other small vessels vnder the fortresse: there fled about 20. French ships to Port Real, and some small Spanish vessels that might passe the sholdes. At our first comming in we sunke with our shot a ship of Raguza of a 1000. tunnes, furnished with 40. pieces of brasse and very richly laden. There came two Gallies more from S. Mary port, and two from Porto Reale, which shot freely at vs, but altogether in vaine: for they went away with the blowes well beaten for their paines.

Before night we had taken 30. of the said ships, and became Masters of the Road, in despight of the Gallies, which were glad to retire them vnder the Fort: in the number of which ships there was one new ship of an extraordinary hugenesse in burthen aboue 1200. tunnes, belonging to the Marquesse of Santa Cruz being at that instant high Admirall of Spaine. Fiue of them were great ships of Biskay, whereof 4. we fired, as they were taking in the Kings prouision of victuals for the furnishing of his Fleet at Lisbon: the fift being a ship about 1000. tunnes in burthen, laden with Iron spikes, nailes, yron hoopes, horse-shooes, and other like necessaries bound for the West Indies we fired in like maner. Also we tooke a ship of 250. tunnes laden with wines for the Kings prouision, which wee caried out to the Sea with vs, and there discharged the said wines for our owne store, and afterward set her on fire. Moreouer we tooke 3. Flyboats of 300. tunnes a piece laden with biscuit, whereof one was halfe vnladen by vs in the Harborow, and there fired, and the other two we tooke in our company to the Sea. Likewise there were fired by vs ten other ships which were laden with wine, raisins, figs, oiles, wheat, and such like. To conclude, the whole number of ships and barkes (as we suppose) then burnt, suncke, and brought away with vs, amounted to 30. at the least, being (in our iudgement) about 10000. tunnes of shipping.

There were in sight of vs at Porto Real about 40. ships, besides those that fled from Cadiz.

We found little ease during our aboad there, by reason of their continuall shooting from the Gallies, the fortresses, and from the shoare: where continually at places conuenient they planted new ordinance to offend vs with: besides the inconuenience which wee suffered from their ships, which, when they could defend no longer, they set on fire to come among vs. Whereupon when the flood came wee were not a little troubled to defend vs from their terrible fire, which neuerthelesse was a pleasant sight for vs to beholde, because we were thereby eased of a great labour, which lay vpon vs day and night, in discharging the victuals, and other prouisions of the enemie. Thus by the assistance of the almightie, and the inuincible courage and industrie of our Generall, this strange and happy enterprize was atchieued in one day and two nights, to the great astonishment of the King of Spaine, which bread such a corrasiue in the heart of the Marques of Santa Cruz high Admiral of Spaine, that he neuer enioyed good day after, but within fewe moneths (as may iustly be supposed) died of extreame griefe and sorrow.

Thus hauing performed this notable seruice, we came out of the Road of Cadiz on the Friday morning the 21. of the said moneth of April, with very small losse not worth the mentioning.

After our departure ten of the Gallies that were in the Road came out, as it were in disdaine of vs, to make some pastime with their ordinance, at which time the wind skanted vpon vs, whereupon we cast about againe, and stood in with the shoare, and came to an anker within a league of the towne: where the said Gallies, for all their former bragging, at length suffred vs to ride quietly.

We now haue had experience of Gally-fight: wherein I can assure you, that onely these 4. of her Maiesties ships will make no accompt of 20. Gallies, if they may be alone, and not busied to guard others. There were neuer Gallies that had better place and fitter opportunitie for their aduantage to fight with ships: but they were still forced to retire, wee riding in a narrow gut, the place yeelding no better, and driuen to maintaine the same, vntill wee had discharged and fired the shippes, which could not conueniently be done but vpon the flood, at which time they might driue cleare off vs. Thus being victualed with bread and wine at the enemies cost for diuers moneths (besides the prouisions that we brought from home) our Generall dispatched Captaine Crosse into England with his letters, giuing him further in charge to declare vnto her Maiestie all the particularities of this our first enterprize.

After whose departure wee shaped our course toward Cape Sacre, and in the way thither wee tooke at seuerall times of ships, barkes, and Carauels well neere an hundred, laden with hoopes, gally-oares, pipe-staues, and other prouisions of the king of Spaine, for the furnishing of his forces intended against England, al which we burned, hauing dealt fauourably with the men and sent them on shoare. We also spoiled and consumed all the fisher-boats and nets thereabouts, to their great hinderance: and (as we suppose) to the vtter ouerthrow of the rich fishing of their Tunies for the same yere. At length we came to the aforesaid Cape Sacre, where we went on land; and the better to enioy the benefite of the place, and to ride in the harborow at our pleasure, we assailed the same castle, and three other strong holds, which we tooke some by force and some by surrender.

Thence we came before the hauen of Lisbon ankering nere vnto Cascais, where the Marques, of Santa Cruz was with his Gallies, who seeing vs chase his ships a shoare, and take and cary away his barks and Carauels, was content to suffer vs there quietly to tary, and likewise to depart, and neuer charged vs with one canon-shot. And when our Generall sent him worde that hee was there ready to exchange certaine bullets with him, the marques refused his chalenge, sending him word, that he was not then ready for him, nor had any such Commission from his King.

[Sidenote: The Carack called the Sanct Philip taken.] Our Generall thus refused by the Marques, and seeing no more good to be done in this place, thought it conuenient to spend no longer time vpon this coast: and therefore with consent of the chiefe of his Company he shaped his course toward the Isles of the Açores, and passing towards the Isle of Saint Michael, within 20. or 30. leagues thereof, it was his good fortune to meete with a Portugale Carak called Sant Philip, being the same shippe which in the voyage outward had carried the 3. Princes of Iapan, that were in Europe, into the Indies. This Carak without any great resistance he tooke, bestowing the people thereof in certaine vessels well furnished with victuals, and sending them courteously home into their Countrey: and this was the first Carak that euer was then comming foorth of the East Indies; which the Portugals tooke for an euil signe, because the ship bare the Kings owne name.

The riches of this prize seemed so great vnto the whole Company (as in trueth it was) that they assured themselues euery man to haue a sufficient reward for his trauel: and thereupon they all resolued to returne home for England: which they happily did, and arriued in Plimouth the same Sommer with their whole Fleete and this rich booty, to their owne profite and due commendation, and to the great admiration of the whole kingdome.

And here by the way it is to be noted, that the taking of this Carak wrought two extraordinary effects in England: first, that it taught others, that Caracks were no such bugs but that they might be taken (as since indeed it hath fallen out in the taking of the Madre de Dios, and fyreing and sinking of others) and secondly in acquainting the English Nation more generally with the particularities of the exceeding riches and wealth of the East Indies: whereby themselues and their neighbours of Holland haue bene incouraged, being men as skilfull in Nauigation and of no lesse courage then the Portugals to share with them in the East Indies: where their strength is nothing so great as heretofore hath bene supposed.

* * * * *

A true discourse written (as is thought) by Colonel Antonie Winkfield emploied in the voiage to Spaine and Portugall, 1589. sent to his particular friend, and by him published for the better satisfaction of all such as hauing bene seduced by particular report, haue entred into conceits tending to the discredite of the enterprise and Actors of the same.

Although the desire of aduancing my reputation caused me to withstand the many perswasions you vsed to hold me at home, and the pursuite of honorable actions drew me (contrary to your expectation) to neglect that aduise, which in loue I know you gaue me: yet in respect of the many assurances you haue yeelded mee of your kindest friendship, I cannot suspect that you will either loue or esteeme me the lesse, at this my returne: and therefore I wil not omit any occasion which may make me appeare thankfull, or discharge any part of that duetie I owe you; which now is none other then to offer you a true discourse how these warres of Spaine and Portugall haue passed since our going out of England the 18 of Aprill, till our returne which was the first of Iuly. Wherein I wil (vnder your fauourable pardon) for your further satisfaction, as well make relation of those reasons which confirmed me in my purpose of going abroad, as of these accidents which haue happened during our aboad there; thereby hoping to perswade you that no light fansie did drawe me from the fruition of your dearest friendship, but an earnest desire by following the warres to make my selfe more woorthy of the same.

Hauing therefore determinately purposed to put on this habite of a souldier, I grew doubtfull whether to employ my time in the wars of the low Countries, which are in auxiliarie maner maintained by her maiestie, or to folow the fortune of this voiage, which was an aduenture of her and many honorable personages, in reuenge of vnsupportable wrongs offered vnto the estate of our countrey by the Castilian king: in arguing whereof, I find that by how much the chalenger is reputed before the defendant, by so much is the iourney to be preferred before those defensiue wars. For had the duke of Parma his turne bene to defend, as it was his good fortune to inuade: from whence could haue proceeded that glorious honor which these late warres haue laid vpon him, or what could haue bene said more of him, then of a Respondent (though neuer so valiant) in a priuate Duell: Euen, that he hath done no more then by his honor he was tied vnto. For the gaine of one towne or any small defeat giueth more renoume to the Assailant, then the defence of a countrey, or the withstanding of twentie encounters can yeeld any man who is bound by his place to guard the same: whereof as well the particulars of our age, especially in the Spaniard, as the reports of former histories may assure us, which haue still laied the fame of all warres vpon the Inuader. And do not ours in these dayes liue obscured in Flanders, either not hauing wherewithall to manage any warre, or not putting on armes, but to defend themselues when the enemie shall procure them? Whereas in this short time of our aduenture, we haue won a towne by escalade, battered and assaulted another, ouerthrowen a mightie princes power in the field, landed our armie in 3 seueral places of his kingdom, marched 7 dayes in the heart of his country, lien three nights in the suburbs of his principall citie, beaten his forces into the gates thereof, and possessed two of his frontier forts, as shall in discourse thereof more particularly appeare: whereby I conclude, that going with an Inuader, and in such an action as euery day giueth new experience, I haue much to vaunt of, that my fortune did rather cary me thither then into the wars of Flanders. Notwithstanding the vehement perswasions you vsed with me to the contrary, the grounds whereof sithence you receiued them from others, you must giue me leaue to acquaint you with the error you were led into by them, who labouring to bring the world into an opinion that it stood more with the safetie of our estate to bend all our forces against the prince of Parma, then to folow this action by looking into the true effects of this iourney, will iudicially conuince themselues of mistaking the matter. For, may the conquest of these countries against the prince of Parma be thought more easie for vs alone now, then the defence of them was 11 yeeres ago, with the men and money of the Queene of England? the power of the Monsieur of France? the assistance of the principal states of Germanie? and the nobilitie of their owne country? Could not an armie of more then 20000 horse, and almost 30000 foot, beat Don Iohn de Austria out of the countrey, who was possessed of a very few frontier townes? and shall it now be laid vpon her maiesties shoulders to remoue so mightie an enemie, who hath left vs but 3 whole parts of 17 vnconquered? It is not a iourney of a few moneths, nor an auxiliarie warre of fewe yeeres that can damnifie the king of Spaine in those places where we shall meet at euery 8 or 10 miles end with a towne, which will cost more the winning then will yeerely pay 4 or 5 thousand mens wages, where all the countrey is quartered by riuers which haue no passage vnfortified, and where most of the best souldiers of Christendom that be on our aduerse party be in pension. But our armie, which hath not cost her maiestie much aboue the third part of one yeres expenses in the Low countries, hath already spoiled a great part of the prouision he had made at the Groine of all sortes, for a new voyage into England; burnt 3 of his ships, whereof one was the second in the last yeres expedition called S. Iuan de Colorado, taken from him aboue 150 pieces of good artillerie; cut off more then 60 hulks and 20 French ships wel manned fit and readie to serue him for men of war against vs, laden for his store with corne, victuals, masts, cables, and other marchandizes; slaine and taken the principal men of war he had in Galitia; made Don Pedro Enriques de Gusman, Conde de Fuentes, Generall of his forces in Portugall, shamefully run at Peniche; laid along of his best Commanders in Lisbon; and by these few aduentures discouered how easily her maiestie may without any great aduenture in short time pull the Tirant of the world vpon his knees, as wel by the disquieting his vsurpation of Portugall as without difficultie in keeping the commoditie of his Indies from him, by sending an army so accomplished, as may not be subiect to those extremities which we haue endured: except he draw, for those defences, his forces out of the Low countries and disfurnish his garisons of Naples and Milan, which with safetie of those places he may not do. And yet by this meane he shall rather be enforced therevnto, then by any force that can be vsed there against him: wherefore I directly conclude that this proceeding is the most safe and necessary way to be held against him, and therefore more importing then the war in the Low countries. Yet hath the iourney (I know) bene much misliked by some, who either thinking too worthily of the Spaniards valure, too indifferently of his purposes against vs, or too vnworthily of them that vndertooke this iourney against him, did thinke it a thing dangerous to encounter the Spaniard at his owne home, a thing needlesse to proceed by inuasion against him, a thing of too great moment for two subiects of their qualitie to vndertake: And therefore did not so aduance the beginnings as though they hoped for any good successe therof.

The chances of wars be things most vncertaine: for what people soeuer vndertake them, they are in deed as chastisements appointed by God for the one side or the other. For which purpose it hath pleased him to giue some victories to the Spaniards of late yeeres against some whom he had in purpose to ruine. But if we consider what wars they be that haue made their name so terrible, we shal find them to haue bin none other then against the barbarous Moores, the naked Indians, and the vnarmed Netherlanders, whose yeelding rather to the name then act of the Spaniards, hath put them into such a conceit of their mightines, as they haue considerately vndertaken the conquest of our monarchie, consisting of a people vnited and always held sufficiently warlike: against whom what successe their inuincible army had the last yeere, as our very children can witness, so I doubt not but this voiage hath sufficiently made knowen what they are euen vpon their owne dunghill, which, had it bene set out in such sort as it was agreed vpon by their first demaund, it might haue made our nation the most glorious people of the world. For hath not the want of 8 of the 12 pieces of artillerie, which were promised vnto the Aduenture, lost her maiestie the possession of the Groine and many other places, as hereafter shall appeare, whose defensible rampires were greater then our batterie (such as it was) cold force: and therefore were left vnattempted?

It was also resolued to haue sent 600 English horses of the Low countries, whereof we had not one, notwithstanding the great charges expended in their transportation hither: and that may the army assembled at Puente de Burgos thanke God of, as well as the forces of Portugall, who foreran vs 6 daies together: Did we not want 7 of the 13 old Companies, which we should haue had from thence; foure of the 10 Dutch Companies; and 6 of their men of war for the sea, from the Hollanders: which I may iustly say we wanted, in that we might haue had so many good souldiers, so many good ships, and so many able bodies more then we had?

Did there not vpon the first thinking of the iourney diuers gallant Courtiers put in their names for aduenturers to the summe of 10000 li. who seeing it went forward in good earnest, aduised themselues better, and laid the want of so much money vpon the iourney?

Was there not moreouer a rounde summe of the aduenture spent in leuying, furnishing, and maintaining 3 moneths 1500 men for the seruice of Berghen, with which Companies the Mutinies of Ostend were suppressed, a seruice of no smal moment?

What misery the detracting of the time of our setting out, which should haue bene the 1 of February, did lay vpon vs, too many can witnes: and what extremitie the want of that moneths victuals which we did eat, during the moneth we lay at Plimouth for a wind, might haue driuen vs vnto, no man can doubt of, that knoweth what men do liue by, had not God giuen vs in the ende a more prosperous wind and shorter passage into Galitia then hath bene often seen, where our owne force and fortune reuictualled vs largely: of which crosse windes, that held vs two dayes after our going out, the Generals being wearie, thrust to Sea in the same, wisely chusing rather to attend the change thereof there, then by being in harborough to lose any part of the better, when it should come by hauing their men on shore: in which two dayes 25 of our companies shipped in part of the fleet were scattered from vs, either not being able or willing to double Vshant.

These burdens layed vpon our Generals before their going out, they haue patiently endured, and I thinke they haue thereby much enlarged their honour: for hauing done thus much with the want of our artillery, 600 horse, 3000 foot, and 20000 li. of their aduenture, and one moneths victuals of their proportion, what may be conjectured they would haue done with their ful complement?

For the losse of our men at sea, since we can lay it on none but the will of God, what can be said more, then that it is his pleasure to turne all those impediments to the honor of them against whom they were intended: and he will still shew himselfe the Lord of hosts in doing great things by them, whom many haue sought to obscure: who if they had let the action fall at the height thereof in respect of those defects, which were such especially for the seruice at land, as would haue made a mighty subiect stoope vnder them, I do not see how any man could iustly haue layd any reproch vpon him who commanded the same, but rather haue lamented the iniquity of this time, wherein men whom forren countries haue for their conduct in seruice worthily esteemed of, should not only in their owne countrey not be seconded in their honorable endeuors, but mightily hindred, euen to the impairing of their owne estates, which most willingly they haue aduentured for the good of their countries: whose worth I will not value by my report, lest I should seem guiltie of flattery (which my soule abhorreth) and yet come short in the true measure of their praise. Onely for your instruction against them who had almost seduced you from the true opinion you hold of such men, you shall vnderstand that Generall Norris from his booke was trained vp in the wars of the Admiral of France, and in very yong yeeres had charge of men vnder the erle of Essex in Ireland: which with what commendations he then discharged, I leaue to the report of them who obserued those seruices. Vpon the breach betwixt Don Iohn and the States, he was made Colonel generall of all the English forces there present, or to come, which he continued 2 yeeres: he was then made Marshal of the field vnder Conte Hohenlo: and after that, General of the army in Frisland: at his comming home in the time of Monsieurs gouernment in Flanders, he was made lord President of Munster in Ireland, which he yet holdeth, from whence within one yere he was sent for, and sent Generall of the English forces which her maiestie then lent to the Low countries, which he held til the erle of Leicesters going ouer. And he was made Marshall of the field in England, the enemy being vpon our coast, and when it was expected the crowne of England should haue bene tried by battel. Al which places of commandement which neuer any Englishman successiuely attained vnto in forren wars, and the high places her maiestie had thought him woorthy of, may suffice to perswade you, that he was not altogether vnlikely to discharge that which he vndertooke.

What fame general Drake hath gotten by his iourney about the world, by his aduentures to the west Indies, and the scourges he hath laid vpon the Spanish nation, I leaue to the Southerne parts to speake of, and refer you to The Booke extant in our own language treating of the same, and beseech you considering the waighty matters they haue in all the course of their liues with wonderfull reputation managed, that you wil esteeme them not wel informed of their proceedings, that thinke them insufficient to passe through that which they vndertooke, especially hauing gone thus far in the view of the world, through so many incombrances, and disappointed of those agreements which led them the rather to vndertake the seruice. But it may be you wil thinke me herein either to much opinionated of the voiage, or conceited of the Commanders, that labouring thus earnestly to aduance the opinion of them both, haue not so much as touched any part of the misorders, weaknes and wants that haue bene amongst vs, whereof they that returned did plentifully report. True it is, I haue conceiued a great opinion of the iourney, and do thinke honorably of the Commanders: for we find in greatest antiquities, that many Commanders haue bene receiued home with triumph for lesse merite, and that our owne countrey hath honored men heretofore with admiration for aduentures vnequal to this: it might therefore in those daies haue seemed superfluous to extend any mans commendations by particular remembrances, for that then all men were ready to giue enery man his due. But I hold it most necessary in these daies, sithence euery vertue findeth her direct opposite, and actions woorthy of all memory are in danger to be enuiously obscured, to denounce the prayses of the action, and actors to the ful, but yet no further then with sinceritie of trueth, and not without grieuing at the iniury of this time, wherein is enforced a necessitie of Apologies for those men and matters, which all former times were accustomed to entertaine with the greatest applause that might be. But to answere the reports which haue bene giuen out in reproach of the actors and action by such as were in the same: let no man thinke otherwise, but that they, who fearing the casuall accidents of war had any purpose of returning, did first aduise of some occasion that should moue them thereunto: and hauing found any whatsoever did thinke it sufficiently iust, in respect of the earnest desire they had to seeke out matter that might colour their coming home.

Of these there were some, who hauing noted the late Flemish warres did finde that many yong men haue gone ouer and safely returned souldiers within fewe moneths, in hauing learned some wordes of Arte vsed in the warres, and thought after that good example to spend like time amongst vs: which being expired they beganne to quarrell at the great mortalitie that was amongst vs.

The neglect of discipline in the Armie, for that men were suffered to be drunke with the plentie of wines.

The scarsitie of Surgions.

The want of carriages for the hurt and sicke: and the penurie of victuals in the Campe:

Thereupon diuining that there would be no good done: And that therefore they could be content to lose their time, and aduenture to returne home againe.

These men haue either conceiued well of their owne wits (who by obseruing the passages of the warre were become sufficient souldiers in these fewe weeks, and did long to be at home, where their discourses might be wondred at) or missing of their Portegues and Milrayes [Footnote: Coins current in Spain and Portugal.] which they dreamed on in Portugall, would rather returne to their former maner of life, then attend the ende of the iourney. For seeing that one hazard brought another; and that though one escaped the bullet this day it might light vpon him to morow, the next day, or any day; and that the warre was not confined to any one place, but that euery place brought foorth new enemies, they were glad to see some of the poore souldiers fal sicke, that fearing to be infected by them they might iustly desire to go home.

[Sidenote: Answere to the first.] The sicknesse I confesse was great, because any is too much. But hath it bene greater then is ordinary among Englishmen at their first entrance into the warres, whithersoeuer they goe to want the fulnesse of their flesh pots? Haue not ours decayed at all times in France, with eating yong fruits and drinking newe wines? haue they not abundantly perished in the Low countreys with cold, and rawnesse of the aire, euen in their garrisons? Haue there not more died in London in sixe moneths of the plague, then double our Armie being at the strongest? And could the Spanish armie the last yeere (who had all prouisions that could be thought on for an Armie, and tooke the fittest season, in the yeere for our Climate) auoyd sicknes among their souldiers? May it then be thought that ours could escape there, where they found inordinate heat of weather, and hot wines to distemper them withall?

But can it be, that we haue lost so many as the common sort perswade themselues wee haue? It hath bene prooued by strickt examinations of our musters, that we were neuer in our fulnesse before our going from Plimouth 11000. souldiers, nor aboue 2500. Marriners. It is also euident that there returned aboue 6000. of all sorts, as appeareth by the seuerall paiments made to them since our comming home. And I haue truely shewed you that of these numbers very neere 3000. forsooke the Armie at the Sea, whereof some passed into France and the rest returned home. So as we neuer being 13000. in all, and hauing brought home aboue 6000. with vs, you may see how the world hath bene seduced, in belieuing that we haue lost 16000. men by sicknes.

[Sidenote: Answere to the second.] To them that haue made question of the gouernment of the warres (little knowing what appertained thereunto in that there were so many drunkards amongst vs) I answere that in their gouernment of shires and parishes, yea in their very housholdes, themselues can hardly bridle their vassals from that vice. For we see it is a thing almost impossible, at any your Faires or publique assemblies to finde any quarter thereof sober, or in your Townes any Ale-poles vnfrequented: And we obserue that though any man hauing any disordered persons in their houses, do locke vp their drincke and set Butlers vpon it, that they will yet either by indirect meanes steale themselues drunke from their Masters tables, or runne abroad to seeke it. If then at home in the eyes of your Iustices, Maiors, Preachers, and Masters, and where they pay for euery pot they take, they cannot be kept from their liquor: doe they thinke that those base disordered persons whom themselves sent vnto vs, as liuing at home without rule, who hearing of wine doe long for it as a daintie that their purses could neuer reach to in England, and having it there without mony euen in their houses where they lie and hold their guard, can be kept from being drunk; and once drunke, held in any order or tune, except we had for euery drunkard an officer to attend him? But who be they that haue runne into these disorders? Euen our newest men, our yongest men, and our idelest men, and for the most part our slouenly prest men, whom the Iustices, (who haue alwayes thought vnwoorthily of any warre) haue sent out as the scumme and dregs of their countrey. And those were they, who distempering themselues with these hote wines, haue brought in that sicknesse, which hath infected honester men then themselues. But I hope, as in other places the recouerie of their diseases doeth acquaint their bodies with the aire of the countries where they be, so the remainder of these which haue either recouered, or past without sicknesse will proue most fit for Martiall seruices.

[Sidenote: Answere to the third.] If we haue wanted Surgeons, may not this rather be laid vpon the captaines (who are to prouide for their seuerall Companies) then vpon the Generals, whose care hath bene more generall. And how may it be thought that euery captaine, vpon whom most of the charges of raising their Companies was laid as an aduenture, could prouide themselues of all things expedient for a war, which was alwaies wont to be maintained by the purse of the prince. But admit euery Captaine had his Surgeon: yet were the want of curing neuer the lesse: for our English Surgeons (for the most part) be vnexperienced in hurts that come by shot;

because England hath not knowen wars but of late, from whose ignorance proceeded this discomfort, which I hope wil warne those that hereafter go to the wars to make preparation of such as may better preserue mens liues by their skill.

[Sidenote: Answere to the fourth.] From whence the want of cariages did proceed, you may conjecture in that we marched through a countrey neither plentifull of such prouisions, nor willing to part from any thing: yet this I can assure you, that no man of worth was left either hurt or sicke in any place vnprouided for. And that the General commanded all the mules and asses that were laden with any baggage to be vnburdened and taken that vse: and the earle of Essex and he for money hired men to cary men vpon pikes. And the earle (whose true vertue and nobilitie, as it doeth in all other his actions appeare, so did it very much in this) threw down his own stuffe, I meane apparel and necessaries which he had there, from his owne cariages, and let them be left by the way, to put hurt and sicke men vpon them. Of whose honourable deseruings I shall not need here to make any particular discourse, for that many of his actions do hereafter giue me occasion to obserue the same.

[Sidenote: Answere to the fift.] And the great complaint that these men make for the want of victuals may well proceed from their not knowing the wants of the war; for if to feed vpon good bieues, muttons and goats, be to want, they haue endured great scarcitie at land, wherunto they neuer wanted, two daies together, wine to mixe with their water, nor bread to eat with their meat (in some quantitie) except it were such as had vowed rather to starue then to stir out of their places for food: of whom we had too many, who if their time had serued for it, might haue seen in many campes in the most plentifull countries of the world for victuals, men daily die with want of bread and drinke in not hauing money to buy, nor the countrey yeelding any good or healthful water in any place; whereas both Spaine and Portugall do in euery place affoord the best water that may be, and much more healthful then any wine for our drinking.

And although some haue most injuriously exclaimed against the smal prouisions of victuals for the sea, rather grounding the same vpon an euill that might haue fallen, then any that did light vpon vs: yet know you this, that there is no man so forgetfull, that will say they wanted before they came to the Groine, that whosoeuer made not very large prouisions for himselfe and his company at the Groine, was very improuident, where was plentiful store of wine, biefe, and fish, and no man of place prohibited to lay in the same into their ships, wherewith some did so furnish themselues, as they did not onely in the journey supplie the wants, of such as were lesse provident then they, but in their returne home made a round commoditie of the remainder thereof. And that at Cascais there came in such store of prouisions into the Fleet out of England, as no man that would haue vsed his diligence could haue wanted his due proportion thereof, as might appeare by the remainder that was returned to Plimmouth, and the plentifull sale thereof made out of the marchants ships after their comming into the Thames.

But least I should seeme vnto you too studious in confuting idle opinions, or answering friuolous questions, I wil adresse me to the true report of those actions that haue passed therein: wherein I protest, I will neither hide any thing that hath hapned against vs, nor attribute more to any man or matter, then the iust occasions thereof lead me vnto: wherein it shall appeare that there hath bene nothing left vndone by the Generals which was before our going out vndertaken by them, but that there hath bene much more done then was at the first required by Don Antonio, who should haue reaped the fruit of our aduenture.

[Sidenote: Our men land within a mile of the Groine the 20 of April.] After 6 daies sailing from the coast of England, and the 5 after we had the wind good being the 20 of April in the euening, we landed in a baie more then an English mile from the Groine, in our long boats and pinnasses without any impeachment: from whence we presently marched toward the towne, within one halfe mile we were encountred by the enemie who being charged by ours, retired into their gates. For that night our armie lay in the villages, houses and mils next adioining, and very neere round about the towne, into the which the Galeon named S. Iohn (which was the second of the last yeeres Fleet agaynst England) one hulke, two smaller ships and two Gallies which were found in the road, did beate vpon vs and vpon our Companies as they passed too and fro that night and the next morning. Generall Norris hauing that morning before day viewed the Towne, found the same defended on the land side (for it standeth vpon the necke of an Iland) with a wall vpon a dry ditch; whereupon he resolued to trie in two places what might bee done against it by escalade, and in the meane time aduised for the landing of some artillery to beat vpon the ships and gallies, that they might not annoy vs: which being put in execution, vpon the planting of the first piece the gallies abandoned the road, and betooke them to Feroll, not farre from thence: and the Armada being beaten with the artillery and musketers that were placed vpon the next shore, left her playing vpon vs. The rest of the day was spent in preparing the companies, and other prouisions ready for the surprise of the base towne which was effected in this sort.

There were appointed to be landed 1200 men vnder the conduct of Colonell Huntley, and Captaine Fenner the Viceadmirall, on that side next fronting vs by water in long boats and pinnesses, wherein were placed many pieces ol artillery to beat vpon the tonne in their aproch: at the corner of the wall which defended the other water side, were appointed Captaine Richard Wingfield Lieutenant Colonell to Generall Norris, and Captaine Sampson Lieutenant Colonell to Generall Drake to enter at low water with 500 men if they found it passable, but if not, to betake them to the escalade, for they had also ladders with them: at the other corner of the wall which joyned to that side that was attempted by water, were appointed Colonell Vmpton, and Colonell Bret with 300 men to enter by escalade. All the companies which should enter by boat being imbarked before the low water, and hauing giuen the alarme, Captaine Wingfield and Captaine Sampson betooke them to the escalade, for they had in commandement to charge all at one instant. The boats landed without any great difficulty: yet had they some men hurt in the landing. Colonell Bret and Colonell Vmpton entred their quarter without encounter, not finding any defence made against them: for Captaine Hinder being one of them that entred by water, at his first entry, with some of his owne company whom he trusted well, betooke himselfe to that part of the wall, which be cleared before that they offered to enter, and so still scoured the wall till hee came on the backe of them who mainteined the fight against Captaine Wingfield and Captaine Sampson; who were twise beaten from their ladders, and found very good resistance, till the enemies perceiuing ours entred in two places at their backs, were driuen to abandon the same. The reason why that place was longer defended then the other, is (as Don Iuan de Luna who commanded the same affirmeth) that the enemy that day had resolued in councell how to make their defences, if they were approched: and therein concluded, that, if we attempted it by water, it was not able to be held, and therefore vpon the discouery of our boats, they of the high towne should make a signall by fire from thence, that all the lowe towne might make their retreat thither: but they (whether troubled with the sudden terror we brought vpon them, or forgetting their decree) omitted the fire, which made them guard that place til we were entred on euery side.

Then the towne being entred in three seuerall places with an huge cry, the inhabitants betooke them to the high towne: which they might with lesse perill doe, for that ours being strangers here, knew not the way to cut them off. The rest that were not put to the sword in fury, fled to the rocks in the Iland, and others hid themselues in chambers and sellers, which were euery day found out in great numbers.

Amongst those Don Iuan de Luna, a man of very good commandement, hauing hidden himselfe in a house, did the next morning yeeld himselfe.

There was also taken that night a commissary of victuals called Iuan de Vera, who confessed that there were in the Groine at our entry 500 souldiours being in seuen companies which returned very weake (as appeareth by the small numbers of them) from the iourney of England, namely:

Vnder Don Iuan de Luna.

Don Diego Barran, a bastard sonne of the Marques of Santa Cruz; his company was that night in the Galeon.

Don Antonio de Herera then at Madrid.

Don Pedro de Manriques brother to the Earle of Paxides.

Don Ieronimo de Mourray of the Order of S. Iuan, with some of the towne were in the fort.

Don Gomez de Caramasal then at Madrid.

Captaine Manço Caucaso de Socas.

Also there came in that day of our landing from Retanzas the companies of Don Iohn de Mosalle, and Don Pedro Poure de Leon.

Also he saith that there was order giuen for baking of 300000 of biscuit, some in Batansas, some in Ribadeo, and the rest there.

There were then in the towne 2000 pipes of wine, and 150 in the ships.

That there were lately come vnto the Marques of Seralba 300000 ducats.

That there were 1000 iarres of oile.

A great quantity of beanes, peaze, wheat, and fish.

That there were 3000 quintals of beefe.

And that not twenty dayes before, there came in three barks laden with match and harquebuzes.

Some others also found fauour to be taken prisoners, but the rest falling into the hands of the common souldiers, had their throats cut, to the number of 500, as I coniecture, first and last, after we had entred the towne; and in the entry thereof there was found euery celler full of wine, whereon our men, by inordinate drinking, both grew themselues for the present senselesse of the danger of the shot of the towne, which hurt many of them being drunke, and tooke the first ground of their sicknesse; for of such was our first and chiefest mortality. There was also abundant store of victuals, salt, and all kinde of prouision for shipping and the warre: which was confessed by the sayd Commissary of victuals there, to be the beginning of a magasin of all sorts of prouision for a new voyage into England: whereby you may conjecture what the spoile thereof hath aduantaged vs, and prejudiced the king of Spaine.

The next morning about eight of the clocke the enemies abandoned their ships. And hauing ouercharged the artillery of the gallion, left her on fire, which burnt in terrible sort two dayes together, the fire and ouercharging of the pieces being so great, as of fifty that were in her, there were not aboue sixteene taken out whole; the rest with ouercharge of the powder being broken, and molten with heat of the fire, were taken out in broken pieces into diuers shippes. The same day was the cloister on the South side of the towne entred by vs, which ioyned very neere to the wall of the towne, out of the chambers and other places whereof we beat into the same with our musquetiers.

The next day in the afternoone there came downe some 2000 men, gathered together out of the countrey, euen to the gates of the towne, as resolutely (ledde by what spirit I know not) as though they would haue entred the same: but at the first defence made by ours that had the guard there, wherein were slaine about eighteene of theirs, they tooke them to their heeles in the same disorder they made their approch, and with greater speed then ours were able to follow: notwithstanding we followed after them more then a mile. The second day Colonell Huntley was sent into the countrey with three or foure hundred men, who brought home very great store of kine and sheepe for our reliefe.

The third day in the night the Generall had in purpose to take a long munition-house builded vpon their wall, opening towards vs, which would haue giuen vs great aduantage against them; but they knowing the commodity thereof for vs, burnt it in the beginning of the euening; which put him to a new councell: for he had likewise brought some artillery to that side of the towne. During this time there happened a very great fire in the lower end of the towne; which, had it not bene by the care of the Generals heedily sene vnto, and the fury thereof preuented by pulling downe many houses which were most in danger, as next vnto them, had burnt all the prouisions we found there, to our woonderfull hinderance.

The fourth day were planted vnder the gard of the cloister two demy-canons, and two coluerings against the towne, defended or gabbioned with a crosse wall, thorow the which our battery lay; the first and second fire whereof shooke all the wall downe, so as all the ordinance lay open to the enemy, by reason whereof some of the Canoniers were shot and some slaine. The Lieutenant also of the ordinance, M. Spencer, was slaine fast by Sir Edward Norris, Master thereof: whose valour being accompanied with an honourable care of defending that trust committed vnto him, neuer left that place, till he receiued direction from the Generall his brother to cease the battery, which he presently did, leauing a gard vpon the same for that day; and in the night following made so good defence for the place of the battery, as after there were very few or none annoyed therein. That day Captaine Goodwin had in commandement from the Generall, that when the assault should be giuen to the towne, he should make a proffer of an escalade on the other side, where he held his guard: but he (mistaking the signall that should haue bene giuen) attempted the same long before the assault, and was shot in the mouth. The same day the Generall hauing planted his ordinance ready to batter, caused the towne to be summoned; in which summons they of the towne shot at our Drum; immediatly after that there was one hanged ouer the wall, and a parle desired; wherein they gaue vs to vnderstand, that the man hanged was he that shot at the Drum before: wherein also they intreated to haue faire warres, with promise of the same on their parts. The rest of the parle was spent in talking of Don Iuan de Luna, and some other prisoners, and somewhat of the rendring of the towne, but not much, for they listened not greatly thereunto.

Generall Norris hauing by his skilfull view of the towne (which is almost all seated vpon a rocke) found one place thereof mineable, did presently set workemen in hand withall; who after three dayes labour (and the seuenth after we were entred the base towne) had bedded their powder, but indeede not farre enough into the wall. Against which time the breach made by the canon being thought assaultable, and companies appointed as well to enter the same, as that which was expected should be blowen vp by the mine: namely, to that of the canon, Captaine Richard Wingfield, and Captaine Philpot who lead the Generals foot-companie, with whom also Captaine Yorke went, whose principall commandment was ouer the horsemen. And to that of the Myne, Captaine Iohn Sampson, and Captaine Anthonie Wingfield Lieutenant Colonell to the Master of the Ordinance, with certaine selected out of diuers Regiments. All these companies being in armes, and the assault intended to be giuen in al places at an instant, fire was put to the traine of the mine; but by reason the powder brake out backewards in a place where the caue was made too high, there could be nothing done in either place for that day. During this time Captaine Hinder was sent with some chosen out of euery company into the countrey for prouisions, whereof he brought in good store, and returned without losse.

The next day Captaine Anthony Sampson was sent out with some 500 to fetch in prouisions for the army, who was encountred by them of the countrey, but he put them to flight, and returned with good spoile. The same night the miners were set to worke againe, who by the second day after had wrought very well into the foundation of the wall. Against which time the companies aforesayd being in readinesse for both places (Generall Drake on the other side, with two or three hundred men in pinnesses, making proffer to attempt a strong fort vpon an Iland before the towne, where he left more then thirty men) fire was giuen to the traine of the mine, which blew vp halfe the tower vnder which the powder was planted. The assailants hauing in charge vpon the effecting of the mine presently to giue the assault, performed it accordingly; but too soone: for hauing entred the top of the breach, the other halfe of the tower, which with the first force of the powder was onely shaken and made loose, fell vpon our men: vnder which were buried about twenty or thirty, then being vnder that part of the tower. This so amazed our men that stood in the breach, not knowing from whence that terror came, as they forsooke their Commanders, and left them among the ruines of the mine. The two Ensignes of Generall Drake and Captaine Anthony Wingfield were shot in the breach, but their colours were rescued: the Generals by Captaine Sampsons Lieutenant, and Captaine Wingfields by himselfe. Amongst them that the wall fell vpon, was Captaine Sydenham pitifully lost; who hauing three or foure great stones vpon his lower parts, was held so fast, as neither himselfe could stirre, nor any reasonable company recouer him. Notwithstanding the next day being found to be aliue, there was ten or twelue lost in attempting to relieue him.

The breach made by the canon was woonderfully well assaulted by them that had the charge thereof, who brought their men to the push of the pike at the top of the breach. And being ready to enter, the loose earth (which was indeed but the rubbish of the outside of the wall) with the weight of them that were thereon slipped outwards from vnder their feet. Whereby did appeare halfe the wall vnbattered. For let no man thinke that culuerin or demy-canon can sufficiently batter a defensible rampire: and of those pieces which we had; the better of the demy-canons at the second shot brake in her carriages, so as the battery was of lesse force, being but of three pieces.

In our retreat (which was from both breaches thorow a narrow lane) were many of our men hurt: and Captaine Dolphin, who serued very well that day, was hurt in the very breach. The failing of this attempt, in the opinion of all the beholders, and of such as were of best judgement, was the fall of the mine; which had doubtlesse succeeded, the rather, because the approch was vnlooked for by the enemy in that place, and therefore not so much defence made there as in the other; which made the Generall grow to a new resolution: for finding that two dayes battery had so little beaten their wall, and that he had no better preparation to batter withall: he knew in his experience, there was no good to be done that way; which I thinke he first put in proofe, to trie if by that terror he could get the vpper towne, hauing no other way to put it in hazzard so speedily, and which in my conscience had obtained the towne, had not the defendants bene in as great perill of their liues by the displeasure of their king in giuing it vp, as by the bullet or sword in defending the same. For that day before the assault, in the view of our army, they burnt a cloister within the towne, and many other houses adioyning to the castle, to make it more defensible: whereby it appeared how little opinion themselues had of holding it against vs, had not God (who would not haue vs suddenly made proud) layed that misfortune vpon vs.

Hereby it may appeare, that the foure canons, and other pieces of battery promised to the iourney, and not performed, might haue made her Maiesty mistresse of the Groine: for though the mine were infortunate, yet if the other breach had bene such as the earth would haue held our men thereon, I doe not thinke but they had entred it thorowly at the first assault giuen: which had bene more then I haue heard of in our age. And being as it was, is no more then the Prince of Parma hath in winning of all his townes endured, who neuer entred any place at the first assault, nor aboue three by assault.

The next day the Generall hearing by a prisoner that was brought in, that the Conde de Andrada had assembled an armie of eight thousand at Puente de Burgos, sixe miles from thence in the way to Petance, which was but the beginning of an armie: in that there was a greater leauie readie to come thither vnder the Conde de Altemira, either in purpose to relieue the Groine, or to encampe themselues neere the place of our embarking, there to hinder the same; for to that purpose had the marquesse of Seralba written to them both the first night of our landing, as the Commissarie taken then confessed, or at the least to stop our further entrance into the countrey, (for during this time, there were many incursions made of three or foure hundred at a time, who burnt, spoyled, and brought in victuals plentifully) the General, I say, hearing of this armie, had in purpose the next day following to visite them, agaynst whom hee caried but nine Regiments: in the vantgard were the Regiment of Sir Roger Williams, Sir Edward Norris, and Colonell Sidney: in the Battaile, that of the Generall, of Colonell Lane, and Colonel Medkerk: and in the Rereward, Sir Henrie Norris, Colonell Huntley, and Colonell Brets Regiments; leauing the other fiue Regiments with Generall Drake, for the guard of the Cloister and Artillerie. About ten of the clocke the next day, being the sixt of May, halfe a mile from the campe, we discouering the enemy, Sir Edward Norris, who commanded the vantgard in chiefe, appointed his Lieutenant Colonell Captaine Anthonie Wingfield to command the shot of the same, who diuided them into three troups; the one he appointed to Captaine Middleton to be conducted in a way on the left hand: another to Captaine Erington to take the way on the right hand, and the body of them (which were Musquetiers) Captaine Wingfield tooke himselfe, keeping the direct way of the march. But the way taken by Captaine Middleton met a little before with the way held by Captaine Wingfield, so as be giuing the first charge vpon the enemy, was in the instant seconded by Captaine Wingfield, who beat them from place to place (they hauing very good places of defence, and crosse walles which they might haue held long) till they betooke them to their bridge, which is ouer a creeke comming out of the Sea, builded of stone vpon arches. On the foot of the further side whereof, lay the Campe of the enemy very strongly entrenched, who with our shot beaten to the further end of the bridge, Sir Edward Norris marching in the point, of the pikes, without stay passed to the bridge, accompanied with Colonell Sidney, Captaine Hinder, Captaine Fulford, and diuers others, who found the way cleare ouer the same, but through an incredible volley of shot; for that the shot of their army flanked vpon both sides of the bridge, the further end whereof was barricaded with barrels: but they who should haue guarded the same, seeing the proud approch we made, forsooke the defence of the barricade, where Sir Edward entred, and charging the first defendant with his pike, with very earnestnesse in ouerthrusting, fell, and was grieuously hurt at the sword in the head, but was most honourably rescued by the Generall his brother, accompanied with Colonell Sidney, and some other gentlemen: Captaine Hinder also hauing his Caske shot off, had fiue wounds in the head and face at the sword: and Captaine Fulford was shot into the left arme at the same encounter: yet were they so thorowly seconded by the Generall, who thrust himselfe so neere to giue encouragement to the attempt (which was of woonderfull difficulty) as their brauest men that defended that place being ouerthrowen, their whole army fell presently into rout, of whom our men had the chase three miles in foure sundry wayes, which they betooke themselues vnto. [Sidenote: The notable ouerthrow giuen to the Spaniards at Puente de Burgos.] There was taken the Standard with the Kings armes, and borne before the Generall. How many two thousand men (for of so many consisted our vantgard) might kill in pursuit of foure sundry parties, so many you may imagine fell before vs that day. And to make the number more great, our men hauing giuen ouer the execution, and returning to their standes, found many hidden in the Vineyards and hedges, which they dispatched. Also Colonell Medkerk was sent with his regiment three miles further to a Cloister, which he burnt and spoiled, wherein he found two hundred more, and put them to the sword. There were slaine in this fight on our side onely Captaine Cooper and one priuate souldier; Captaine Barton was also hurt vpon the bridge in the eye. But had you seene the strong baricades they had made on either side of the bridge, and how strongly they lay encamped thereabouts, you would haue thought it a rare resolution of ours to giue so braue a charge vpon an army so strongly lodged. After the furie of the execution, the Generall sent the vantgard one way, and the battell another, to burne and spoile; so as you might haue seene the countrey more then three miles compasse on fire. There was found very good store of munition and victuals in the Campe, some plate and rich apparell, which the better sort left behinde, they were so hotly pursued. Our sailers also landed in an Iland next adioyning to our ships, where they burnt and spoiled all they found. Thus we returned to the Groine, bringing small comfort to the enemy within the same, who shot many times at vs as we marched out; but not once in our comming backe againe.

The next day was spent in shipping our artillery landed for the battery, and of the rest taken at the Groine, which had it bene such as might haue giuen vs any assurance of a better battery, or had there bene no other purpose of our iourney but that, I thinke the Generall would haue spent some more time in the siege of the place.

The last two nights, there were that vndertooke to fire the higher towne in one place, where the houses were builded vpon the wall by the water side: but they within suspecting as much, made so good defence against vs, as they preuented the same. In our departure there was fire put into euery house of the low towne, insomuch as I may iustly say, there was not one house left standing in the base towne, or the cloister.

The next day being the eight of May, we embarked our army without losse of a man, which (had we not beaten the enemy at Puente de Burgos) had bene impossible to haue done; for that without doubt they would haue attempted something against vs in our imbarking: as appeared by the report of the Commissary aforesayd, who confessed, that the first night of our landing the Marques of Seralba writ to the Conde de Altemira, the Conde de Andrada, and to Terneis de Santisso, to bring all the forces against vs that they could possible raise, thinking no way so good to assure that place, as to bring an army thither, where withall they might either besiege vs in their base towne, if we should get it, or to lie betweene vs and our place of imbarking, to fight with us vpon the aduantage; for they had aboue 15000 souldiers vnder their commandements.

After we had put from thence, we had the winde so contrary, as we could not vnder nine dayes recouer the Burlings: in which passage on the thirteenth day the Earle of Essex, and with him M. Walter Deuereux his brother (a Gentleman of woonderfull great hope) Sir Roger Williams Colonell generall of the footmen, Sir Philip Butler, who hath alwayes bene most inward with him, and Sir Edward Wingfield, came into the fleet. The Earle hauing put himselfe into the iourney against the opinion of the world, and as it seemed to the hazzard of his great fortune, though to the great aduancement of his reputation, (for as the honourable cariage of himselfe towards all men doth make him highly esteemed at home; so did his exceeding forwardnesse in all seruices make him to bee woondered at amongst vs) who, I say, put off in the same winde from Falmouth, that we left Plimmouth in, where he lay, because he would auoid the importunity of messengers that were dayly sent for his returne, and some other causes more secret to himselfe, not knowing (as it seemed) what place the Generals purposed to land in, had bene as farre as Cadiz in Andaluzia, and lay vp and downe about the South Cape, where he tooke some ships laden with corne, and brought them vnto the fleet. Also in his returne from thence to meet with our fleet, he fell with the Ilands of Bayon; and on that side of the riuer which Cannas standeth vpon, he, with Sir Roger Williams, and those Gentlemen that were with him went on shore, with some men out of the ship he was in, whom the enemy, that held guard vpon that coast, would not abide, but fled vp into the countrey.

The 16 day we landed at Peniche in Portugall, vnder the shot of the castle, and aboue the waste in water, more then a mile from the towne, wherein many were in perill of drowning, by reason the winde was great, and the sea went high, which ouerthrew one boat, wherein fiue and twenty of Captaine Dolphins men perished. The enemy being fiue companies of Spaniards vnder the commandement of the Conde de Fuentes, sallied out of the towne against vs, and in our landing made their approch close by the water side. But the Earle of Essex with Sir Roger Williams, and his brother, hauing landed sufficient number to make two troups, left one to holde the way by the water side, and led the other ouer the Sandhils; which the enemy seeing, drew theirs likewise further into the land; not, as we coniectured, to encounter vs, but indeed to make their speedy passage away: notwithstanding, they did it in such sort, as being charged by ours which were sent out by the Colonell generall vnder Captaine Iackson, they stood the same euen to the push of the pike: in which charge and at the push, Captaine Robert Piew was slaine. The enemy being fled further then we had reason to follow them, all our companies were drawn to the towne; which being vnfortified in any place, we found vndefended by any man against vs. And therefore the Generall caused the castle to be summoned that night; which being abandoned by him that commanded it, a Portugall named Antonio de Aurid, being possessed thereof, desired but to be assured that Don Antonio was landed, whereupon he would deliuer the same; which he honestly performed. [Sidenote: Peniche taken.] There was taken out of the castle some hundred shot and pikes, which Don Emanuel furnished his Portugals withall, and twenty barrels of powder: so as possessing both the towne and the castle, we rested there one day: wherein some Friers and other poore men came vnto their new king, promising in the name of their countrey next adioyning, that within two dayes he should haue a good supply of horse and foote for his assistance. That day we remained there, the Generals company of horses were vnshipped.

The Generals there fully resolued, that the armie should march ouer land to Lisbone vnder the conduct of Generall Norris; and that Generall Drake should meete him in the riuer therof with the Fleete; and there should be one Company of foote left in the garde of the Castle, and sixe in the ships: also that the sicke and hurt should remaine there with prouisions for their cures. The Generall, to trie the euent of the matter by expedition, the next day beganne to march in this sort: his owne Regiment, and the Regiment of Sir Roger Williams, Sir Henrie Norris, Colonell Lane, and Colonell Medkerk, in the vantgard: Generall Drake, Colonell Deuereux, Sir Edward Norris, and Colonell Sidneis in the battel: Sir Iames Hales, Sir Edward Wingfield, Colonell Vmptons, Colonell Huntlies, and Colonell Brets in the arrereward. By that time our army was thus marshalled, Generall Drake, although hee were to passe by Sea, yet to make knowen the honourable desire he bad of taking equall part of all fortunes with vs, stood vpon the ascent of an hill, by the which our battalions must of necessity march and with a pleasing kindnesse tooke his leaue seuerally of the Commanders of euery regiment, wishing vs all most happy successe in our iourney ouer the land, with a constant promise that he would, if the injury of the weather did not hinder him, meet vs in the riuer of Lisbon with our fleet. The want of cariages the first day was such, as they were enforced to cary their munition vpon mens backs, which was the next day remedied.

In this march captaine Crispe the Prouost Marshall caused one who (contrary to the Proclamation published at our arriuall in Portugall) had broken vp an house for pillage, to be hanged, with the cause of his death vpon his brest, in the place where the act was committed: which good example prouidently giuen in the beginning of our march, caused the commandement to be more respectiuely regarded all the iourney after, by them whom feare of punishment doeth onely holde within compasse. The campe lodged that night at Lorinha: the next day we had intelligence all the way, that the enemy had made head of horse and foot against vs at Torres Vedras, which we thought they would haue held: but comming thither the second day of our march, not two houres before our vantgard came in, they left the towne and the castle to the possession of Don Antonio.

There began the greatest want we had of victuals, especially of bread, vpon a commandement giuen from the Generall, that no man should spoile the countrey, or take any thing from any Portugall: which was more respectiuely obserued, then I thinke would haue bene in our owne countrey, amongst our owne friends and kindred: but the countrey (contrary to promise) wholly neglected the prouision of victuals for vs, whereby we were driuen for that time into a great scarsity. Which mooued the Colonell generall to call all the Colonels together, and with them to aduise for some better course for our people: who thought it best, first to aduertise the king what necessity we were in, before we should of our selues alter the first institution of abstinence. The Colonell generall hauing acquainted the Generall herewith, with his very good allowance thereof, went to the king: who after some expostulations vsed, tooke the more carefull order for our men, and after that our army was more plentifully relieued.

The third day we lodged our army in three sundry villages, the one battalion lying in Exarama de los Caualleros, another in Exarama do Obispo, and the third in San Sebastian.

Captaine Yorke who commanded the Generals horse company, in this march made triall of the valour of the horsemen of the enemy; who by one of his Corporals charged with eight horses thorow 40 of them, and himselfe thorow more than 200 with forty horses: who would abide him no longer then they could make way from him.

The next day we marched to Lores, and had diuers intelligences that the enemy would tary vs there: for the Cardinall had made publique promise to them of Lisbon, that he would fight with vs in that place, which he might haue done aduantageously; for we had a bridge to passe ouer in the same place: but before our comming he dislodged, notwithstanding it appeared vnto vs that he had in purpose to encampe there; for we found the ground staked out where their trenches should haue bene made: and their horsemen with some few shot shewed themselues vpon an hill at our comming into that village; whom Sir Henry Norris (whose regiment had the point of the vantgard) thought to draw vnto some fight, and therefore marched without sound of drumme, and somewhat faster then ordinary, thereby to get neere them, before he were discouered, for he was shadowed from them by an hil that was betweene him and them: but before he could draw his companies any thing neere, they retired.

General Drakes regiment that night, for the commodity of good lodging, drew themselues into a village, more than one English mile from thence, and neere the enemy: who not daring to do any thing against vs in foure dayes before, tooke that occasion, and in the next morning fell downe vpon that regiment, crying, Viua el Rey Don Antonio, which was a generall salutation thorow all the Countrey, as they came: whom our yoong shouldiers (though it were vpon their guard, and before the watch was discharged) began to entertaine kindly, but hauing got within their guard, they fell to cut their throats: but the alarme being taken inwards, the officers of the two next Companies, whose Captaines (Captaine Sydnam and Captaine Young) were lately dead at the Groine, brought downe their colours and pikes vpon them in so resolute manner, as they presently draue them to retire with losse: they killed of ours at their first entrance foarteene, and hurt sixe or seuen.

The next day we lodged at Aluelana within three miles of Lisbon, where many of our souldiers drinking in two places of standing waters by the way were poisoned, and thereon presently; died. Some do think it came rather by eating hony, which they found in the houses plentifully. But whether it were by water or by hony, the poor men were poisoned.

That night the Earle of Essex, and Sir Rodger Williams went out about eleuen of the clock with 1000 men to lie in ambuscade neere the town, and hauing layed the same very neere, sent some to giue the alarme vnto the enemy: which was well performed by them that had the charge thereof, but the enemy refused to issue after them, so as the Earle returned assone as it was light without doing any thing, though he had in purpose, and was ready to haue giuen an honourable charge on them.

The 25 of May in the evening we came to the suburbs of Lisbon at the very entrance whereof Sir Rodger Williams calling Captaine Anthony Wingfield with him, tooke thirty shot or thereabouts, and first scowred all the streets till they came very neere the town; where they found none but old folks and beggars, crying, Viua el Rey Don Antonio, and the houses shut vp: for they had caried much of their wealth into the towne, and had fired some houses by the water side, full of corne and other prouisions of victuals, least we should be benefited thereby, but yet left behinde them great riches in many houses.

The foure regiments that had the vantgard that day, which were Colonell Deuereux, Sir Edward Norris, Colonell Sidneys, and Generall Drakes (whom I name as they marched) the Colonell generall caused to hold guard in the neerest street of the Suburbs: the battell and arreward stood in armes all the night in the field neere to Alcantara. Before morning Captaine Wingfield, by direction from the Colonell generall Sir Roger Williams, held guard with Sir Edward Norris his regiment in three places very neere the town wall, and so held the same till the other regiments came in the morning. About midnight they within the towne burnt all their houses that stood upon their wall either within or without, least we possessing them, might thereby greatly haue annoyed the towne.

The next morning Sir Roger Williams attempted (but not without peril) to take a church called S. Antonio, which ioyned to the wall of the towne, and would haue bene a very euill neighbor to the towne: but the enemy hauing more easie entry into it then we gained it before vs. The rest of that morning was spent in quartering the battell and arrereward in the Suburbs called Bona Vista, and in placing Musquetiers in houses, to front their shot vpon the wall, who from the same scowred the great streets very dangerously.

By this time our men being thorowly weary with our six days march, and the last nights watch, were desirous of rest; whereof the enemy being aduertised, about one or two of the clocke sallied out of the towne, and made their approach in three seuerall streets vpon vs, but chiefly in Colonell Brets quarter: who (as most of the army was) being at rest, with as much speed as he could, drew his men to armes, and made head against them so thorowly, as himselfe was slaine in the place, Captaine Carsey shot thorow the thigh, of which hurt he died within foure dayes after, Captaine Carre slaine presently, and Captaine Caue hurt (but not mortally) who were all of his regiment.

This resistance made aswell here, as in other quarters where Colonell Lane and Colonell Medkerk commanded, put them to a sudden foule retreat; insomuch, as the Earle of Essex had the chase of them euen to the gates of the towne, wherein they left behinde them many of their best Commanders: their troupe of horsemen also came out, but being charged by Captaine Yorke, withdrew themselues again. Many of them also left the streets, and betooke them to houses which they found open: for the Sergeant maior Captaine Wilson slew with his owne hands three or foure, and caused them that were with him to kill many others. Their losse I can assure you did triple ours, as well in quality as in quantity.

During our march to this place, Generall Drake with the whole fleet was come into Cascais, and possessed the towne without any resistance: many of the inhabitants at their discouery of our nauy, fledde with their baggage into the mountaines, and left the towne for any man that would possesse it, till Generall Drake sent vnto them by a Portugall Pilot which he had on boord, to offer them all peaceable kindnesse, so farre foorth as they would accept of their King, and minister necessaries to all the army he had brought; which offer they ioyfully imbraced, and presently sent two chiefe men of their towne, to signifie their loyalty to Don Antonio, and their honest affections to our people. Whereupon the Generall landed his companies not farre from the Cloister called San Domingo, but not without perill of the shot of the castle, which being guarded by 65 Spaniards, held still against him.

As our fleet were casting ancre when the camne first into that road, there was a small ship of Brasil that came from thence, which bare with them, and seemed by striking her sailes, as though she would also haue ancred: but taking her fittest occasion hoised againe, and would haue passed vp the riuer, but the Generall presently discerning her purpose, sent out a pinnesse or two after her, which forced her in such sort, as she ran herselfe vpon the Rocks: all the men escaped out of her, and the lading (being many chests of sugar) was made nothing woorth, by the salt water. In his going thither also, he tooke ships of the port of Portugall, which were sent from thence, with fifteene other from Pedro Vermendes Xantes Sergeant maior of the same place, laden with men and victuals to Lisbon: the rest that escaped put into Setuuel.

The next day it pleased Generall Norris to call all the Colonels together, and to aduise with them, whether it were more expedient to tary there to attend the forces of the Portugall horse and foot, whereof the King had made promise, and to march some conueuient number to Cascais to fetch our artillery and munition, which was all at our ships, sauing that which for the necessity of the seruice was brought along with vs: whereunto, some caried away with the vaine hope of Don Antonio, that most part of the towne stood for vs, held it best to make our abode there, and to send some 3000 for our artillery; promising to themselues, that the enemy being wel beaten the day before, would make no more sallies: some others (whose vnbeliefe was very strong of any hope from the Portugall) perswaded rather to march wholly away, then to be any longer carried away with the opinion of things, whereof there was so little appearance. The Generall not willing to leaue any occasion of blotte to be layed vpon him for his speedy going from thence, nor to lose any more time by attending the hopes of Don Antonio; tolde them that though the expedition of Portugall were not the onely purpose of their iourney, but an aduenture therein (which if it succeeded prosperously, might make them sufficiently rich, and woonderfull honourable) and that they had done so much already in triall thereof, as what end soeuer happened, could nothing impaire their credits: yet in regard of the Kings last promise, that he should haue that night 3000 men armed of his owne Countrey, he would not for that night dislodge. And if they came thereby to make him so strong, that he might send the like number for his munition, he would resolue to trie his fortune for the towne. But if they came not, he found it not conuenient to diuide his forces, by sending any to Cascais, and keeping a remainder behinde, sithence he saw them the day before so boldly sally vpon his whole army, and knew that they were stronger of Souldiours armed within the towne, then he was without: and that before our returne could be from Cascais, they expected more supplies from all places, of Souldiours: for the Duke of Bragança, and Don Francisco de Toledo were looked for with great reliefe. Whereupon his conclusion was, that if the 3000 promised came not that night, to march wholly away the next morning.

It may be here demanded, why a matter of so great moment should be so slenderly regarded, as that the Generall should march with such an army against such an enemy, before he knew either the fulnesse of his owne strength, or certaine meanes how he should abide the place when he should come to it. Wherein I pray you remember the Decrees made in the Councell at Peniche, and confirmed by publique protestation the first day of our march, that our nauy should meet vs in the riuer of Lisbon, in the which was the store of all our prouisions, and so the meane of our tariance in that place, which came not, though we continued till we had no munition left to entertaine a very small fight. We are also to consider, that the King of Portugall (whether carried away with imagination by the aduertisements he receiued from the Portugals, or willing by any promise to bring such an army into his Countrey, thereby to put his fortune once more in triall) assured the Generall, that vpon his first landing, there would be a reuolt of his subiects: whereof there was some hope giuen at our first entry to Peniche, by the maner of the yeelding of that towne and fort, which made the Generall thinke it most conuenient speedily to march to the principall place, thereby to giue courage to the rest of the Countrey. The Friers also and the poore people that came vnto him, promised, that within two dayes the gentlemen and others of the Countrey would come plentifully in: within which two dayes came many more Priests, and some very few gentlemen on horsebacke; but not til we came to Torres Vedras: where they that noted the course of things how they passed, might somewhat discouer the weaknesse of that people. There they tooke two dayes more: and at the end thereof referred him till our comming to Lisbon, with assurance, that so soone as our army should be seene there, all the inhabitants would be for the King and fall vpon the Spaniards.

After two nights tariance at Lisbon, the King, as you haue heard, promised a supply of 3000 foot, and some horse: but all his appointments being expired, euen to the last of a night, all his horse could not make a cornet of 40, nor his foot furnish two ensignes fully, although they caried three, or foure colours: and these were altogether such as thought to inrich themselues by the ruine of their neighbours: for they committed more disorders in euery place where we came by spoile, then any of our owne.

The Generall, as you see, hauing done more then before his comming out of England was required by the King, and giuen credit to his many promises, euen to the breach of the last, he desisted not to perswade him to stay yet nine dayes longer: in which time he might haue engaged himselfe further, then with any honour he could come out of againe, by attempting a towne fortified, wherein were more men armed against vs, then we had to oppugne them withall, our artillery and munition being fifteene miles from vs, and our men then declining; for there was the first shew of any great sickenesse amongst them. Whereby it seemeth, that either his prelacy did much abuse him in perswading him to hopes, whereof after two or three dayes he saw no semblance: or he like a silly louer, who promiseth himselfe fauor by importuning a coy mistresse, thought by our long being before his towne, that in the end taking pity on him, they would let him in.

What end the Friers had by following him with such deuotion, I know not, but sure I am, the Laity did respite their homage till they might see which way the victory would sway; fearing to shew themselues apparently vnto him, least the Spaniard should after our departure (if we preuailed not) call them to account: yet sent they vnder hand messages to him of obedience, thereby to saue their owne, if he became King; but indeed very well contented to see the Spaniards and vs try by blowes, who should carry away the crowne. For they be of so base a mould, as they can very wel subiect themselues to any gouernment, where they may liue free from blowes, and haue liberty to become rich, being loth to endure hazzard either of life or goods. For durst they haue put on any minds thorowly to reuolt, they had three woonderfull good occasions offered them during our being there.

Themselues did in generall confesse, that there were not aboue 5000 Spaniards in that part of the Countrey, of which number the halfe were out of the towne till the last day of our march: during which time, how easily they might haue preuailed against the rest, any man may conceiue. But vpon our approch they tooke them all in, and combined themselues in generall to the Cardinall.

The next day after our comming thither, when the sally was made vpon vs by their most resolute Spaniards, how easily might they haue kept them out, or haue giuen vs the gate which was held for their retreat, if they had had any thought thereof?

And two dayes after our comming to Cascais, when 6000 Spaniards and Portugals came against vs as farre as S. Iulians by land, as you shal presently heare (all which time I thinke there were not many Spaniards left in the towne) they had a more fit occasion to shew their deuotion to the King, then any could be offered by our tarying there. And they could not doubt, that if they had shut them out, but that we would haue fought with them vpon that aduantage, hauing sought them in Galitia vpon disaduantage to beat them: and hauing taken so much paines to seeke them at their owne houses, whereof we gaue sufficient testimony in the same accident. But I thinke the feare of the Spaniard had taken so deepe impression within them, as they durst not attempt any thing against them vpon any hazzard.

For, what ciuill countrey hath euer suffered themselues to be conquered so few men as they were; to be depriued of their naturall King, and to be tyrannized ouer thus long, but they? And what countrey, liuing in slauery vnder a stranger whom they naturally hate, hauing an army in the field to fight for them and their liberty, would lie still with the yoke vpon their necks, attending if any strangers would vnburthen them, without so much as rousing themselues vnder it, but they? They will promise much in speeches, for they be great talkers, whom the Generall had no reason to distrust without triall, and therefore marched on into their countrey: but they performed little in action, whereof we could haue had no proofe without this thorow triall. Wherein he hath discouered their weaknesse, and honorably performed more then could be in reason expected of him: which had he not done, would not these maligners, who seeke occasions of slander, haue reported him to be suspicious of a people, of whose infidelity he had no testimony: and to be fearefull without cause, if he had refused to giue credit to their promises without any aduenture? Let no friuolous questionist therefore further enquire why he marched so many dayes to Lisbon, and taried there so small a while.

The next morning, seeing no performance of promise kept, he gaue order for our marching away; himselfe, the Earle of Essex, and Sir Roger Williams remaining with the stand that was made in the high street, till the whole army was drawen into the field, and marched out of the towne, appointing Captaine Richard wingfield, and Captaine Anthony Wingfield in the arrereward of them with the shot; thinking that the enemy (as it was most likely) would haue issued out vpon our rising; but they were otherwise aduised. When we were come into the field, euery battalion fell into that order which by course appertained vnto them, and so marched that night vnto Cascais. Had we marched thorow this Countrey as enemies, our Souldiours had beene well supplied in all their wants: but had we made enemies of the Suburbs of Lisbon, we had beene the richest army that euer went out of England: for besides the particular wealth of euery house, there were many Warehouses by the water side full of all sorts of rich marchandizes.

In our march that day the gallies which had somewhat, but not much, annoyed vs at Lisbon, (for that our way lay along the riuer) attended vs till we were past S. Iulians, bestowing many shot amongst vs, but did no harme at all, sauing that they strooke off a gentlemans legend, and killed the Sergeant majors moile vnder him. The horsemen also followed vs afarre off, and cut off as many sicke men as were not able to holde in marche, nor we had cariage for.

After we had bene two dayes at Cascais, we had intelligence by a Frier, that the enemy was marching strongly towards vs, and then came as farre as S. Iulian: which newes was so welcome to the Earle of Essex and the Generals, as they offered euery one of them to giue the messenger an hundred crownes if they found them in the place; for the Generall desiring nothing more then to fight with them in field roome, dispatched that night a messenger with a trumpet, by whom he writ a cartell to the Generall of their army, wherein he gaue them the lie, in that it was by them reported that we dislodged from Lisbon in disorder and feare of them (which indeed was most false) for that it was fiue of the clocke in the morning before we fell into armes, and then went in such sort, as they had no courage to follow out vpon vs. Also he challenged him therein, to meet him the next morning with his whole army, if he durst attend his comming, and there to try out the iustnesse of their quarrel by battell: by whom also the Earle of Essex (who preferring the honor of the cause, which was his countreys, before his owne safety) sent a particular cartel, offering himselfe against any of theirs, if they had any of his quality; or if they would not admit of that; sixe, eight, or tenne, or as many as they would appoint, should meet so many of theirs in the head of our battell to trie their fortunes with them; and that they should haue assurance of their returne and honourable intreaty.

The Generall accordingly made all his army ready by three of the clocke in the morning and marched euen to the place where they had encamped, but they were dislodged in the night in great disorder, being taken with a sudden feare that we had bene come vpon them, as the Generall was the next day certainly informed: so as the Trumpet followed them to Lisbon, but could not get other answere to either of his letters, but threatening to be hanged, for daring to bring such a message. Howbeit the Generall had caused to be written vpon the backside of their passport, that if they did offer any violence vnto the messengers, he would hang the best prisoners he had of theirs: which made them to aduise better of the matter, and to returne them home; but without answere.

After our army came to Cascais, and the castle summoned, the Castellan thereof granted, that vpon fiue or sixe shot of the canon he would deliuer the same, but not without sight thereof. The Generall thinking that his distresse within had bene such for want of men or victuals as he could not holde it many dayes, because he saw it otherwise defensible enough, determined rather to make him yeeld to that necessity then to bring the cannon, and therefore onely set a gard vpon the same, lest any supply of those things which he wanted should be brought vnto them. But he still standing vpon those conditions, the Generall about two dayes before he determined to goe to Sea, brought three or foure pieces of battery against it: vpon the first fire whereof he surrendered, and compounded to go away with his baggage and armies; he had one canon, two culuerings, one basiliske, and three or foure other field pieces, threescore and fiue Souldiours, very good store of munition and victualles enough in the Castle: insomuch as he might haue held the same longer then the Generall had in purpose to tarry there. One company of footmen was put into the guard thereof, till the artillery was taken out, and our army embarked; which without hauing that fort, we could not without great peril haue done. When we were ready to set saile (one halfe of the fort being by order from the Generall blowen vp by mine) the company was drawne away.

During the time we lay in the road, our fleet began the second of Iune, and so continued six dayes after to fetch in some hulks to the number of threescore, of Dansik, Stetin, Rostock, Lubeck and Hamburgh, laden with Spanish goods, and as it seemed for the kings prouision, and going for Lisbon: their principall lading was Corne, Masts, Cables, Copper, and waxe: amongst which were some of great burthen woonderful well builded for sailing, which had no great lading in them, and therefore it was thought that they were brought for the kings prouision, to reinforce his decayed nauy: whereof there was the greater likelyhood, in that the owner of the greatest of them which caried two misnes, was knowen to be very inward with the Cardinall, who rather then he would be taken with his ships, committed himself vnto his small boat, wherein he recouered S. Sebastians: into the which our men, that before were in flieboats, were shipped, and the flieboats sent home with an offer of corne, to the value of their hire. But the winde being good for them for Rochel, they chuse rather to lose their corne then the winde, and so departed. The Generall also sent his horses with them, and from thence shipped them into England.

The third of Iune, Colonell Deuereux and Colonell Sidney, being both very sicke, departed for England, who in the whole iourney had shewed themselues very forward to all seruices, and in their departure very vnwilling to leave vs: that day we imbarked all our army, but lay in the road vntill the eight thereof.

The sixt day the Earle of Essex, vpon receit of letters from her Maiesty, by them that brought in the victuals, presently departed towards England, with whom Sir Roger Williams was very desirous to go, but found the Generalls very vnwilling he should do so, in that he bare the next place vnto them, and if they should miscarry, was to command the army. And the same day there came vnto vs two small barks that brought tidings of some other shippes come out of England with victuals, which were passed vpwards to the Cape: for meeting with whom, the second day after we set saile for that place, in purpose after our meeting with them to go with the Iles of Açores, the second day, which was the ninth, we met with them comming backe againe towards vs, whose prouision little answered our expectation. Notwithstanding we resolued to continue our course for the Ilands.

About this time was the Marchant Royall, with three or foure other ships, sent to Peniche, to fetch away the companies that were left there; but Captaine Barton hauing receiued letters from the Generals that were sent ouerland, was departed before not being able by reason of the enemies speedy marching thither either to bring away the artillery, or all his men, according to the direction those letters gaue him; for he was no sooner gone than the enemy possessed both town and castle, and shot at our ships as they came into the road.

At this time also was the Ambassador from the Emperor of Marocco, called Reys Hamet Bencasamp, returned, and with him M. Ciprian, a gentleman of good place and desert, was sent from Don Antonio, and Captaine Ousley from the Generals to the Emperor.

The next morning the nine gallies which were sent not fiue dayes before out of Andaluzia for the strengthening of the riuer of Lisbon (which being ioyned with the other twelue that were there before, though we lay hard by them at S. Iulians, durst neuer make any attempt against vs) vpon our departure from thence returning home, and in the morning being a very dead calme, in the dawning thereof, fell in the winde of our fleet, in the vttermost part whereof they assailed one stragling barke of Plimmouth, of the which Captaine Cauerly being Captaine of the land company, with his Lieutenant, the Master and some of the Mariners abandoned the ship, and betooke them to ship-boats, whereof one, in which the Master and Captaine were, was ouerrunne with the gallies, and they drowned. There were also two hulks stragled farre from the strength of the other ships, which were so calmed, as neither they could get to vs, or we to them, though all the great shippes towed with their boats to haue releiued them, but could not be recouered; in one of which was Captaine Minshaw with his company, who fought with them to the last, yea after his ship was on fire, which whether it was fired by himselfe or by them we could not well discerne, but might easily iudge by his long and good fight, that the enemy could not but sustaine much loose: who setting also vpon one other hulke wherein was but a Lieutenant, were by the valour of the Lieutenant put off although they had first beaten her with their artillery, and attempted to boord her. And seeing also another hulke a league off, a sterne off vs, they made towards her; but finding that she made ready to fight with them, they durst not further attempt her: whereby it seemed, their losse being great in other fights, they were loth to proceed any further.

From that day till the 19 of Iune, our direction from the Generall was, that if the wind were Northerly, we should plie for the Açores; but if Southerly, for the Iles of Bayon. We lay with contrary windes, about that place and the Rocke, till the Southerly winde preuailing carried vs to Bayon: part of our ships to the number of 25, in a great winde which was two dayes before, hauing lost the Admirals and the fleet, according to their direction, fell in the morning of that day with Bayon, among whom was Sir Henry Norris in the Ayde; who had in purpose (if the Admirals had not come in) with some 500 men out of them all to haue landed, and attempted the taking of Vigo. The rest of the fleet held with Generall Drake, who though he were two dayes before put vpon those Ilands, cast off againe to sea for the Açores: but remembering how vnprouided he was for iourney and seeing that he had lost company of his great ships, returned for Bayon, and came in there that night in the euening where he passed vp the riuer more than a mile aboue Vigo.

[Sidenote: Vigo taken.] The next morning we landed as many as were able to fight, which were not in the whole aboue 2000 men (for in the 17 dayes we continued on boord we had cast many of our men ouerboord) with which number the Colonell generall marched to the towne of Vigo, neere the which when he approched, he sent Captaine Anthony Wingfield with a troupe of shot to enter one side of the same, who found vpon euery streets end a strong barricade, but altogether abandoned; for hauing entered the towne, he found but one man therein, but might see them making way before him to Bayon. On the other side of the towne entred Generall Drake with Captaine Richard Wingfield, whose approch on that side (I thinke) made them leaue the places they had so artificially made for defence: there were also certaine shippes sent with the Vice-admirall to lie close before the towne to beat vpon the same with their artillery.

In the afternoone were sent 300 vnder the conduct of Captaine Petuin and Captaine Henry Poure, to burne another village betwixt that and Bayon, called Borsis, and as much of the country as the day would giue them leaue to do; which was a very pleasant rich valley: but they burnt it all, houses and corne, as did others on the other side of the towne, both that and the next day, so as the countrey was spoiled seuen or eight miles in length. There was found great store of wine in the towne, but not any thing els: for the other dayes warning of the shippes that came first in, gaue them a respit to cary all away.

[Sidenote: Vigo burned.] The next morning by breake of the day the Colonell generall (who in the absence of the Generalls that were on boord their ships, commanded that night on shore) caused all our companies to be drawen out of the towne, and sent in two troups to put fire in euery house of the same: which done, we imbarked againe.

This day there were certaine Mariners which (without any direction) put themselues on shore, on the contrary side of the riuer from vs for pillage; who were beaten by the enemy from their boats, and punished by the Generals for their offer, in going without allowance.

The reasons why we attempted nothing against Bayon were before shewed to be want of artillery, and may now be alledged to be the small number of our men: who should haue gone against so strong a plade, manned with very good souldiers, as was shewed by Iuan de Vera taken at the Groine, who confessed that there were sixe hundred olde Souldiers in garrison there of Flanders, and the Tercios of Naples, lately also returned out of the iourney of England,

Vnder the leading of

Capitan Puebla,
Christofero Vasques de Viralta a souldier of Flanders.
Don Pedro Camascho, del tercio de Napoles.
Don Francisco de Cespedes.
Cap. Iuan de Solo, del tercio de Naples.
Don Diego de Cassaua.
Cap. Sauban.

Also he sayth there be 18 pieces of brasse, and foure of yron, lately layed vpon the walles of the towne, besides them that were there before.

The same day the Generals seeing what weake estate our army was drawn into by sicknesse, determined to man and victuall twenty of the best ships for the Ilands of Açores with Generall Drake, to see if he could meet with the Indian fleet, and Generall Norris to returne home with the rest: And for the shifting of men and victualles accordingly, purposed the next morning to fall downe to the Ilands of Bayon againe, and to remaine there that day. But Generall Drake, according to their apointment, being vnder saile neuer strooke at the Ilands, but put straight to sea; whom all the fleet followed sauing three and thirty, which being in the riuer further then he, and at the entrance out of the same, finding the winde and tide too hard against them, were inforced to cast ancre there for that night; amongst whom, by good fortune, was the Foresight, and in her Sir Edward Norris. And the night folowing, Generall Norris being driuen from the rest of the Fleet by a great storme, (for all that day was the greatest storme we had all the time we were out) came againe into the Ilands, but not without great perill, he being forced to trust to a Spanish Fisherman (who was taken two dayes before at sea) to bring him in.

The next morning he called a council of as many as he found there, holding the purpose he had concluded with sir Francis Drake the day before, and directed all their courses for England, tarrying there all that day to water and helpe such with victuall, as were left in wonderfull distresse by hauing the victuals that came last, caried away the day before to sea.

[Sidenote: Their returne to Plimmouth.] The next day he set saile, and the 10 day after, which was the 2 of Iuly came into Plimmouth, where he found sir Francis Drake and all the Queens ships, with many of the others but not all; for the Fleet was dispersed into other harbors, some led by a desire of returning from whence they came, and some being possessed of the hulks sought other Ports from their Generals eie, where they might make their priuate commoditie of them, as they haue done to their great aduantage.

Presently vpon their arriual there, the Generals dissolued all the armie sauing 8 companies which are yet held together, giuing euery souldier fiue shillings in money, and the armies hee bare to make money of, which was more then could by any means be due vnto them: for they were not in seruice three moneths, in which time they had their victuals, which no man would value at lesse then halfe their pay, for such is the allowance in her maiesties ships to her mariners, so as there remained but 10 shillings a moneth more to be paid, for which there was not any priuate man but had apparel and furniture to his owne vse, so as euery common souldier discharged, receiued more in money, victuals, apparel and furniture, then his pay did amount vnto.

Notwithstanding, there be euen in the same place where those things haue passed, that either do not or will not conceiue the souldiers estate, by comparing their pouertie and the shortness of the time together, but lay some iniuries vpon the Generals and the action. Where, and by the way, but especially here in London, I find there haue bene some false prophets gone before vs, telling strange tales. For as our countrey doeth bring foorth many gallant men, who desirous of honour doe put themselues into the actions thereof, so doeth it many more dull spirited, who though their thoughts reach not so high as others, yet doe they listen how other mens acts doe passe, and either beleeuing what any man will report vnto them, are willingly caried away into errors, or tied to some greater mans faith, become secretaries against a noted trueth. The one sort of these doe take their opinions from the high way side, or at the furthest go no further then Pauls to enquire what hath bene done in this voiage; where if they meet with any, whose capacitie before their going out could not make them liue, nor their valour maintaine their reputation, and who went onely for spoile, complaining on the hardnesse and misery thereof, they thinke they are bound to giue credite to these honest men who were parties therein, and in very charitie become of their opinions. The others to make good the faction they had entred into, if they see any of those malecontents (as euery iourney yeeldeth some) doe runne vnto them like tempting spirits to confirme them in their humour, with assurance that they foresaw before our going out what would become thereof.

Be ye not therefore too credulous in beleeuing euery report: for you see there haue bene many more beholders of these things that haue passed, then actors in the same; who by their experience, not hauing the knowledge of the ordinary wants of the warre, haue thought, that to lie hard, not to haue their meat well dressed, to drinke sometimes water, to watch much, or to see men die and be slaine, was a miserable thing; and not hauing so giuen their mindes to the seruice, as they are any thing instructed thereby, doe for want of better matter discourse ordinarily of these things: whereas the iourney (if they had with that iudgement seene into it, which their places required) hath giuen them far more honorable purpose and argument of discourse.

[Sidenote: A worthy question dilated.] These mens discontentments and mislikings before our comming home haue made mee labour thus much to instruct you in the certaintie of euery thing, because I would not willingly haue you miscaried in the indgements of them, wherein you shall giue me leaue somewhat to dilate vpon a question, which I onely touched in the beginning of my letter, namely, whether it bee more expedient for our estate to maintain an offensiue war against the king of Spaine in the Low countries, or as in this iourney, to offend him in his neerer territories, seeing the grounds of arguing thereof are taken from the experience which the actions of this iourney haue giuen vs.

There is no good subiect that will make question, whether it be behoofeful for vs to hold friendship with these neighbours of ours or no, as well in respect of the infinite proportion of their shipping, which must stand either with vs or against vs; as of the commoditie of their harbors, especially that of Vlishing, by the fauour whereof our Nauie may continually keepe the Narrow seas, and which would harbour a greater Fleete agaynst vs, then the Spaniard shall need to annoy vs withall, who being now distressed by our common enemie, I thinke it most expedient for our safetie to defend them, and if it may be, to giue them a reentrie into that they haue of late yeeres lost vnto him. The one without doubt her maiestie may do without difficultie, and in so honorable sort as he shal neuer be able to dispossesse her or them of any the townes they now hold. But if any man thinke that the Spaniard may be expelled from thence more speedily or conueniently by keeping an armie there, then by sending one against him into his owne countrey: let him foresee of how many men and continuall supplies that armie must consist, and what intollerable expenses it requireth. And let him thinke by the example of the duke of Alua, when the prince of Orenge had his great armie agaynst him; and of Don Iuan, when the States had their mightie assembly against him; how this wise enemie, with whom we are to deale, may but by prolonging to fight with vs, leaue vs occasions enough for our armie within few moneths to mutine and breake; or by keeping him in his townes leaue vs a spoyled field: where though our prouision may bee such of our owne as we starue ['staure' in source text—KTH] not, yet is our weaknesse in any strange country such, as with sicknes and miserie we shal be dissolued. And let him not forget what a continual burthen we hereby lay vpon vs, in that to repossesse those countreys which have been lately lost, wil be a warre of longer continuance then we shall be able to endure.

In the very action whereof, what should hinder the king of Spaine to bring his forces home vnto vs? For it is certaine he hath long since set downe in councell, that there is no way for him wholy to recouer those Low countries, but by bringing the warre vpon England it selfe, which hath alwayes assisted them against him: and that being determined, and whereunto he hath bene vehemently urged by the last yeeres losse he sustained vpon our coasts, and the great dishonor this iourney hath laid vpon him; no doubt if we shall giue him respite to doe it, but he will mightily advance his purpose, for he is richly able thereunto, and wonderfull desirous of reuenge.

To encounter wherewith, I wish euen in true and honest zeale to my Countrey, that we were all perswaded that there is no such assured meanes for the safetie of our estate, as to busy him with a well furnished armie in Spaine, which hath so many goodly Bayes open, as we may land without impeachment as many men as shall be needfull for such an inuasion. And hauing an armie of 20000 roially furnished there, we shall not need to take much care for their payment: for shal not Lisbon be thought able to make so few men rich, when the Suburbs thereof were found so abounding in riches, as had we made enemie of them, they had largely enriched vs all? Which with what small losse it may be won, is not here to shew; but why it was not won by vs, I haue herein shewed you. Or is not the spoyle of Siuil sufficient to pay more then shall bee needful to bee sent against it, whose defence (as that of Lisbone) is onely force of men, of whom how many may for the present be raised, is not to be esteemed, because wee haue discouered what kind of men they be, euen such as will neuer abide ours in field, nor dare withstand any resolute attempt of ours agaynst them: for during the time we were in many places of their countrey, they cannot say that euer they made 20 of our men turne their faces from them. And be there not many other places of lesse difficultie to spoyle, able to satisfie our forces?

But admit, that if vpon this alarme that we haue giuen him, he tendering his naturall and neerest soile before his further remooued off gouernments, do draw his forces of old souldiers out of the Low countreys for his owne defence, is not the victory then won by drawing and holding them from thence, for the which we should haue kept an armie there at a charge by many partes greater then this, and not stirred them?

Admit further our armie be impeached from landing there, yet by keeping the Sea and possessing his principall roades, are we not in possibilitie to meet with his Indian merchants, and very like to preuent him of his prouisions comming out of the East countreys; without the which, neither the subiect of Lisbon is long able to liue, nor the king able to maintaine his Nauie? For though the countrey of Portugall doe some yeeres find themselues corne, yet are they neuer able to victuall the least part of that Citie. And albeit the king of Spaine be the richest prince in Christendome, yet can he neither draw cables, hewe masts, nor make pouder out of his mettals, but is to be supplied of them all from thence. Of whom (some will hold opinion) it is no reason to make prize, because they bee not our enemies: and that our disagreeance with them will impeach the trade of our marchants, and so impouerish our countrey, of whose mind I can hardly be drawn to be: For if my enemie fighting with me doe breake his sword, so as I thereby haue the aduantage against him; what shall I thinke of him that putteth a new sword into his hand to kill me withall? And may it not bee thought more fitting for vs in these times to loose our trades of Cloth, then by suffering these mischiefes, to put in hazard whether we shall haue a countrey left to make cloth in or no? And yet though neither Hamburgh, Embden, nor Stode doe receiue our cloth, the necessary vse thereof in all places is such, as they will find means to take it from vs with our sufficient commoditie.

And admit (which were impossible) that we damnifie him neither at sea nor land (for vnlesse it be with a much more mightie armie then ours, he shall neuer be able to withstand vs) yet shall we by holding him at his home, free our selues from the warre at our owne wals; the benefit whereof let them consider that best can iudge, and haue obserued the difference of inuading, and being inuaded; the one giuing courage to the souldier, in that it doeth set before him commoditie and reputation; the other a fearefull terror to the countrey-man, who if by chance he play the man yet is he neuer the richer: and who knowing many holes to hide himselfe in, will trie them all before he put his life in perill by fighting: whereas the Inuader casteth vp his account before hee goeth out, and being abroad must fight to make himselfe way, as not knowing what place or strength to trust vnto. I will not say what I obserued in our countrey-men when the enemy offred to assaile vs here: but I wish that all England knew what terror we gaue to the same people that frighted vs, by visiting them at their owne houses.

Were not Alexanders fortunes great against the mightie Darius, onely in that his Macedonians thirsted after the wealth of Persia, and were bound to fight it out to the last man, because the last man knew no safer way to saue himselfe then by fighting? Whereas the Persians either trusting to continue stil masters of their wealth by yeelding to the Inuader, began to practise against their owne king: or hauing more inward hopes, did hide themselues euen to the last, to see what course the Conquerour would take in his Conquest. And did not the aduise of Scipio, though mightily impugned at the first, prooue very sound and honourable to his countrey? Who seeing the Romans wonderfully amazed at the neerenesse of their enemies Forces, and the losses they daily sustained by them, gaue counsell rather by way of diuersion to cary an army into Afrike, and there to assaile, then by a defensiue warre at home to remaine subiect to the common spoiles of an assailing enemie. Which being put in execution drew the enemie from the gates of Rome, and Scipio returned home with triumph: albeit his beginnings at the first were not so fortunate against them, as ours haue bene in this smal time against the Spaniard. The good successe whereof may encourage vs to take armes resolutely against him. And I beseech God it may stirre vp all men that are particularly interested therein, to bethinke themselues how small a matter will assure them of their safetie, by holding the Spaniard at a Baie, so farre off: whereas, if we giue him leaue quietly to hatch and bring foorth his preparations, it will be with danger to vs all.

He taketh not armes against vs by any pretense of title to the crowne of this realme, nor led altogether with an ambicious desire to command our countrey, but with hatred towrrds our whole Nation and religion. Her maiesties Scepter is already giuen by Bull to another, the honours of our Nobilitie are bestowed for rewards vpon his attendants, our Clergie, our Gentlemen, our Lawyers, yea all the men of what conditon soeuer are offered for spoyle vnto the common souldier. Let euery man therefore, in defence of the liberty and plentie he hath of long enjoyed, offer a voluntarie contribution of the smallest part of their store for the assurance of the rest. It were not much for euery Iustice of peace, who by his blew coat proteceth the properest and most seuiceable men at euery muster from the warres, to contribute the charge that one of these idle men doe put him to for one yeere: nor for the Lawyer, who riseth by the dissensions of his neighbours, to take but one yeeres gifts (which they call fees) out of his coffers. What would it hinder euery officer of the Exchequer, and other of her Maiesties courts, who without checks doe suddenly grow to great wealth, honestly to bring foorth the mysticall commoditie of one yeeres profits? Or the Clergie, who looke precisely for the Tenths of euery mans increase, simply to bring forth the Tenth of one yeeres gathering, and in thankfulnesse to her Maiestie (who hath continued for all our safeties a most chargeable warre both at land & sea) bestow the same for her honor & their own assurance, vpon an army which may make this bloody enemy so to know himselfe and her Maiesties power, as he shall bethinke him what it is to mooue a stirring people? Who, though they haue receiued some small checke by the sicknesse of this last iourney, yet doubt I not, but if it were knowen, that the like voyage were to bee supported by a generalitie, (that might and would beare the charge of a more ample prouision) but there would of all sortes most willingly put themselues into the same: some caried with an honourable desire to be in action, and some in loue of such would affectionately folow their fortunes; some in thirsting to reuenge the death and hurts of their brethren, kinred, and friends: and some in hope of the plentifull spoyles to be found in those countreys, hauing bene there already and returned poore, would desire to goe againe, with an expectation to make amends for the last: and all, in hatred of that cowardly proud Nation, and in contemplation of the true honour of our owne, would with courage take armes to hazard their liues agaynst them, whom euery good Englishman is in nature bound to hate as an implacable enemie to England, thirsting after our blood, and labouring to ruine our land, with hope to bring vs vnder the yoke of perpetuall slauerie.

Against them is true honour to be gotten, for that we shall no sooner set foot in their land, but that euery step we tread will yeeld vs new occasion of action, which I wish the gallantrie of our Countrey rather to regard then to folow those soft vnprofitable pleasures wherein they now consume their time and patrimonie. And in two or three townes of Spaine is the wealth of all Europe gathered together, which are the Magasins of the fruits and profits of the East and West Indies, whereunto I wish our yong able men, who (against the libertie they are borne vnto) terme themselues seruing men, rather to bend their desires and affections, then to attend their double liuerie and 40 shillings by the yeere wages, and the reuersion of the old Copy-hold, for carying a dish to their masters table. But let me here reprehend my selfe and craue pardon for entring into a matter of such state and consequence, the care whereof is already laid vpon a most graue and honorable counsell, who will in their wisdoms foresee the dangers that may be threatned agaynst vs. And why do I labour to disquiet the securitie of these happy gentlemen, and the trade of those honest seruing men, by perswading them to the warres when I see the profession thereof so slenderly esteemed? For though all our hope of peace be frustrate, and our quarels determinable by the sword: though our enemie hath by his owne forces, and his pensionaries industry, confined the united Prouinces into a narow roume, and almost disunited the same: if he be now in a good way to harbor himselfe, in the principall hauens of France, from whence he may front vs at pleasure: yea though we are to hope for nothing but a bloodie warre, nor can trust to any helpe but Armes; yet how far the common sort are from reuerencing or regarding any persons of condition, was too apparant in the returne of this our iourney, wherein the base and common souldier hath bene tollerated to speake against the Captaine, and the souldier and Captaine against the Generals, and wherein mechanicall and men of base condicion doe dare to censure the doings of them, of whose acts they are not woorthy to talke.

The ancient graue degree of the Prelacie is vpheld, though Martin raile neuer so much, and the Lawyer is after the old maner worshipped, whosoeuer inueigh against him. But the ancient English honour is taken from our men of war, and their profession in disgrace, though neuer so necessary. Either we commit idolatry to Neptune, and will put him alone stil to fight for vs as he did the last yeere, or we be inchanted with some diuelish opinions, that trauell nothing more then to diminish the reputation of them, vpon whose shoulders the burden of our defence against the enemie must lie when occasion shall be offred. For whensoeuer he shall set foote vpon our land, it is neither the preaching of the Clergie that can turne him out againe, nor the pleading of any Lawyers that can remoue him out of possession: no, then they will honour them whom now they thinke not on, and then must those men stand betweene them and their perils, who are now thought vnwoorthy of any estimation.

May the burning of one towne (which cost the king then being six times as much as this hath done her maiestie, wherein were lost seuen times as many men as in any one seruice of this iourney, and taried not the tenth part of our time in the enemies Countrey) be by our elders so highly reputed and sounded out by the historie of the Realme: and can our voyage be so meanly esteemed, wherein we burned both townes and Countreys without the losse of fortie men in any such attempt?

Did our kings in former times reward some with the greatest titles of honour for ouerthrowing a number of poore Scots, who, after one battell lost, were neuer able to reenforce themselues against him; and shall they in this time who haue ouerthrowen our mightie enemie in battell, and taken his roiall Standerd in the field, besieged the marquesse of Saralba 15 dayes together, that should haue bene the Generall of the Armie against vs, brought away so much of his artillerie (as I haue before declared) be vnwoorthily esteemed of?

It is possible that some in some times should receiue their reward for looking vpon an enemie, and ours in this time not receiue so much as thanks for hauing beaten an enemie at handie strokes?

But is it true that no man shall bee a prophet in his Countrey: and for my owne part I will lay aside my Armes till that profession shal haue more reputation, and liue with my friends in the countrey, attending either some more fortunate time to vse them, or some other good occasion to make me forget them.

But what? shall the blind opinion of this monster, a beast of many heads, (for so hath the generaltie of old bene termed) cause me to neglect the profession from whence I chalenge some reputation, or diminish my loue to my countrey, which hitherto hath nourished me? No, it was for her sake I first tooke armes, and for her sake I will handle them so long as I shall be able to vse them: not regarding how some men in private conuenticles do measure mens estimations by their owne humors; nor how euery popular person doeth giue sentence on euery mans actions by the worst accidents. But attending the gracious aspect of our dread Soueraigne, who neuer yet left vertue vnrewarded: and depending vpon the iustice of her most rare and graue aduisors, who by their heedie looking into euery mans worth, do giue encouragement to the vertuous to exceed others in vertue: and assuring you that there shall neuer any thing happen more pleasing vnto me, then that I may once againe bee a partie in some honorable journey against the Spaniard in his owne countrey, I will cease my complaint: and with them that deserue beyond me, patiently endure the vnaduised censure of our malicious reproouers.

If I haue seemed in the beginning hereof troublesome vnto you, in the discouering of those impediments, and answering the slanders which by the vulgar malicious and mutinous sort are laid as blemishes vpon the iourney, and reprochse vpon the Generals (hauing indeed proceeded from other heads:) let the necessitie of conseruing the reputation of the action in generall, and the honors of our Generals in particular, bee my sufficient excuse: the one hauing by the vertue of the other made our countrey more dreaded and renowmed, then any act that euer England vndertooke before. Or if you haue thought my perswasible discourse long in the latter end; let the affectionate desire of my countreys good be therein answerable for me. And such as it is I pray you accept it, as only recommended to your selfe, and not to be deliuered to the publique view of the world, lest any man take offence thereat: which some particular men may seeme iustly to do, in that hauing deserued very well, I should not herein giue them their due considerations: whereas my purpose in this priuate discourse hath bene onely to gratifie you with a touch of those principall matters that haue passed, wherein I haue onely taken notes of those men who either commaunded euery seruice, or were of chiefest marke: if therefore you shall impart the same to one, and he to another, and so it passe through my hands, I know not what constructions would be made thereof to my preiudice; for that the Hares eares may happily be taken for hornes. Howbeit I hold it very necessary (I must confesse) that there should be some true manifestation made of these things: but be it far from me to be the author thereof, as very vnfit to deliuer my censure of any matter in publique, and most vnwilling to haue my weaknesse discouered in priuate. And so I doe leaue you to the happy successe of your accustomed good exercises, earnestly wishing that there may be some better acceptance made of the fruits of your studies, then there hath bene of our hazards in the wars. From London the 30 of August 1589.

* * * * *

The escape of the Primrose a tall ship of London, from before the towne of Bilbao in Biscay: which ship the Corrigidor of the same Prouince, accompanied with 97 Spaniards, offered violently to arrest, and was defeated of his purpose, and brought prisoner into England.

Whereunto is added the Kings Commission for a generall imbargment or arrest of all English, Netherlandish, and Easterlings ships, written in Barcelona the 19 of May 1585.

It is not vnknowen vnto the world what danger our English shippes haue lately escaped, how sharpely they haue beene intreated, and howe hardly they haue beene assaulted: so that the valiancie of those that mannaged them is worthy remembrance. And therefore in respect of the couragious attempt and valiant enterprise of the ship called the Primrose of London, which hath obteined renowne, I haue taken in hande to publish the trueth thereof, to the intent that it may be generally knowen to the rest of the English ships, that by the good example of this the rest may in time of extremitie aduenture to doe the like: to the honor of the Realme, and the perpetuall remembrance of themselues: The maner whereof was at followeth.

Vppon Wednesday being the sixe and twentieth day of May 1585, the shippe called the Primrose being of one hundred and fiftie tunnes, lying without the bay of Bilbao, hauing beene there two dayes, there came a Spanish pinnesse to them, wherein was the Corrigidor and sixe others with him: these came aboord the Primrose, seeming to be Marchantes of Biscay, or such like, bringing Cherries with them, and spake very friendly to the Maister of the ship, whose name was Foster, and he in courteous wise, bad them welcome, making them the best cheere that he could with beere, beefe, and bisket, wherewith that ship was well furnished: and while they were thus in banquetting with the Maister, foure of the seuen departed in the sayd Pinnesse, and went backe againe to Bilbao: the other three stayed, and were very pleasant for the time. But Master Foster misdoubting some danger secretly gaue speech that he was doubtfull of these men what their intent was; neuerthelesse he sayd nothing, nor seemed in any outward wise to mistrust them at all. Foorthwith there came a ship-boate wherein were seuentie persons being Marchants and such like of Biscay: and besides this boate, there came also the Pinnesse which before had brought the other three, in which Pinnesse there came foure and twentie, as the Spaniards themselues since confessed. These made towards the Primrose, and being come thither, there came aboord the Corrigidor with three or foure of his men: but Master Foster seeing this great multitude desired that there might no more come aboord, but that the rest should stay in their boates, which was granted: neuerthelesse they tooke small heede of these wordes; for on a suddaine they came foorth of the boate, entring the shippe, euery Spaniarde taking him to his Rapier which they brought in the boate, with other weapons, and a drumme wherewith to triumph ouer them. Thus did the Spaniards enter the shippe, plunging in fiercely vpon them, some planting themselues vnder the decke, some entring the Cabbens, and the multitude attending their pray. Then the Corrigidor hauing an officer with him which bore a white wand in his hand, sayd to the master of the ship: Yeeld your selfe, for you are the kings prisoner: whereat the Maister sayd to his men, We are betrayed. Then some of them set daggers to his breast, and seemed in furious manner as though they would haue slaine him, meaning nothing lesse then to doe any such act, for all that they sought was to bring him and his men safe aliue to shore. Whereat the Maister was amazed, and his men greatly discomfited to see themselues readie to be conueyed euen to the slaughter: notwithstanding some of them respecting the daunger of the Maister, and seeing how with themselues there was no way but present death if they were once landed among the Spaniards, they resolued themselues eyther to defend the Maister, and generally to shunne that daunger, or else to die and be buried in the middest of the sea, rather then to suffer themselues to come into the tormentors hands: and therefore in very bold and manly sort some tooke them to their iauelings, lances, bore-speares, and shot, which they had set in readinesse before, and hauing fiue Calieuers readie charged, which was all the small shot they had, those that were vnder the hatches or the grate did shoote vp at the Spaniards that were ouer their heads, which shot so amazed the Spaniards on the suddaine, as they could hardly tell which way to escape the daunger, fearing this their small shot to be of greater number then it was: others in very manlike sort dealt about among them, shewing themselues of that courage with bore-speares and lances, that they dismayed at euery stroke two or three Spaniards. Then some of them desired the Maister to commaund his men to cease and holde their handes, but hee answered that such was the courage of the English Nation in defence of their owne liues, that they would slay them and him also: and therefore it lay not in him to doe it. Now did their blood runne about the ship in great quantitie, some of them being shot in betweene the legges, the bullets issuing foorth at their breasts, some cut in the head, some thrust into the bodie, and many of them very sore wounded, so that they came not so fast in on the one side, but now they tumbled as fast ouer boord on both sides with their weapons in their handes, some falling into the sea, and some getting into their boates, making haste towardes the Citie. And this is to be noted, that although they came very thicke thither, there returned but a small companie of them, neither is it knowen as yet how many of them were slaine or drowned, onely one English man was then slaine, whose name was Iohn Tristram, and sixe other hurt. It was great pitie to behold how the Spaniards lay swimming in the sea, and were not able to saue their liues. Foure of them taking hold of the shippe were for pities sake taken vp againe by Maister Foster and his men, not knowing what they were: all the Spaniards bosomes were stuft with paper, to defend them from the shot, and these foure hauing some wounds were dressed by the surgion of the shippe. One of them was the Corrigidor himselfe, who is gouernour of a hundred Townes and Cities in Spaine, his liuing by his office being better then sixe hundred pound yerely. This skirmish happened in the euening about sixe of the clocke, after they had laden twenty Tunne of goods and better out of the sayd ship: which goods were deliuered by two of the same ship, whose names were Iohn Burrell and Iohn Brodbanke, who being on shore were apprehended and stayed.

[Sidenote: The Corrigidor of Bilbao taken and brought to London.] After this valiant enterprise of eight and twentie English men against 97 Spaniards, they saw it was in vaine for them to stay, and therefore set vp sayles, and by Gods prouidence auoyded all daunger, brought home the rest of their goods, and came thence with all expedition: and (God be thanked) arriued safely in England neere London on Wednesday being the 8 day of Iune 1585. In which their returne to England the Spaniards that they brought with them offered fiue hundred crownes to be set on shore in any place: which, seeing the Maister would not doe, they were content to be ruled by him and his companie, and craued mercie at their hands. And after Master Foster demaunded why they came in such sort to betray and destroy them, the Corrigidor answered, that it was not done onely of themselues, but by the commandement of the king himselfe; and calling for his hose which were wet, did plucke foorth the kings Commission, by which he was authorized to doe all that he did: the Copie whereof followeth, being translated out of Spanish.

The Spanish kings commision for the generall imbargment or arrest of the English, &c.

Licentiat de Escober, my Corigidor of my Signorie of Biskay, I haue caused a great fleete to be put in readinesse in the hauen of Lisbone, and the riuer of Siuill. There is required for the Souldiers, armour, victuals, and munition, that are to be imployed in the same great store of shipping of all series against the time of seruice, and to the end there may be choise made of the best, vpon knowledge of their burden and goodnesse; I doe therefore require of you, that presently vpon the arriuall of this carrier, and with as much dissimulation as may be (that the matter may not be knowen vntill it be put into execution) you take order for the staying and arresting (with great foresight) of all the shipping that may be found vpon the coast, and in the portes of the sayd Signorie, excepting none of Holand, Zeland, Easterland, Germanie, England, and other Prouinces that are in rebellion against mee, sauing those of France which being litle, and of small burden and weake, are thought vnfit to serue the turne. And the stay being thus made, you shall haue a speciall care that such marchandize as the sayd shippes or hulkes haue brought, whether they be all or part vnladen, may bee taken out, and that the armour, munition, tackels, sayles, and victuals

- 50 -

may be safely bestowed, as also that it may be well foreseene, that none of the shippes or men escape away. Which things being thus executed, you shall aduertise me by an expresse messenger, of your proceeding therein: And send me a plaine and distinct declaration of the number of shippes that you shall haue so stayed in that coast and partes, whence euery one of them is, which belong to my Rebels, what burden and goods there are, and what number of men is in euery of them, and what quantitie they haue of armour, ordinance, munition, victuals, tacklings and other necessaries, to the end that vpon sight hereof, hauing made choise of such as shall be fit for the seruice, we may further direct you what ye shall do. In the meane time you shall presently see this my commandment put in execution, and if there come thither any more ships, you shall also cause them to be stayed and arrested after the same order, vsing therein such care and diligence, as may answere the trust that I repose in you, wherein you shall doe me great seruice. Dated at Barcelona the 29 of May, 1585.

And thus haue you heard the trueth and manner thereof, wherein is to be noted the great courage of the maister, and the louing hearts of the seruants to saue their master from the daunger of death: yea, and the care which the master had to saue so much of the owners goods as hee might, although by the same the greatest is his owne losse in that he may neuer trauell to those parts any more without the losse of his owne life, nor yet any of his seruantes: for if hereafter they should, being knowen they are like to taste of the sharpe torments which are there accustomed in their Holy-house. And as for their terming English shippes to be in rebellion against them, it is sufficiently knowen by themselues, and their owne consciences can not denie it, but that with loue, vnitie, and concord, our shippes haue euer beene fauoruable vnto them, and as willing to pleasure their King, as his subiectes any way willing to pleasure English passengers.

* * * * *

The voiage of the right honorable George Erle of Cumberland to the Azores, &c. Written by the excellent Mathematician and Enginier master Edward Wright.

The right honorable the Erle of Cumberland hauing at his owne charges prepared his small Fleet of foure Sailes onely, viz. The Victorie one of the Queenes ships royall; the Meg and Margaret small ships, (one of which also he was forced soone after to send home againe, finding her not able to endure the Sea) and a small Carauell, and hauing assembled together about 400 men (or fewer) of gentlemen, souldiers, and saylers, embarked himself and them, and set saile from the Sound of Plimmouth in Deuonshire, the 18 day of Iune 1589, being accompanied with these captaines and gentlemen which hereafter folow.

Captaine Christopher Lister a man of great resolution, captaine Edward Carelesse, *aliàs* Wright, who in sir Francis Drakes West Indian voyage to S. Domingo and Carthagena, was captaine of the Hope. Captaine Boswell, M. Meruin, M. Henry Long, M. Partridge, M. Norton, M. William Mounson captaine of the Meg, and his viceadmirall, now sir William Mounson, M. Pigeon captaine of the Carauell.

About 3 dayes after our departure from Plimmouth we met with 3 French ships, whereof one was of Newhauen, another of S. Malos, and so finding them to be Leaguers and lawful Prises, we tooke them and sent two of them for England with all their loding, which was fish for the most part from New-found-land, sauing that there was part thereof distributed amongst our small Fleet, as we could find Stowage for the same: and in the third, all their men were sent home into France. The same day and the day folowing we met with some other ships, whom (when after some conference had with them, we perceiued plainly to bee of Roterodam and Emden, bound for Rochell) we dismissed.

The 28 and 29 dayes we met diuers of our English ships, returning from the Portugall voiage which my lord relieued with victuals. The 13 day of Iuly being Sonday in the morning, we espied 11 ships without sight of the coast of Spaine, in the height of 39 degrees, whom wee presently prepared for, and prouided to meet them, hauing first set forth Captaine Mounson in the Meg, before vs, to descry whence they were. The Meg approching neere, there passed some shot betwixt them, whereby, as also by their Admiral and Vice-admirall putting foorth their flags, we perceiued that some fight was likely to follow. Having therefore fitted our selues for them, we made what hast we could towards them with regard alwayes to get the wind of them, and about 10 or 11 of the clocke, we came vp to them with the Victory. But after some few shot and some litle fight passed betwixt vs, they yeelded themselues, and the masters of them all came aboord vs, shewing their seuerall Pasports from the cities of Hamburg and Lubeck, from Breme, Pomerania and Calice.

They had in them certaine bags of Pepper and Synamon, which they confessed to be the goods of the Iew in Lisbon, which should haue bene carried by them into their countrey to his Factor there, and so finding it by their owne confession to be lawful Prise, the same was soone after taken and diuided amongst our whole company, the value wherof was esteemed to be about 4500 pounds, at two shillings the pound.

The 17 day the foresaid ships were dismissed, but 7 of their men that were willing to go along with vs for sailers, we tooke to help vs, and so held on our course for the Azores.

The 1 of August being Friday in the morning, we had sight of the Iland of S. Michael, being one of the Eastermost of the Azores toward which we sailed all that day, and at night hauing put foorth a Spanish flag in our main-top, that so they might the lesse suspect vs, we approched neere to the chiefe towne and road of that Iland, where we espied 3 ships riding at anker and some other vessels: all which we determined to take in the darke of the night, and accordingly attempted about 10 or 11 of the clocke, sending our boats well manned to cut their cables and hausers, and let them driue into the sea. Our men comming to them, found the one of those greatest ships was the Falcon of London being there vnder a Scottish Pilot who bare the name of her as his own. [Sidenote: 3 ships forcibly towed our of harbour.] But 3 other smal ships that lay neere vnder the castle there, our men let loose and towed them away vnto vs, most of the Spaniards that were in them leaping ouer-boord and swimming to shore with lowd and lamentable outcries, which they of the towne hearing were in an vprore, and answered with the like crying. The castle discharged some great shot at our boats, but shooting without marke by reason of the darknesse they did vs no hurt. The Scots likewise discharged 3 great pieces into the aire to make the Spaniards thinke they were their friends and our enemies, and shortly after the Scottish master, and some other with him, came aboord to my lord doing their dutie, and offering their seruice, &c. These 3 ships were fraught with wine and Sallet-oile from Siuil.

The same day our Carauel chased a Spanish Carauel to shore at S. Michael, which caried letters thither, by which we learned that the Caraks were departed from Tercera 8 dayes before.

The 7 of August we had sight of a litle ship which wee chased towards Tercera with our pinasse (the weather being calme) and towards euening we ouertooke her, there were in her 30 tunnes of good Madera wine, certaine woollen cloth, silke, taffata, &c. The 14 of August we came to the Iland of Flores, where we determined to take in some fresh water and fresh victuals, such as the Iland did affoord. So we manned our boats with some 120 men and rowed towards the shore; whereto when we approched the inhabitants that were assembled at the landing place, put foorth a flag of truce, whereupon we also did the like.

When we came to them, my Lord gaue them to vnderstand by his Portugall interpreter, that he was a friend to their king Don Antonio, and came not any way to iniury them, but that he meant onely to haue some fresh water and fresh victuals of them, by way of exchange for some prouision that he had, as oile, wine, or pepper, to which they presently agreed willingly, and sent some of their company for beeues and sheepe, and we in the meane season marched Southward about a mile to Villa de Santa Cruz, from whence all the inhabitants yong and old were departed, and not any thing of value left. We demanding of them what was the cause hereof, they answered, Feare; as their vsuall maner was when any ships came neere their coast.

We found that part of the Iland to be full of great rockie barren hils and mountains, litle inhabited by reason that it is molested with ships of war which might partly appeare by this towne of Santa Cruz (being one of their chiefe townes) which was all ruinous, and (as it were) but the reliques of the ancient towne which had bene burnt about two yeeres before by certaine English ships of war, as the inhabitants there reported.

At euening as we were in rowing towards the Victory, an huge fish pursued vs for the space of well nigh of two miles together, distant for the most part from the boats sterne not a speares length, and sometimes so neere that the boat stroke vpon him, the tips of whose finnes about the ghils (appearing oft times aboue the water) were by estimation 4 or 5 yards asunder, and his iawes gaping a yard and a halfe wide, which put vs in feare of ouerturning the pinnasse, but God be thanked (rowing as hard as we could) we escaped.

When we were about Flores a litle ship called the Drake, brought vs word that the Caraks were at Tercera, of which newes we were very glad, and sped vs thitherward with all the speed we could: and by the way we came to Fayal road the seuen and twentieth day of August after sunne set, where we espied certaine shippes ryding at anker, to whom we sent in our Skiffe with Captaine Lister and Captaine Monson in her to discouer the roaders: and least any daunger should happen to our boate, we sent in likewise the Sawsie Iack and the small Carauell; but the wind being off the shoare, the shippes were not able to fet it so nigh as the Spaniards ride, which neuerthelesse the boate did, and clapped a shippe aboord of two hundred and fiftie tunnes, which caried in her fourteene cast peeces, and continued fight alone with her for the space of one houre vntill the comming vp of other boates to the reskue of her, which were sent from the shippes, and then a fresh boording her againe one boate in the quarter, another in the hause, we entred her on the one side, and all the Spaniards lept ouerboord on the other, saue Iuan de Palma the Captaine of her and two or three more, and thus we became possessors of her. This shippe was mored to the Castle which shot at vs all this while: the onely hurt which we receiued of all this shot was this, that the master of our Carauell had the calfe of his legge shot away. This shippe was laden with Sugar, Ginger, and hides lately come from S. Iuan de Puerto Rico; after we had towed her cleare off the castle, we rowed in againe with our boats, and fetched out fiue small ships more, one laden with hides, another with Elephants teeth, graines, coconuts, and goates skins come from Guinie, another with woad, and two with dogge-fish, which two last we let driue into the sea making none account of them. The other foure we sent for England the 30 of August.

At the taking of these Prizes were consorted with vs some other small men of warre, as Maister Iohn Dauis with his shippe, Pinnesse, and Boate, Captaine Markesburie with his ship, whose owner was Sir Walter Ralegh, the
Barke of Lime, which was also consorted with vs before.

[Sidenote: An eescape of 8 Englishmen from Tercera.] The last of August in the morning we came in sight of Tercera, being about some nine or ten leagues from shoare, where we espied comming toward vs, a small boat vnder saile, which seemed somewhat strange vnto vs, being so farre from lande, and no shippe in sight, to which they might belong; but comming neere, they put vs out of doubt, shewing they were English men (eight in number) that had lately bene prisoners in Tercera, and finding opportunitie to escape at that time, with that small boat committed themselues to the sea, vnder Gods prouidence, hauing no other yard for their maine saile, but two pipe staues tyed together by the endes, and no more prouision of victuals, then they could bring in their pockets and bosomes. Hauing taken them all into the Victorie, they gaue vs certaine intelligence, that the Carackes were departed from thence about a weeke before.

Thus beeing without any further hope of those Caraks, we resolued to returne for Fayall, with intent to surprize the towne, but vntill the ninth of September, we had either the winde so contrary, or the weather so calme, that in all that time, we made scarce nine or ten leagues way, lingring vp and downe not farre from Pico.

The tenth of September being Wednesday in the afternoone, wee came again to Fayal roade. Whereupon immediatly my Lord sent Captaine Lister, with one of Graciosa (whom Capatine Munson had before taken) and some others, towards Fayal, whom certaine of the Inhabitants met in a boat, and came with Captaine Lister to my Lord, to whom hee gaue this choice: either to suffer him quietly to enter into the platforme there without resistance, where he and his companie would remaine a space without offering any iniurie to them, that they (the Inhabitants) might come vnto him and compound for the ransome of the Towne; or else to stand to the hazard of the warre.

With these words they returned to the towne: but the keepers of the platforme answered, that it was against their oath and allegeance to king Philip to giue ouer without fight. Whereupon my Lord commanded the boates of euery ship, to be presently manned, and soone after landed his men on the sandie shoare, vnder the side of an hill, about halfe a league to the Northwards from the platforme: vpon the toppe of which hill certaine horsemen and footmen shewed themselues, and other two companies also appeared, with ensignes displayed, the one before the towne vpon the shore by the sea side, which marched towards our landing place, as though they would encounter vs; the other in a valley to the Southwards of the platforme, as if they would haue come to helpe the Townesmen: during which time they in the platforme also played vpon vs with great Ordinance. [Sidenote: The taking of the towne and platforme of Fayal.] Notwithstanding my L. (hauing set his men in order) marched along the sea shore, vpon the sands, betwixt the sea and the towne towards the platforme for the space of a mile or more, and then the shore growing rockie, and permitting no further progresse without much difficultie, he entred into the towne and passed through the street without resistance, vnto the platforme; for those companies before mentioned at my Lo. approching, were soone dispersed, and suddenly vanished.

Likewise they of the platforme, being all fled at my Lordes comming thither, left him and his company to scale the walles, to enter and take possession without resistance.

In the meane time our shippes ceased not to batter the foresaid Towne and Platforme with great shotte, till such time as we saw the Red-Crosse of England flourishing vpon the Forefront thereof.

[Sidenote: A description of the towne of Faial.] This Fayal is the principal towne in all that is land, and is situate directly ouer against the high and mighty mountaine Pico, lying towards the West Northwest from that mountaine, being deuided therefrom by a narrow Sea, which at that place is by estimation about some two or three leagues in bredth betweene the Isles of Fayal and Pico.

The towne conteyned some three hundred housholds, their houses were faire and strongly builded of lime and stone, and double couered with hollow tyles much like our roofe tyles, but that they are lesse at the one end then at the other.

Euery house almost had a cisteme or well in a garden on the backe side: in which gardens grew vines (with ripe clusters of grapes) making pleasant shadowes, and Tabacco nowe commonly knowen and vsed in England, wherewith their women there dye their faces reddish, to make them seeme fresh and young: Pepper Indian and common; figge-trees bearing both white and red figges: Peach trees not growing very tall: Orenges, Limons, Quinces, Potato-roots, &c. Sweete wood (Cedar I thinke) is there very common, euen for building and firing.

My Lord hauing possessed himselfe of the towne and platforme, and being carefull of the preseruation of the towne, gaue commandement, that no mariner or souldier should enter into any house, to make any spoyle thereof. But especially he was carefull that the Churches and houses of religion there should be kept inuiolate, which was accordingly performed, through his appointment of guarders and keepers for those places: but the rest of the towne eyther for want of the former inhibition, or for desire of spoyle and prey, was rifled, and ransacked by the souldiers and mariners, who scarcely left any house vnsearched, out of which they tooke such things as liked them, as chestes of sweete wood, chaires, cloth, couerlets, hangings, bedding, apparell: and further ranged into the countrey, where some of them also were hurt by the inhabitants. The Friery there conteyning and maintayning thirty Franciscan Friars (among whom we could not finde any one able to speake true Latine) was builded by a Fryer of Angra in Tercera of the same order, about the yeare of our Lord one thousand fiue hundred and sixe. The tables in the hall had seates for the one side onely, and were alwayes couered, as readie at all times for dinner or supper.

From Wednesday in the afternoone, at which time we entred the towne, til Saturday night, we continued there, vntill the Inhabitants had agreed and payed for the ransome of the towne, two thousand duckats, most part whereof was Church-plate.

We found in the platfonne eight and fiftie yron peeces of Ordinance, whereof three and twentie (as I remember) or more were readie mounted vpon their carriages, betweene Barricadoes, vpon a platforme towardes the sea-side, all which Ordinance we tooke, and set the platforme on fire, and so departed: My Lord hauing inuited to dinner in the Victorie, on the Sunday following, so many of the Inhabitants as would willingly come (saue onely Diego Gomes the Gouernour, who came but once onely to parle about the ransome) onely foure came and were well entertained, and solemnely dismissed with sound of drumme and trumpets, and a peale of Ordinance: to whom my Lord deliuered his letter subscribed with his owne hand, importing a request ['repuest' in source text—KTH] to all other Englishmen to abstaine from any further molesting them, saue onely for fresh water, and victuals necessary for their intended voyage. During our abode here (viz. the 11 of September) two men came out of Pico which had beene prisoners there: Also at Fayal we set at libertie a prisoner translated from S. Iago who was cousin to a seruant of Don Anthonio king of Portugall in England: These prisoners we detyned with vs.

On Munday we sent our boates ashore for fresh water, which (by reason of the raine that fell the former night) came plentifully running downe the hilles, and would otherwise haue beene hard to be gotten there. On Tuesday likewise hauing not yet suffiently serued our turnes, we sent againe for fresh water, which was then not so easie to be gotten as the day before, by reason of a great winde: which in the afternoone increased also in such sort, that we thought it not safe to ride so neere the land; whereupon we weyed anker and so departed Northwest and by west, alongst the coast of Fayal Island. Some of the Inhabitants comming aboord to vs this day, tolde vs that always about that time of the yeere such windes West Southwest blew on that coast.

This day, as we sayled neere Saint Georges Island, a huge fish lying still a litle vnder water, or rather euen therewith, appeared hard by a head of vs, the sea breaking vpon his backe, which was blacke coloured, in such sort as deeming at the first it had beene a rocke, and the ship stemming directly with him, we were put in a sudden feare for the time: till soone after we saw him moue out of the way.

The 16 of September in the nigh it lightened much, whereupon there followed great winds and raine which continued the 17 18 19-20 and 21 of the same. The 23 of September we came againe into Faial road to weigh an anker which (for haste and feare of foule weather) wee had left there before, where we went on shore to see the towne, the people (as we thought) hauing now setled themselues there againe, but notwithstanding many of them through too much distrustfulnesse, departed and prepared to depart with their packets at the first sight of vs: vntill such time as they were assured by my Lord, that our comming was not any way to iniury them, but especially to haue fresh water, and some other things needeful for vs, contenting them for the same.

So then we viewed the Towne quietly, and bought such things as we desired for our money as if we had bene in England. And they helped to fill vs in fresh water, receiuing for their paines such satisfaction as contented them.

The 25 day we were forced againe to depart from thence, before we had sufficiently watered, by reason of a great tempest that suddenly arose in the night, in so much, that my Lord himselfe soone after midnight raysed our men out of itheir Cabines to wey anker, himselfe also together with them haling at the Capsten, and after chearing them vp with wine.

The next day we sent our Carauel and the Sawsie-Iack to the road of Saint Michael, to see what they could espie: we following after them vpon the 27 day, plying to and fro, came within sight of S. Michael, but by contrary windes the 28 29 and 30 dayes wee were driuen to leewarde, and could not get neere the Island.

The first of October wee sayled alongst Tercera, and euen against Brasill (a promontorie neere to Angra the strongest Towne in that Island) wee espied some boates comming to the Towne, and made out towardes them: but being neere to the lande they ranne to shoare and escaped vs.

In the afternoone we came neere to Graciosa, whereupon my Lord foorthwith sent Captain Lister to the Ilanders, to let them vnderstand that his desire was onely to haue water and wine of them, and some fresh victuals, and not any further to trouble them. They answered they could giue no resolute answere to this demande, vntill the Gouernors of the Iland had consulted therevpon, and therefore desired him to send againe to them the next day.

Vpon the second day of October eariy in the morning, we sent forth our long boat and Pinnesse, with emptie Caske, and about some fiftie or sixty men together with the Margaret, and Captaine Dauis his shippe: for we now wanted all the rest of our consortes. But when our men would haue landed, the Ilanders shot at them, and would not suffer them. And troupes of men appeared vpon land, with ensignes displayed to resist vs: So our boates rowed alongst the shoare, to finde some place where they might land, not with too much disaduantage: our shippes and they still shooting at the Ilanders: but no place could be founde where they might land without great perill of loosing many of their liues, and so were constrayned to retire without receiuing any answere, as was promised the day before. We had three men hurt in this conflict, whilest our boates were together in consulting what was best to be done: two of them were stroken with a great shot (which the Ilanders drew from place to place with Oxen) wherewith the one lost his hand, and the other his life within two or three dayes after: the third was shot into his necke with a small shot, without any great hurt.

With these newes our company returned backe againe at night, whereupon preparation was made to goe to them againe the next day: but the daye was farre spent before we could come neere them with our ship: neither could we finde any good ground to anker in, where we might lye to batter the Towne, and further we could finde no landing place, without great danger to loose many men: which might turne not only to the ouerthrow of our voiage, but also put the Queenes ship in great perill for want of men to bring her home. Therefore my Lord thought it best to write to them to this efiect: That he could not a litle maruell at their inhumanitie and crueltie which they had shewed towards his men, seeing they were sent by him vnto them in peaceable manner to receiue their answere which they had promised to giue the day before: and that were it not for Don Antonio their lawful king his sake, he could not put vp so great iniury at their hands, without iust reuengement vpon them: notwithstanding for Don Antonio his sake, whose friend he was, he was yet content to send to them once againe for their answere: At night Captaine Lister returned with this answere from them. That their Gunner shot off one of their pieces, which was charged with pouder onely, and was stopped; which our men thinking it had bin shot at them, shot againe, and so beganne the fight: and that the next morning they would send my Lord a resolute answere to his demaunde, for as yet they could not knowe their Gouernours minde herein. The next morning there came vnto vs a boate from the shoare with a flagge of truce, wherein were three of the chiefe men of the Island, who agreed with my Lorde that hee should haue of them sixtie buttes of wine, and fresh victuals to refresh himselfe and his companie withall: but as for fresh water, they could not satisfie our neede therein, hauing themselues little or none, sauing such as they saued in vessels or cistrnes when it rayned, and that they had rather giue vs two tunnes of wine then one of water: but they requested that our souldiers might not come on shoare, for they themselues would bring all they had promised to the water-side, which request was graunted, we keeping one of them aboord with vs, untill their promise was performed, and the other we sent to shoare with our emptie Caske, and some of our men to helpe to fill, and bring them away with such other prouision as was promised: so the Margaret, Captaine Dauis his shippe, and another of Weymouth stayed ryding at anker before the Towne, to take in our prouision. This shippe of Weymouth came to vs the day before, and had taken a rich Prize (as it was reported) worth sixteene thousand pound, which brought vs newes that the West-Indian Fleete was not yet come, but would come very shortly. But we with the Victorie put off to sea, and vpon Saturday the fourth of October, we tooke a French shippe of Saint Malo (a citie of the vnholy league) loden with fish from Newfoundland: which had beene in so great a tempest, that she was constrayned to cut her mayne mast ouerboord for her safetie, and was now comming to Graciosa, to repaire her selfe. But so hardly it befell her, that she did not onely not repaire her former losses, but lost all that remayned vnto vs. The chiefe of our men we tooke into our ship, and sent some of our men, mariners, and souldiers into her to bring her into England.

Vpon the Sunday following at night, all our promised prouision was brought vnto vs from Gratiosa: and we friendly dismissed the Ilanders with a peale of Ordinance.

Vpon Munday, Tuesday, and Wednesday, we plyed to and fro about those Islandes, being very rough weather. And vpon Thursday at night, being driuen some three or foure leagues from Tercera, we saw fifteene saile of the West-Indian Fleete comming into the Hauen at Angra in Tercera. But the winde was such, that for the space of foure dayes after, though wee lay as close by the winde as was possible, yet we could not come neere them. In this time we lost our late French Prize, not being able to lie so neere the winde as we, and heard no more of her till we came to England where shee safely arrriued. Vpon Munday we came very neere the Hauens month, being minded to haue runne in amongst them, and to haue fetched out some of them if it had beene possible: But in the end this enterprise was deemed too daungerous, considering the strength of the place where they rode, being haled and towed in neerer the towne, at the first sight of our approching, and lying vnder the protection of the Castle of Brasil, on the one side (hauing in it fiue and twentie peeces of Ordinance) and a fort on the other side wherein were 13 or 14 great brasse pieces. Besides, when we came neere land the winde prooued too scant for vs to attempt any such enterprise.

Vpon Tuesday the fourteenth of October we sent our boate to the roade to sound the depth, to see if there were any ankoring place for vs, where we might lie without shot of the Castle and Fort, and within shot of some of those shippes, that we might either make them come out to vs, or sinke them where they lay. Our boate returned hauing found out such a place as we desired, but the winde would not suffer vs to come neere it, and againe if we could haue ankered there, it was thought likely that they would rather runne themselues a ground to saue their liues and liberties, and some of their goods, then come foorth to loose their liberties and goods to vs their enemies. So we shot at them to see if we could reach them, but it fell farre short. And thus we departed, thinking it not probable that they would come foorth so long as we watched for them before the hauens mouth, or within sight of them. For the space of fiue dayes after we put off to sea, and lay without sight of them, and sent a pinnesse to lie out of sight close by the shore, to bring vs word if they should come foorth. After a while the Pinnesse returned and told vs that those shippes in the Hauen had taken downe their sayles, and let downe their toppe mastes: so that wee supposed they would neuer come foorth, till they perceiued vs to bee quite gone.

Wherefore vpon the 20 of October, hearing that there were certaine Scottish ships at Saint Michael, we sayled thither, and found there one Scottish roader, and two or three more at Villa Franca, the next road a league or two from the towne of S. Michael, to the Eastwards: of whom we had for our reliefe some small quantitie of wine (viz. some fiue or sixe buttes of them all) and some fresh water, but nothing sufficient to serue our turne.

Vpon Tuesday the one and twentieth of October, we sent our long boate to shore for fresh water at a brooke a little to the Westwards from Villa Franca.

But the Inhabitants espying vs came downe with two Ensignes displayed, and about some hundred and fiftie men armed, to withstand our landing. So our men hailing spent all their pouder vpon them in attempting to land, and not being able to preuaile at so great oddes, returned frustrate.

From thence we departed towards Saint Maries Iland, minding to water there, and then to goe for the coast of Spaine. For we had intelligence that it was a place of no great force, and that we might water there very well: therefore vpon Friday following, my Lord sent Captaine Lister, and

Captaine Amias Preston now Sir Amias Preston (who not long before came to vs out of his owne shippe, and she loosing vs in the night, hee was forced to tarry still with vs) with our long boate and Pinnesse, and some sixtie or seuentie shotte in them, with a friendly letter to the Ilanders, that they would grant vs leaue to water, and we would no further trouble them.

So we departed from the Victorie for the Iland, about nine of the clocke in the afternoone, and rowed freshly vntill about 3 a clocke afternoone. At which time our men being something weary with rowing, and being within a league or two of the shore, and 4 or 5 leagues from the Victorie, they espied (to their refreshing), two shippes ryding at anker hard vnder the the towns, whereupon hauing shifted some 6 or 7 of our men into Captaine Dauis his boate, being too much pestered in our owne, and retayning with vs some 20 shot in the pinnesse, we made way towardes them with all the speede we could.

By the way as we rowed we saw boates passing betwixt the roaders and the shore, and men in their shirtes swimming and wading to shoare, who as we perceiued afterwardes, were labouring to set those shippes fast on ground, and the Inhabitants as busily preparing themselues for the defence of those roaders, their Iland, and themselues. When we came neere them, Captaine Lister commaunded the Trumpets to be sounded, but prohibited any shot to be discharged at them, vntill they had direction from him: But some of the companie, either not well perceiuing or regarding what he sayd, immediately vpon the sound of the Trumpets discharged their pieces at the Islanders; which for the most part lay in trenches and fortefied places vnseene, to their owne best aduantage: who immediatly shot likewise at vs, both with small and great shot, without danger to themselues: Notwithstanding Captaine Lister earnestly hastened forward the Saylers that rowed, who beganne to shrinke at that shot, flying so fast about their eares, and himselfe first entring one of the shippes that lay a litle further from shoare then the other, we spedily followed after him into her, still plying them with our shot And hauing cut in sunder her Cables and Hausers, towed her away with our Pinnesse. In the meane time Captaine Dauis his boate ouertooke vs and entred into the other shippe, which also (as the former) was forsaken by all her men: but they were constrayned to leaue her and to come againe into their boate (whilest shot and stones from shoare flew fast amongst them) finding her to sticke so fast a grounde, that they could not stire her: which the Townesmen also perceiuing, and seeing that they were fewe in number, and vs (busied about the other ship) not comming to ayde them, were preparing to haue come and taken them. But they returned vnto vs, and so together we came away towards the Victory, towing after vs the Prize that we had now taken, which was lately come from Brasil, loden with Sugar.

In this fight we had two men slaine and 16 wounded: and as for them, it is like they had little hurt, lying for the most part behind stone walles, which were builded one aboue another hard by the sea side, vpon the end of the hill whereupon the Towne stoode betwixt two vallies. Vpon the toppe of the hill lay their great Ordinance (such as they had) wherewith they shot leaden bullets, whereof one pierced through our Prizes side, and lay still in the shippe without doing any more harme.

The next day we went againe for water to the same Iland, but not knowing before the inconuenience and disuaduantage of the place where we attempted to land, we returned frustrate.

The same night the 25 of October we departed for S. Georges Iland for fresh water, whither we came on Munday following October 27, and hauing espied where a spout of water came running downe: the pinnesse and long boate were presently manned and sent vnder the conduct of Captaine Preston, and Captaine Munson, by whom my Lord sent a letter to the Ilanders as before, to grant vs leaue to water onely, and we would no further trouble them: notwithstanding our men comming on shoare found some of the poore Ilanders, which for feare of vs hid themselues amongst the rockes.

And on Wednesday following our boats returned with fresh water, whereof they brought only sixe tunnes for the Victorie, alleaging they could get no more, thinking (as it was supposed) that my Lord hauing no more prouision of water and wine, but onely 12 tunnes, would not goe for the coast of Spaine, but straight for the coast of England, as many of our men greatly desired: notwithstanding my Lord was vnwilling so to doe, and was minded the next day to haue taken in more water: but through roughnesse of the seas and winde, and vnwillingnesse of his men it was not done. Yet his Hon. purposed not to returne with so much prouision vnspent, and his voyage (as he thought) not yet performed in such sort as mought giue some reasonable contentment or satisfaction to himselfe and others.

Therefore because no more water could now conueniently be gotten, and being vncertaine when it could be gotten, and the time of our staying aboord also vncertaine, the matter being referred to the choyse of the whole companie, whither they would tarrie longer, till wee might be more sufficiently prouided of fresh water, or goe by the coast of Spaine for England, with halfe so much allowance of drinke as before, they willingly agreed that euery mease should bee allowed at one meale but halfe so much drinke as they were accustomed (except them that were sicke or wounded) and so to goe for England, taking the coast of Spaine in our way, to see if we could that way make vp our voyage.

Vpon Saturday Octob. 31 we sent the Margaret (because she leaked much) directly for England, together with the Prize of Brasile which we tooke at S. Marie, and in them some of our hurt and wounded men or otherwise sicke were sent home as they desired for England: but Captaine Monson was taken out of the Megge into the Victorie.

So we held on our course for the coast of Spaine with a faire winde and a large which before we seldome had. And vpon Twesday following being the 4 of Nouemb. we espied a saile right before vs, which we chased till about three a clocke in the afternoone, at which time we ouertaking her, she stroke sayle, and being demaunded who was her owner and from whence she was, they answered, a Portugall, and from Pernanbucke in Brasile. She was a ship of some 110 tuns burden, fraighted with 410 chestes of Sugar, and 50 Kintals, of Brasill-wood, euery Kintall contayning one hundred pound weight: we tooke her in latitude nine and twentie degrees, about two hundred leagues from Lisbone westwards: Captaine Preston was presently sent vnto her, who brought the principall of her men aboord the Victorie, and certaine of our men, mariners and souldiers were sent aboord her. The Portugals of this Prize told vs that they saw another ship before them that day about noone. Hauing therefore dispatched all things about the Prize aforesaid and left our long boat with Captaine Dauis, taking his lesser boat with vs, we made way after this other ship with all the sayles we could beare, holding on our course due East, and giuing order to Captaine Dauis his ship and the Prize that they should follow vs due East, and that if they had sight of vs the morning following they should follow vs still: if not they should goe for England.

The next morning we espied not the sayle which we chased, and Captaine Dauis his ship and the Prize were behinde vs out of sight: but the next Thursday the sixt of Nouember (being in latitude 38 degrees 30 minutes, and about sixtie leagues from Lisbone westwards) early in the morning Captaine Preston descried a sayle some two or three leagues a head of vs, after which we presently hastened our chase, and ouertooke her about eight or nine of the clocke before noone. She came lately from Saint Michaels roade, hauing beene before at Brasill loden with Sugar and Brasile. Hauing sent our boat to them to bring some of the chiefe of their men aboord the Victorie, in the meane time whilest they were in comming to vs one out of the maine toppe espied another saile a head some three or foure leagues from vs. So immediately vpon the returne of our boate, hauing sent her backe againe with some of our men aboord the prize, we pursued speedily this new chase, with all the sayles we could packe on, and about two a clocke in the afternoone ouertooke her: she had made prouision to fight with vs, hauing hanged the sides of the shippe so thicke with hides (wherewith especially she was loden) that musket shot could not haue pearced them: but yer we had discharged two great peeces of our Ordinance at her, she stroke sayle, and approching neerer, we asking of whence they were, they answered from the West-Indies, from Mexico, and Saint Iohn de Lowe (truely called Vlhua.) This ship was of some three or foure hundred tunnes, and had in her seuen hundred hides worth tenne shillings a peece: sixe chests of Cochinell, euery chest houlding one hundred pound weight, and euery pound worth sixe and twenty shillings and eight pence, and certaine chests of Sugar and China dishes, with some plate and siluer.

The Captaine of her was an Italian, and by his behauiour seemed to be a graue, wise, and ciuill man: he had put an aduenture in this shippe fiue and twentie thousand Duckats, Wee tooke him with certaine other of her chiefest men (which were Spaniards) into the Victorie: and Captaine Lister with so manie other of the chiefest of our Mariners, souldiers, and saylers as were thought sufficient, to the number of 20. or thereabouts, were sent into her. In the meane time (we staying) our other prizes which followed after, came vp to vs. And nowe wee had our hands full and with ioy shaped our course for England, for so it was thought meetest, hauing now so many Portugals, Spaniards and Frenchmen amongst vs, that if we should haue taken any more prizes afterwards, wee had not bene well able to haue manned them without endangering our selues. So about six of the clocke in the afternoone (when our other prize had ouertaken vs) wee set saile for England. But our prizes not being able to beare vs company without sparing them many of our sailes, which caused our ship to route and wallow, in such sort that it was not onely very troublesome to vs, but, as it was thought, would also haue put the maine Maste in danger of falling ouerboord: hauing acquainted them with these inconueniences, we gaue them direction to keepe their courses together, folowing vs, and so to come to Portsmouth. We tooke this last prize in the latitude of 39. degrees, and about 46. leagues to the Westwards from the Rocke.

She was one of those 16. ships which we saw going into the hauen at Angra in Tercera, October 8. Some of the men that we tooke out of her tolde vs, that whilest wee were plying vp and downe before that hauen, as before was shewed, expecting the comming foorth of those shippes, three of the greatest and best of them, at the appointment of the Gouernour of Tercera were vnloden of their treasure and marchandize. And in euery of them were put three hundred Souldiers, which were appointed to haue come to lay the Victory aboord in the night, and take her: but when this should haue bene done the Victory was gone out of their sight.

Now we went meerily before the winde with all the sailes we could beare, insomuch that in the space of 24. houres, we sailed neere 47. leagues, that is seuenscore English miles, betwixt Friday at noone and Saturday at noone (notwithstanding the shippe was very foule, and much growne with long being at Sea) which caused some of our company to make accompt they would see what running at Tilt there should bee at Whitehall vpon the Queenes day. Others were imagining what a Christmas they would keepe in England with their shares of the prizes we had taken. But so it befell, that we kept a colde Christmas with the Bishop and his clearks (rockes that lye to the Westwards from Sylly, and the Westerne parts of England:) For soone after the wind scanting came about to the Eastwards (the worst part of the heauens for vs, from which the winde could blow) in such sort, that we could not fetch any part of England. And hereupon also our allowance of drinke, which was scant ynough before, was yet more scanted, because of the scarcitie thereof in the shippe. So that now a man was allowed but halfe a pinte at a meale, and that many times colde water, and scarce sweete. Notwithstanding this was an happie estate in comparison of that which followed: For from halfe a pinte we came to a quarter, and that lasted not long either, so that by reason of this great scarsitie of drinke, and contrarietie of winde, we thought to put into Ireland, there to relieue our wants. But when wee came neere thither, lying at hull all night (tarrying for the daylight of the next morning, whereby we might the safelyer bring our ship into some conuenient harbour there) we were driuen so farre to lee-ward, that we could fetch no part of Ireland, so as with heauie hearts and sad cheare, wee were constreined to returne backe againe, and expect till it should please God to send vs a faire winde either for England or Ireland. In the meane time we were allowed euery man three or foure spoones full of vineger to drinke at a meale: for other drinke we had none, sauing onely at two or three meales, when we had in stead hereof as much wine, which was wringed out of Winelees that remained. With this hard fare (for by reason of our great want of drinke, wee durst eate but very litle) wee continued for the space of a fortnight or thereabouts: Sauing that now and then wee feasted for it in the meane time: And that was when there fell any haile or raine: the haile-stones wee gathered vp and did eate them more pleasantly then if they had bene the sweetest Comfits in the world; The raine drops were so carefully saued, that so neere as wee coulde, not one was lost in all our shippe. Some hanged vp sheetes tied with cordes by the foure corners, and a weight in the midst that the water might runne downe thither, and so be receiued into some vessel set or hanged vnderneth: Some that wanted sheetes, hanged vp napkins, and cloutes, and watched them till they were thorow wet, then wringing and sucking out the water. And that water which fell downe and washed away the filth and soiling of the shippe, trod vnder foote, as bad as running downe the kennell many times when it raineth, was not lost. I warrant you, but watched and attended carefully (yea sometimes with strife and contention) at euery scupper hole, and other place where it ranne downe, with dishes, pots, cannes, and Iarres, whereof some dranke hearty draughts, euen as it was, mud and all, without tarrying to clense or settle it: Others. cleansed it first but not often, for it was so thicke and went so slowly thorow, that they might ill endure to tary so long, and were loth to loose too much of such precious stuffe: some licked with their tongues (like dogges) the boards vnder feete, the sides, railes, and Masts of the shippe: others that were more ingenious, fastened girdles or ropes about the Mastes, dawbing tallow betwixt them and the Maste (that the raine might not runne downe betweene) in such sort, that those ropes or girdles hanging lower on the one side then of the other, a spout of leather was fastened to the lowest part of them, that all the raine drops that came running downe the Maste, might meete together at that place, and there be receiued.

Hee that got a canne of water by these meanes was spoken of, sued to, and enuied as a rich man. Quàm pulchrum digito monstrari et dicier hic est? Some of the poore Spaniards that we had taken (who notwithstanding had the same allowance that our owne men had) would come and craue of vs, for the loue of God, but so much water as they could holde in the hollow of their hand: and they had it, notwithstanding our great extremitie, to teach them some humanitie instead of their accustomed barbaritie, both to vs and other nations heretofore. They put also bullets of lead into their mouthes to slake their thirst.

Now in euery corner of the shippe were heard the lamentable cries of sicke and wounded men sounding wofully in our eares crying out and pitifully complaining for want of drinke, being ready to die, yea many dying for lacke thereof, so as by reason of this great extremite we lost many more men, then wee had done all the voyage before: hauing before this time bene so well and sufficiently prouided for, that we liued in maner as well and healthfully, and died as few as if we had bene in England, whereas now lightly euery day some were cast ouerboord.

But the second day of December 1589. was a festiuall day with vs, for then it rained a good pace, and wee saued some pretie store of raine water (though we were well wet for it, and that at midnight) and filled our skins full besides: notwithstanding it were muddie and bitter with washing the shippe, but (with some sugar which we had to sweeten it withall) it went merrily downe, yet remembred we and wished for with all our hearts, many a Conduit, pumpe, spring, and streame of cleare sweete running water in England: And how miserable wee had accompted some poore soules whom we had seene driuen for thirst to drinke thereof, and how happy we would now haue thought our selues if we might haue had our fills of the same: yet should we haue fared the better with this our poore feasting, if we might haue had our meat and drinke (such and so much as it was) stand quietly before vs: but beside all the former extremities, wee were so tossed and turmoiled with such horrible stormie and tempestuous weather, that euery man had best holde fast his Canne, cup, and dish in his hands, yea and himselfe too, many times, by the ropes, railes, or sides of the ship or else he should soone finde all vnder feet.

Herewith our maine saile was torne from the yarde and blowne ouerboord quite away into the sea without recouery, and our other sailes so rent and torne (from side to side some of them) that hardly any of them escaped hole. The raging waues and foming surges of the sea came rowling like mountaines one after another, and ouerraked the waste of the shippe like a mightie riuer running ouer it, whereas in faire weather it was neere 20. foote aboue the water, that nowe wee might cry out with the princely Prophet Psalme 107. vers. 26. They mount vp to heauen, and descend to the deepe, so that their soule melteth away for trouble: they reele too and fro, and stagger like a drunken man, and all their cunning is gone. With this extremitie of foule weather the ship was so tossed and shaken, that by the craking noise it made, and by the leaking which was now much more than ordinary, wee were in great feare it would haue shaken in sunder, so that now also we had iust cause to pray a litle otherwise than the Poet, though marring the verse, yet mending the meaning.

  Deus maris et Coeli, quid enim nisi vota supersunt,
    Soluere quassatae parcito membra ratis.

Notwithstanding it pleased God of his great goodnesse to deliuer vs out of this great danger. Then forthwith a new maine saile was made and fastened to the yard, and the rest repaired as time and place would suffer: which we had no sooner done, but yet againe wee were troubled with as great an extremitie as before so that againe we were like to haue lost our new maine saile, had not Master William Antony the Master of the ship himselfe (when none else would or durst) ventured with danger of drowning by creeping along vpon the maine yarde (which was let downe close to the railes) to gather it up out of the sea, and to fasten it thereto, being in the meane while oft-times ducked ouer head and eares into the sea.

These stormes were so terrible, that there were some in our company which confessed they had gone to seas for the space of 20. yeeres, and had neuer seene the like, and vowed that if euer they returned safe home, they would neuer come to sea againe.

The last of Nouember at night we met with an English ship, out of which (because it was too late that night) it was agreed that we should haue had the next morning two or three Tunnes of wine, which, as they said, was al the prouision of drink they had, saue only a But or two, which they must needs reserue for their owne vse: but after that, we heard of them no more, till they were set on ground vpon the coast of Ireland, where it appeared that they might haue spared vs much more then they pretended they could, so as they might wel haue relieued our great necessities, and haue had sufficient for themselues besides, to bring them into England.

The first of December at night we spake with another English ship, and had some beere out of her, but not sufficient to cary vs into England, so that wee were constrained to put into Ireland, the winde so seruing.

The next day we came to an anker, not far from the S. Kelmes vnder the land and winde, where we were somewhat more quiet, but (that being no safe harbour to ride in) the next morning wee went about to weigh anker, but hauing some of our men hurt at the Capsten, wee were faine to giue ouer and leaue it behinde, holding on our course to Ventrie hauen, where wee safely arriued the same day, that place being a very safe and conuenient harbor for vs, that now wee might sing as we had iust cause, They that go downe to the sea, &c.

So soone as we had ankered here my Lord went foorthwith to shoare, and brought presently fresh water and fresh victuals, as Muttons, pigges, hennes, &c. to refresh his company withall. Notwithstanding himselfe had lately bene very weake, and tasted of the same extremitie that his Company did: For in the time of our former want, hauing a little fresh water left him remaining in a pot, in the night it was broken, and the water drunke and dried vp. Soone after the sicke and wounded men were carried to the next principall Towne, called Dingenacush, being about three miles distant from the foresaide hauen, where our shippe roade, to the Eastwards, that there they might be the better refreshed, and had the Chirurgians dayly to attend vpon them. Here we wel refreshed our selues whilest the Irish harpe sounded sweetely in our eares, and here we, who for the former extremities were in maner halfe dead, had our liues (as it were) restored vnto vs againe.

This Dingenacush is the chiefe Towne in al that part of Ireland, it consisteth but of one maine streete, from whence some smaller doe proceede on either side. It hath had gates (as it seemeth) in times past at either ende to open and shut as a Towne of warre, and a Castle also. The houses are very strongly built with thicke stone walles, and narrow windowes like vnto Castles: for as they confessed, in time of trouble, by reason of the wilde Irish or otherwise, they vsed their houses for their defence as Castles. The castle and all the houses in the Towne, saue foure, were won, burnt, and ruinated by the Erle of Desmond.

These foure houses fortified themselues against him, and withstood him and all his power perforce, so as he could not winne them.

There remaineth yet a thicke stone wall that passeth ouerthwart the midst of the streete which was a part of their fortification. Notwithstanding whilest they thus defended themselues, as some of them yet aliue confessed, they were driuen to as great extremities as the Iewes, besieged by Titus the Romane Emperour, insomuch that they were constrained to eat dead mens carcases for hunger. The towne is nowe againe somewhat repaired, but in effect there remaine but the ruines of the former Towne. Commonly they haue no chimnies in their houses, excepting them of the better sort, so that the smoake was very troublsom to vs, while we continued there; Their fewell is turfes, which they haue very good, and whinnes or furres. There groweth little wood thereabouts, which maketh building chargeable there: as also want of lime (as they reported) which they are faine to fetch from farre, when they haue neede thereof. But of stones there is store ynough, so that with them they commonly make their hedges to part ech mans ground from other: and the ground seemeth to be nothing else within but rockes and stones; Yet it is very fruitfull and plentifull of grasse and graine, as may appeare by the abundance of kine and cattell there: insomuch that we had good muttons (though somewhat lesse then ours in England) for two shillings or fiue groates a piece, good pigges and hennes for 3 pence a piece.

The greatest want is industrious, painefull, and husbandly inhabitants to till and trimme the ground: for the common sort, if they can prouide sufficient to serue from hand to mouth, take no further care.

Of money (as it seemeth) there is very store amongst them, which perhaps was the cause that made them double and triple the prizes of many things we bought of them, more then they were before our comming thither.

Good land was here to be had for foure pence the Acre yeerely rent. [Sidenote: Mines in Ireland.] There are Mines of Alome, Tinne, brasse, and yron. Stones wee sawe there as cleare as Christall, naturally squared like Diamonds.

That part of the Countrey is al full of great mountaines and hills, from whence came running downe the pleasant streames of sweete fresh running water. The natural hardnesse of the Nation appeareth in this, that their small children runne vsually in the middest of Winter vp and downe the streetes bare-foote and bare-legged, with no other apparell (many times) saue onely a mantle to couer their nakednesse.

The chiefe Officer of their Towne they call their Soueraigne, who hath the same office and authoritie among them that our Maiors haue with vs in England, and hath his Sergeants to attend vpon him, and beare the Mace before him as our Maiors.

We were first intertained at the Soueraignes house, which was one of those 4. that withstood the Erle of Desmond in his rebellion. They haue the same forme of Common prayer word word in Latin, that we haue here in

England. Vpon the Sunday the Soueraigne commeth into the Church with his Sergeant before him, and the Sheriffe and others of the Towne accompany him, and there they kneele downe euery man by himselfe priuately to make his prayers. After this they rise and go out of the Church againe to drinke, which being done, they returne againe into the Church, and then the Minister beginneth prayers.

Their maner of baptizing differeth something from ours: part of the seruice belonging therto is repeated in Latin, and part in Irish. The minister taketh the child in his hands, and first dippeth it backwards, and then forwards, ouer heads and eares into the cold water in the midst of Winter, whereby also may appeare their naturall hardnesse, (as before was specified.) They had neither Bell, drum, nor trumpet, to call the Parishioners together, but they expect till their Soueraigne come, and then they that haue any deuotion follow him.

They make their bread all in cakes, and, for the tenth part, the bakers bake for all the towne.

We had of them some 10. or 11. Tunnes of beere for the Victory, but it proued like a present purgation to them that tooke it, so that we chose rather to drinke water then it.

The 20 of December we loosed from hence, hauing well prouided ourselues of fresh, water, and other things necessary, being accompanied with sir Edw. Dennie, his Lady, and two yong sonnes.

This day in the morning my Lord going ashoare to despatch away speedily some fresh water that remained for the Victory, the winde being very faire for vs, brought vs newes that their were 60. Spanish prizes taken and brought to England. For two or three dayes wee had a faire winde, but afterwards it scanted so, that (as I said before) we were faine to keepe a cold Christmas with The Bishop and his clearkes.

[Sidenote: Captaine Lister drowned.] After this we met with an English ship, that brought vs ioyful newes of 91. Spanish prizes that were come to England: and sorrowfull newes withall, that the last and best prize we tooke, had suffered shipwracke at a place vpon the coast of Cornwal which the Cornish men cals Als Efferne, that is, Helcliffe, and that Captaine Lister and all the men in the ship were drowned, saue 5. or 6. the one halfe English, the other Spanish that saued themselues with swimming; but notwithstanding much of the goods were saued, and reserued for vs, by sir Francis Godolphin and the worshipful gentlemen of the Countrey there. My Lord was very sorry for Captaine Listers death, wishing that he had lost his voyage to haue saued his life.

The 29. of December we met with another shippe, that tolde vs the same newes, and that sir Martin Frobisher, and Captaine Reymond had taken the Admirall and Vice-Admirall of the Fleet that we espied going to Terçera hauen. But the Admirall was sunke with much leaking, neere to the Idy Stone, a rocke that lieth ouer against Plimouth sound, and the men were saued.

This ship also certified vs that Captaine Prestons ship had taken a prize loden with siluer. My Lord entred presently into this ship, and went to Falmouth, and we held on our course for Plimouth. At night we came neere to the Ram-head (the next Cape Westwards from Plimouth sound) but we were afraid to double it in the night, misdoubting the scantnesse of the winde. So we stood off to Sea halfe the night, and towards morning had the winde more large, and made too little spare thereof, that partly for this cause, and partly through mistaking of the land, wee were driuen so much to lee-wards, that we could not double that Cape: Therefore we returned backe againe, and came into Falmouth hauen, where wee strucke on ground in 17. foote water: but it was a low ebbe, and ready againe to flowe, and the ground soft, so as no hurt was done. Here with gladnesse wee set foote againe vpon the English ground (long desired) and refreshed ourselues with keeping part of Christmas vpon our natiue soile.

* * * * *

The valiant fight performed by 10. Merchants ships of London, against 12. Spanish gallies in the Straights of Gibraltar, the 24. of April 1590.

It is not long since sundry valiant ships appertaining to the Marchants of London, were fraighted and rigged forth, some for Venice, some for Constantinople, and some to sundry other places of trafique, among whom these ensuing met within the Straights of Gibraltar, as they were taking their course homewards, having before escaped all other danger. [Sidenote: February 1590] The first whereof was the Salomon appertaining to M. Alderman Barnam of London, and M. Bond, and M. Twyd of Harwich: which went foorth the first day of February last. The second was the Margaret and Iohn belonging to M. Wats of London: The thirde was the Minion: The fourth was the Ascension. The fifth was the Centurion of Master Cordal: the sixt the Violet: the seuenth the Samuel; the eight the Crescent: the ninth the Elizabeth: and the 10. was the Richard belonging to M. Duffield. All these ships being of notable and approued seruice comming neere to the mouth of the Straights hard by the coast of Barbary, descried twelue tall Gallies brauely furnished and strongly prouided with men and munition, ready to seaze vpon these English ships: which being perceiued by the Captaines and Masters thereof, wee made speedy preparation for the defence of our selues, still waiting all the night long for the approching of the enemie. In the morning early being the Tuesday in Easter weeke, and the 24 of April 1590 according to our vsual customes, we said Seruice and made our prayers vnto Almightie God, beseeching him to saue vs from the hands of such tyrants as the Spaniards, whom we iustly imagined to be, and whom we knew and had found to be our most mortall enemies vpon the Sea. And hauing finished our prayers, and set ourselues in a readinesse, we perceiued them to come towards vs, and that they were indeede the Spanish Gallies that lay vnder the conduct of Andre Doria, who is Vice-roy for the King of Spaine in the Straights of Gibraltar, and a notable knowne enemie to all Englishmen. So when they came somewhat neerer vnto vs, they waued vs a maine for the King of Spaine, and wee waued them a maine for the Queene of England, at which time it pleased Almightie God greatly to encourage vs all in such sort, as that the neerer they came the lesse we feared their great multitudes and huge number of men, which were planted in those Gallies to the number of two or three hundred men in ech Gallie. And it was thus concluded among vs, that the foure first and tallest ships should be placed hindmost, and the weaker and smallest ships formost, and so it was performed, every man being ready to take part of such successe as it should please God to send.

And the first encounter the Gallies came vpon vs very fiercely, yet God so strengthened vs, that if they had bene ten times more, we had not feared them at all. Whereupon the Salomon being a hot shippe, and hauing sundry cast pieces in her, gaue the first shotte in such a sowre sort, as that it shared away so many men as sate on the one side of a Gallie, and pierced her through in such maner, as that she was readie to sinke, which made them to assault vs the more fiercely. [Sidenote: A fight of six houres long.] Whereupon the rest of our shippes, especially the foure chiefest, namely, the Margaret and Iohn, the Minion, and the Ascension followed, and gaue a hot charge vpon them, and they at vs, where began a hot and fierce battaile with great valiancie the one against the other, and so continued for the space of six houres. [Sidenote: A faint hearted Fleming.] About the beginning of this our fight there came two Flemings to our Fleet, who seeing the force of the Gallies to be so great, the one of them presently yeelded, strooke his sailes, and was taken by the Gallies, whereas if they would haue offered themselues to haue fought in our behalfe and their owne defence, they needed not to haue bene taken so cowardly as they were to their cost. The other Fleming being also ready to performe the like piece of seruice began to vaile his sailes, and intended to haue yeelded immediatly. But the Trumpetter in that shippe plucked foorth his faulchion and stepped to the Pilote at the helme, and vowed that if he did not speedily put off to the English Fleete, and so take part with them, he would presently kill him: which the Pilote for feare of death did, and so by that meanes they were defended from present death, and from the tyrannie of those Spaniards, which doubtlesse they should haue found at their handes.

Thus we continued in fight six houres and somewhat more, wherein God gaue vs the vpper hand, and we escaped the hands of so many enemies, who were constrained to flie into harbour and shroude themselues from vs, and with speed to seeke for their owne safetie. This was the handie worke of God, who defended vs all from danger in such sort, as that there was not one man of vs slaine. And in all this fierce assault made vpon vs by the Spanish power, wee sustained no hurt or damage at all more then this, that the shrouds and backe-stay of the Salomon, who gaue the first and last shot, and galled the enemie shrewdly all the time of the battell, were cleane stricken off.

The battel being ceased, we were constrained for want of wind to stay and waft vp and downe, and then went backe againe to Tition in Barbary, which is six leagues off from Gibraltar, and when we came thither we found the people wonderous fauourable to vs, who being but Moores and heathen people shewed vs where to haue fresh water and al other necessaries for vs. And there we had such good intertainment, as if we had bene in any place of England.

The gouernour was one that fauoured vs greatly, whom wee in respect of his great friendship presented with giftes and such commodities as we had in our custodie, which he wonderfully wel accepted of: and here we stayed foure dayes.

After the battell was ceased, which was on Easter Tuesday, we stayed for want of winde before Gibraltar, vntill the next morning, where we were becalmed, and therefore looked euery houre when they would haue sent foorth some fresh supply against vs, but they were farre vnable to doe it, for all their Gallies were so sore battered, that they durst not come foorth of the harbour, by reason of our hot resistance which they so lately before had receiued. Yet were they greatly vrged thereunto by the Gouernour of the said Towne of Gibraltar.

At our being at Tition in Barbary, there we heard report of the hurt that wee had done to the Gallies, for at our comming from them wee could not well discerne any thing at all by reason of the smoake which the powder had made: there we heard that we had almost spoiled those twelue Gallies by shooting them cleane through, that two of them were ready to sinke, and that wee had slaine of their men such great abundance, as that they were not able to furnish forth any more Gallies at all for that yeere.

Thus after we came from Tition, we assayed to depart the Straight three seuerall times, but could not passe, yet, God be thanked, the fourth time wee came safely away, and so sailed with a pleasant winde vntil wee came vpon the coast of England, which was in the beginning of the moneth of Iuly 1590.

* * * * *

The valiant fight performed in the Straight of Gibraltar, by the Centurion of London, against the fiue Spanish Gallies, in the moneth of April 1591.

In the moneth of Nouember 1590, there were sundry shippes appertaining to seuerall Marchants of London, which were rigged and fraught foorth with marchandize, for sundry places within the Straight of Gibraltar: who, together hauing winde and weather, which ofttime fell out very vncertaine, arriued safely in short space, at such places as they desired. Among whom was the Centurion of London, a very tall shippe of burden, yet but weakely manned, as appeareth by this discourse following.

This aforesaid shippe called The Centurion safely arriued at Marseils, where after they had deliuered their goods, they stayed about the space of fiue weekes, and better, and then tooke in lading, intending to returne to England.

Now when the Centurion was ready to come away from Marseils, there were sundry other shippes of smaller burden which entreated the Master thereof, (whose name is Robert Bradshaw, dwelling at Lime-house) to stay a day or two for them, vntill they were in a readinesse to depart with them, thereby perswading them, that it would be farre better for them to stay and goe together in respect of their assistance, then to depart of themselues without company, and so happily for want of aide fall into the hands of their enemies in the Spanish Gallies. Vpon which reasonable perswasion, notwithstanding that this shippe was of such sufficiencie as they might hazard her in the danger of the Sea, yet they stayed for those litle shippes; according to their request, who together did put to Sea from Marseils, and vowed in generall not to flie one from another, if they should happen to meete with any Spanish Gallies.

These small shippes, accompanied with the Centurion, sayling along the coast of Spaine, were ypon Easter day in the Straight of Gibraltar suddenly becalmed, where immediatly they saw sundry Gallies make towards them, in very valiant and couragious sort: the chiefe Leaders and souldiers in those Gallies brauely apparelled in silke coates, with their siluer whistles about their neckes, and great plumes of feathers in their hattes, who with their Caliuers shot at the Centurion so fast as they might: so that by 10. of the clocke and somewhat before, they had boorded the Centurion, who before their comming had prepared for them, and intended to giue them so soure a welcome as they might. And thereupon hauing prepared their close fights, and all things in a readinesse, they called vpon God, on whom onely they trusted: and hauing made their prayers, and cheered vp one another to fight so long as life endured, they beganne to discharge their great Ordinance vpon the Gallies, but the little shippes durst not come forward, but lay aloofe, while fiue Gallies had boorded them, yea and with their grapling irons made their Gallies fast to the said shippe called the Centurion.

The Gallies were grapled to the Centurion in this maner, two lay on one side and two on another, and the Admirall lay full in the stern, which galled and battered the Centurion so sore, that her maine Maste was greatly weakened, her sailes filled with many holes, and the Mizzen and sterne made almost vnseruiceable.

During which time there was a sore and deadly fight on both sides, in which the Trumpet of the Centurion sounded foorth the deadly points of warre, and encouraged them to fight manfully against their aduersaries: on the contrary part, there was no warlike Musicke in the Spanish Gallies, but onely their whistles of siluer, which they sounded foorth to their owne contentment: in which fight many a Spaniard was turned into the Sea, and they in multitudes came crauling and hung vpon the side of the shippe, intending to haue entred into the same, but such was the courage of the Englishmen, that so fast as the Spaniards did come to enter, they gaue them such entertainment, that some of them were glad to tumble aliue into the Sea, being remedilesse for euer to get vp aliue. In the Centurion there were in all, of men and boyes, fourtie and eight, who together fought most valiantly, and so galled the enemie, that many a braue and lustie Spaniard lost his life in that place.

The Centurion was fired seuerall times, with wilde fire and other prouision, which the Spaniards, threw in for that purpose: yet, God be thanked, by the great and diligent foresight of the Master it did no harme at all.

In euery of the Gallies there were about 200. souldiers: who together with the shot, spoiled, rent, and battered the Centurion very sore, shot through her maine Maste, and slew 4. of the men in the said shippe, the one of them being the Masters mate.

Ten other persons were hurt, by meanes of splinters which the Spaniards shotte: yea, in the ende when their prouision was almost spent, they were constrained to shoote at them hammers, and the chaines from their slaues, and yet God bee thanked, they receiued no more domage: but by spoyling and ouer-wearying of the Spaniards, the Englishmen constrained them to vngrapple themselues, and get them going: and sure if there had bene any other fresh shippe or succour to haue relieued and assisted the Centurion, they had slaine, suncke, or taken all those Gallies and their Souldiers.

The Dolphin lay a loofe off and durst not come neere, while the other two small shippes fledde away, so that one of the Gallies went from the Centurion and set vpon the Dolphin, which shippe immediatly was set on fire with their owne powder, whereby both men and shippe perished: but whether it was with their good wills or no, that was not knowen vnto the Centurion, but sure, if it had come forward, and bene an aide vnto the Centurion, it is to bee supposed that it had not perished.

Fiue houres and a halfe this fight continued, in which time both were glad to depart onely to breath themselues, but when the Spaniards were gone, they neuer durst returne to fight, yet the next day six other Gallies came and looked at them, but durst not at any hand meddle with them.

Thus God deliuered them from the handes of their enemies, and gaue them the victorie: For which they heartily praised him, and not long after safely arriued in London.

[Symbol: fist] There were present at this fight Master Iohn Hawes Marchaht, and sundry other of good accompt.

* * * * *

A report of the trueth of the fight about the Iles of Açores, the last of
  August 1591, betwixt the Reuenge one of her Maiesties shippes, and an
  Armada of the king of Spaine; penned by the honourable Sir Walter Ralegh
  knight.

Because the rumours are diuersely spred, as well in England as in the Lowe countries and elsewhere, of this late encounter betweene her Maiesties ships and the Armada of Spaine; and that the Spaniards according to their vsuall maner fill the world with their vaine-glorious vaunts, making great apparance of victories, when on the contrary, themselues are most commonly and shamefully beaten and dishonoured; thereby hoping to possesse the ignorant multitude by anticipating and forerunning false reports: It is agreeable with all good reason, for manifestation of the truth, to ouercome falshood and vntrueth; that the beginning, continuance and successe of this late honourable encounter of Sir Richard Greenuil, and other her Maiesties Captaines, with the Armada of Spaine; should be truely set downe and published without partialitie or false imaginations. And it is no marueile that the Spaniard should seeke by false and slanderous pamphlets, aduisoes and Letters, to couer their owne losse, and to derogate from others their due honors, especially in this fight being performed far off: seeing they were not ashamed in the yeere 1588. when they purposed the inuasion of this land, to publish in sundry languages in print, great victories in wordes, which they pleaded to haue obtained against this

Realme; and spred the same in a most false sort ouer all parts of France, Italy, and elsewhere. When shortly after it was happily manifested in very deed to al Nations, how their Nauy which they termed inuincible, consisting of 140. saile of shippes, not onely of their owne kingdome, but strengthened with the greatest Argosies, Portugal Caracks, Florentines, and huge hulks of other Countreis, were by 30. of her Majesties owne ships of war, and a few of our owne Marchants, by the wise, valiant, and aduantagious conduct of the L. Charles Howard high Admirall of England, beaten and shuffled together; euen from the Lizard in Cornwall first to Portland, where they shamefully left Don Pedro de Valdes, with his mighty ship; from Portland to Cales, where they lost Hugo de Moncado, with the Gallies of which he was Captaine, and from Cales, driuen with squibs from their anchors, were chased out of the sight of England, round about Scotland and Ireland. Where for the sympathie of their barbarous religion, hoping to finde succour and assistance, a great part of them were crusht against the rocks, and those other that landed, being very many in number, were notwithstanding broken, slaine, and taken, and so sent from village to village coupled in halters, to be shipped into England. Where her Maiestie of her Princely and inuincible disposition, disdaining to put them to death, and scorning either to retaine or entertaine them: they were all sent backe againe to their countreys, to witnes and recount the worthy achieuements of their inuincible and dreadfull Nauy: Of which the number of Souldiers, the fearefull burthen of their shippes, the commanders names of euery squadron, with all other their magasines of prouisions, were put in print, as an Army and Nauy vnresistable, and disdaining preuention. With all which so great and terrible an ostentation, they did not in all their sailing round about England, so much as sinke or take one shippe, Barke, Pinnesse, or Cockbote of ours: or euer burnt so much as one sheepecote of this land. When as on the contrarie, Sir Francis Drake, with onely 800. souldiers not long before, landed in their Indies, and forced Sant-Iago, Santo Domingo, Cartagena, and the forts of Florida.

And after that, Sir Iohn Norris marched from Peniche in Portugall, with a handfull of souldiers, to the gates of Lisbone, being aboue 40 English miles. Where the Earle of Essex himselfe and other valiant Gentlemen braued the Citie of Lisbone, encamped at the very gates; from whence, after many dayes abode, finding neither promised partie, nor provision to batter; they made retrait by land, in despight of all their Garrisons, both of horse and foote. In this sort I haue a little digressed from my first purpose, onely by the necessarie comparison of theirs and our actions: the one couetous of honour without vaunt of ostentation; the other so greedy to purchase the opinion of their owne affaires, and by false rumors to resist the blasts of their owne dishonours, as they, will not onely not blush to spread all manner of vntruthes: but euen for the least aduantage, be it but for the taking of one poore aduenturer of the English, will celebrate the victory with bonefires in euery towne, alwayes spending more in faggots, then the purchass was worth they obtained. When as we neuer thought it worth the consumption of two billets, when we haue taken eight or ten of their Indian shippes at one time, and twentie of the Brasill fleete. Such is the difference betweene true valure, and ostentation: and betweene honorable actions, and friuolous vaineglorious vaunts. But now to returne to my purpose.

The L. Thomas Howard with sixe of her Maiesties shippes, sixe victuallers of London, the Barke Ralegh, and two or three other Pinnases riding at anker neere vnto Flores, one of the Westerly Ilands of the Azores, the last of August in the afternoone, had intelligence by one Captaine Middleton of the approch of the Spanish Armada. Which Middteton being in a very good sailer had kept them company three dayes before, of good purpose, both to discouer their forces the more, as also to giue aduise to my L. Thomas of their approch. Hee had no sooner deliuered the newes but the fleete was in sight: many of our shippes companies were on shore in the Ilande; some providing ballast for their ships; others filling of water and refreshing themselues from the land with such things as they could either for money, or by force recouer. By reason whereof our ships being all pestered and romaging euery thing out of order, very light for want of balast, and that which was most to our disadvantage, the one halfe part of the men of euery shippe sicke, and vtterly vnseruiceable: for in the Reuenge there were ninety diseased: in the Bonauenture not so many in health as could handle her maine saile. For had not twenty men beene taken out of a Barque of sir George Careys, his being commaunded to be sunke, and those appointed to her, she had hardly euer recouered England. The rest, for the most parte, were in little better state. The names of her Maiesties shippes were these as followeth, the Defiance, which was Admiral, the Reuenge Vice-admirall, the Bonauenture commaunded by Captaine Crosse, the Lion by George Fenner, the Foresight by M. Thomas Vauasour, and the Crane by Duffild. The Foresight and the Crane being but smal ships; only the other were of the middle size; the rest, besides the Barke Ralegh, commanded by Captaine Thin, were victuallers, and of small force or none. The Spanish Fleet hauing shrouded their approch by reason of the Island; were now so soone at hand, as our shippes had scarce time to way their anchors, but some of them were driuen to let slippe their Cables and set saile. Sir Richard Grinuile was the last that wayed, to recouer the men that were vpon the Island, which otherwise had bene lost. The L. Thomas with the rest very hardly recouered the winde, which Sir Richard Grinuile not being able to doe, was perswaded by the Master and others to cut his maine sayle, and cast about, and to trust to the sayling of the ship; for the squadron of Siuil were on his weather bow. But Sir Richard vtterly refused to turne from the enemie, alleaging that hee would rather choose to die, then to dishonour himselfe, his countrey, and her Maiesties shippe, perswading his companie that hee would passe through the two squadrons, in despight of them, and enforce those of Siuil to giue him way. Which hee performed vpon divers of the formost, who, as the Mariners terme it, sprang their luffe, and fell vnder the lee of the Reuenge. But the other course had beene the better, and might right well haue bene answered in so great an impossibility of preuailing. Notwithstanding out of the greatnesse of his minde, he could not be perswaded. In the meane while as hee attended those which were nearest him, the great San Philip being in the winde of him, and comming towards him, becalmed his sailes in such sort, as the shippe could neither make way, nor feele the helme: so huge and high carged [Footnote: From the French, *carguer* to furl.] was the Spanish ship, being of a thousand and fiue hundreth tuns. Who after layd the Reuenge aboord. When he was thus bereft of his sailes, the ships that were vnder his lee luffing vp, also layd him aboord: of which the next was the Admiral of the Biscaines, a very mighty and puissant shippe commanded by Brittandona. The sayd Philip carried three tire of ordinance on a side, and eleuen pieces in euery tire. She shot eight forth right out of her chase, besides those of her sterne ports.

After the Reuenge was entangled with this Philip, foure other boorded her: two on her larbood, and two on her starboord. The fight thus beginning at three of the clock in the afternoone, continued very terrible all that euening. But the great San Philip hauing receiued the lower tire of the Reuenge, discharged with crosse bar-shot, shifted her selfe with all diligence from her sides, vtterly misliking her first entertainement. Some say that the shippe foundred, but we cannot report it for truth, vnlesse we were assured. The Spanish ships were filled with companies of souldiers, in some two hundred besides the mariners; in some fiue, in others eight hundreth. In ours there were none at all besides the mariners; but the seruants of the commanders and some few voluntary gentlemen onely. After many interchanged volies of great ordinance and small shot, the Spaniards deliberated to enter the Reuenge, and made diuers attempts, hoping to force her by the multitudes of her armed souldiers and Musketters, but were still repulsed againe and againe, and at all times beaten backe into their owne ships, or into the seas. In the beginning of the fight, the George Noble of London hauing receiued some shot thorow her by the Armadas, fell vnder the lee of the Reuenge, and asked Sir Richard what he would command him, being but one of the victuallers, and of small force: Sir Richard bid him saue himselfe, and leaue him to his fortune. After the fight had thus, without intermission, continued while the day lasted and some houres of the night, many of our men slaine and hurte, and one of the great Gallions of the Armada, and the Admirall of the Hulkes both sunke, and in many other of the Spanish shippes great slaughter was made. Some write that Sir Richard was very dangerously hurt almost in the beginning of the fight, and lay speechlesse for a time ere hee recovered. But two of the Reuenges owne company, brought home in a ship of Lime from the Ilandes, examined by some of the Lordes, and others, affirmed that hee was neuer so wounded as that hee forsooke the vpper decke, till an houre before midnight; and then being shot into the bodie with a Musket as hee was a dressing, was againe shot into the head, and withall his Chirurgion wounded to death. This agreeth also with an examination taken by sir Francis Godolphin, of foure other mariners of the same shippe being returned, which examination, the said sir Francis sent vnto master William Killegrue, of her Maiesties priuy Chamber.

But to returne to the fight, the Spanish ships which attempted to bord the Reuenge, as they were wounded and beaten off, so alwayes others came in their places, she hauing neuer lesse then two mighty Gallions by her sides, and aboard her: So that ere the morning, from three of the clocke the day before, there had fifteene seuerall Armadas assayled her; and all so ill approued their entertainment, as they were by the breake of day, far more willing to harken to a composition, then hastily to make any more assaults or entries. But as the day encreased, so our men decreased: and as the light grew more and more, by so much more grewe our discomforts. For none appeared in sight but enemies, sauing one small ship called the Pilgrim, commaunded by Iacob Whiddon, who houered all night to see the successe: but in the morning bearing with the Reuenge, was hunted like a hare amongst many rauenous houndes, but escaped.

All the powder of the Reuenge to the last barrell was now spent, all her pikes broken, fortie of her best men slaine, and the most part of the rest hurt. In the beginning of the fight shee had but one hundreth free from sicknes, and fourescore and ten sicke, laid in hold vpon the Ballast. A small troup to man such a ship, and a weake garrison to resist so mighty an army. By those hundred al was susteined, the voleis, boordings, and entrings of fifteen ships of warre, besides those which beat her at large. On the contrary, the Spanish were always supplied with souldiers brought from euery squadron: all maner of Armes and powder at will. Vnto ours there remained no comfort at all, no hope, no supply either of ships, men, or weapons; the Mastes all beaten ouer board, all her tackle cut asunder, her vpper worke altogether rased, and in effect euened shee was with the water, but the very foundation or bottome of a ship, nothing being left ouer head either for flight or defence. [Sidenote: The Spanish 53 saile.] Sir Richard finding himselfe in this distress, and vnable any longer to make resistance, hauing endured in this fifteene houres fight, the assault of fifteene seuerall Armadas, all by turnes aboord him, and by estimation eight hundred shotte of great Artillerie, besides many assaults and entries; and that himselfe and the shippe must needes be possessed by the enemy, who were now all cast in a ring round about him (The Reuenge not able to moue one way or the other, but as she was moued with the waues and billow of the sea) commanded the Master gunner, whom hee knew to be a most resolute man, to split and sinke the shippe; that thereby nothing might remaine of glory or victory to the Spaniards: seeing in so many houres fight, and with so great a Nauie they were not able to take her, hauing had fifteene houres time, aboue ten thousand men, and fiftie and three saile of men of warre to performe it withall: and perswaded the company, or as many as hee could induce, to yeelde themselues vnto God, and to the mercie of none else; but as they had, like valiant resolute men, repulsed so many enemies, they should not nowe shorten the honour of their Nation, by prolonging their owne liues for a few houres, or a fewe dayes. The Master gunner readily condescended and diuers others; but the Captaine and the Master were of another opinion, and besought Sir Richard to haue care of them: alleaging that the Spaniard would be as ready to entertaine a composition, as they were willing to offer the same: and that there being diuers sufficient and valiant men yet liuing, and whose wounds were not mortal, they might do their Countrey and prince acceptable seruice hereafter. And whereas Sir Richard had alleaged that the Spaniards should neuer glory to haue taken one shippe of her Maiestie, seeing they had so long and so notably defended themselues; they answered, that the shippe had sixe foote water in holde, three shot vnder water, which were so weakely stopped, as with the working of the sea, she must needs sinke, and was besides so crusht and brused, as shee could neuer be remoued out of the place.

And as the matter was thus in dispute, and Sir Richard refusing to hearken to any of those reasons: the Master of the Reuenge (while the Captaine wanne vnto him the greater party) was conuoyd aboord the Generall Don Alfonso Baçan: Who (finding none ouer hastie to enter the Reuenge againe, doubting least Sir Richard would haue blowne them vp and himselfe, and perceiuing by report of the Master of the Reuenge his dangerous disposition) yeelded that all their liues should be saued, the company sent for England, and the better sort to pay such reasonable ransome as their estate would beare, and in the meane season to be free from Gally or imprisonment. To this he so much the rather condescended as wel, as I haue said, for feare of further losse and mischiefe to themselues, as also for the desire he had to recouer Sir Richard Greenuil; whom for his notable valure he seemed greatly to honour and admire.

When this answere was returned, and that safetie of life was promised, the common sort being now at the ende of their perill, the most drew backe from Sir Richard and the Master gunner, being no hard matter to disswade men from death to life. The Master gunner finding himselfe and Sir Richard thus preuented and mastered by the greater number, would haue slaine himselfe with a sword, had he not bene by force with-held and locked into his Cabben. Then the Generall sent many boates aboord the Reuenge, and diuers of our men fearing Sir Richards disposition, stole away aboord the Generall and other shippes. Sir Richard thus ouermatched, was sent vnto by Alfonso Baçan to remooue out of the Reuenge, the shippe being marueilous vnsauorie, filled with blood and bodies of dead, and wounded men like a slaughter house. Sir Richard answered that hee might doe with his body what he list, for hee esteemed it not, and as he was carried out of the shippe hee swounded, and reuiuing againe desired the company to pray for him. The Generall vsed Sir Richard with all humanitie, and left nothing vnattempted that tended to his recouery, highly commending his valour and worthinesse, and greatly bewailing the danger wherein he was, being vnto them a rare spectacle, and a resolution seldome approoued, to see one shippe turne toward so many enemies, to endure the charge and boording of so many huge Armadas, and to resist and repell the assaults and entries of so many souldiers. All which and more is confirmed by a Spanish Captaine of the same Armada, and a present actor in the fight, who being seuered from the rest in a storme, was by the Lion of London a small ship taken, and is now prisoner in London.

The generall commander of the Armada, was Don Alphonso Baçan, brother to the Marques of Santa Cruz. The admiral of the Biscaine squadron, was Britandona. Of the squadron of Siuil, the Marques of Arumburch. The Hulkes and Flybotes were commanded by Luis Coutinho. There were slaine and drowned in this fight, well neere one thousand of the enemies, and two speciall commanders Don Luis de sant Iohn, and Don George de Prunaria de Mallaga, as the Spanish captaine confesseth, besides diuers others of speciall account, whereof as yet report is not made.

The Admirall of the Hulkes and the Ascension of Siuil were both sunke by the side of the Reuenge; one other recouered the rode of Saint Michael, and sunke also there; a fourth ranne her self with the shore to saue her men. Sir Richard died as it is sayd, the second or third day aboord the Generall, and was by them greatly bewailed. What became of his body, whether it were buried in the sea or on the land we know not: the comfort that remayneth to his friends is, that hee hath ended his life honourably in respect of the reputation wonne to his nation and countrey, and of the same to his posteritie, and that being dead, he hath not outliued his owne honour.

For the rest of her Maiesties ships that entred not so farre into the fight as the Reuenge, the reasons and causes were these. There were of them but sixe in all, whereof two but small ships; the Reuenge ingaged past recouery: The Iland of Flores was on the one side, 53 saile of the Spanish, diuided into squadrons on the other, all as full filled with souldiers as they could containe: Almost the one halfe of our men sicke and not able to serue: the ships growne foule, vnroomaged, and scarcely able to beare any saile for want of ballast, hauing bene sixe moneths at the sea before. If all the rest had entred, all had bene lost: for the very hugenes of the Spanish fleete, if no other violence had beene offered, would haue crusht them betweene them into shiuers. Of which the dishonour and losse to the Queene had bene farre greater then the spoyle or harme that the enemie could any way haue receiued. Notwithstanding it is very true, that the Lord Thomas would haue entred betweene the squadrons, but the rest would not condescend; and the master of his owne ship offred to leape into the sea, rather then to conduct that her Maiesties ship and the rest to bee a pray to the enemie, where there was no hope nor possibilitie either of defence or victory. Which also in my opinion had ill sorted or answered the discretion and trust of a Generall, to commit himselfe and his charge to an assured destruction, without hope or any likelyhood of preuailing: thereby to diminish the strength of her Maiesties Nauy, and to enrich the pride and glory of the enemie. The Foresight of the Queenes commaunded by M. Thomas Vauisor performed a very great fight, and stayed two houres as neere the Reuenge as the weather would permit him, not forsaking the fight, till he was like to be encompassed by the squadrons, and with great difficultie cleared himselfe. The rest gaue diuers voleis of shot, and entred as farre as the place permitted, and their owne necessities, to keepe the weather gage of the enemie, vntill they were parted by night. A fewe dayes after the fight was ended, and the English prisoners dispersed into the Spanish and Indie ships, there arose so great a storme from the West and Northwest; that all the fleete was dispersed, as well the Indian fleete which were then come vnto them, as the rest of the Armada that attended their arriual, of which 14. saile together with the Reuenge, and in her 200. Spaniards, were cast away vpon the Isle of S. Michael. So it pleased them to honor the buriall of that renowmed ship the Reuenge, not suffering her to perish alone, for the great honour she atchieued in her life time. On the rest of the Ilandes there were cast away in this storme, 15 or 16 more of the ships of warre: and of an hundred and odde saile of the Indie fleete, expected this yeere in Spaine, what in this tempest, and what before in the bay of Mexico, and about the Bermudas, there were 70 and odde consumed and lost, with those taken by our shippes of London, besides one very rich Indian ship, which set herselfe on fire, beeing boarded by the Pilgrim, and fiue other taken by master Wats his ships of London, between the Hauana and Cape S. Antonio. The fourth of this moneth of Nouember we receiued letters from the Tercera, affirming that there are 3000 bodies of men remaining in that Iland, saued out of the perished ships: and that by the Spaniards owne confession, there are 10000 cast away in this storme, besides those that are perished betweene the Ilands and the maine. Thus it hath pleased God to fight for vs and to defend the iustice of our cause, against the ambicious and bloody pretenses of the Spaniard, who seeking to deuoure all nations, are themselues deuoured. A manifest testimony how iniust and displeasing, their attempts are in the sight of God, who hath pleased to witnes by the successe of their affaires, his mislike of their bloody and iniurious designes, purposed and practised against all Christian princes, ouer whom they seeke vnlawfull and vngodly rule and Empery.

One day or two before this wracke happened to the Spanish fleete, when as some of our prisoners desired to be set on shore vpon the Ilandes, hoping to be from thence transported into England, which libertie was formerly by the Generall promised: One Morice Fitz Iohn, sonne of olde Iohn of Desmond, a notable traytour, cousin german to the late Earle of Desmond, was sent to the English from shippe to shippe, to perswade them to serue the King of Spaine. The arguments hee vsed to induce them were these. The increase of pay which he promised to be trebled: aduancement to the better sort: and the exercise of the true Catholique Religion, and safetie of their soules to all. For the first, euen the beggerly and vnnaturall behauiour of those English and Irish rebels, that serued the King in that present action, was sufficient to answere that first argument of rich pay. For so poore and beggerly they were, as for want of apparell they stripped their poore Countrey men prisoners out of their ragged garments, worne to nothing by six months seruice, and spared not to despoyle them euen of their bloody shirtes, from their wounded bodies, and the very shooes from their feete; A notable testimonie of their rich entertainment and great wages. The second reason was hope of aduancement if they serued well, and would continue faithfull to the King. But what man can be so blockishly ignorant euer to expect place or honour from a forraine King, hauing no other argument or perswasion then his owne disloyaltie; to be vnnatural to his owne Countrey that bred him; to his parents that begat him, and rebellious to his true Prince, to whose obedience he is bound by oath, by nature, and by Religion? No, they are onely assured to be employed in all desperate enterprises, to bee helde in scorne and disdaine euer among those whom they serue. And that euer traitour was either trusted or aduanced I could neuer yet reade, neither can I at this time remember any example. And no man coulde haue lesse becommed the place of an Orator for such a purpose, then this Morice of Desmond. For the Erle his cosen being one of the greatest subiects in that kingdom of Ireland, hauing almost whole Countreis in his possession; so many goodly Manners, castles, and lordships; the Count Palatine of Kerry, fiue hundred gentlemen of his owne name and family to follow him, besides others (all which he possessed in peace for three or foure hundred yeeres) was in lesse then three yeeres after his adhering to the Spaniards and rebellion, beaten from all his holdes, not so many as ten gentlemen of his name left liuing, himselfe taken and beheaded by a souldier of his owne nation, and his land giuen by a Parliament to her Maiestie, and possessed by the English: His other cosen Sir Iohn of Desmond taken by Master Iohn Zouch, and his body hanged ouer the gates of his natiue Citie to be deuoured by rauens: the thirde brother Sir Iames hanged, drawne, and quartered in the same place. If hee had withall vaunted of his successe of his owne house, no doubt the argument would haue mooued much, and wrought great effect: which because, hee for that present forgot, I thought it good to remember in his behalfe. For matter of Religion it would require a particular volume, if I should set downe how irreligiously they couer their greedy and ambicious pretenses, with that veile of pietie. But sure I am, that there is no kingdome or commonwealth in all Europe, but if they be reformed, they then inuade it for religion sake: if it bee, as they terme Catholique, they pretend title; as if the Kings of Castile were the naturall heires of all the world: and so betweene both, no kingdome is vnsought. Where they dare not with their owne forces to inuade, they basely entertaine the traitours and vagabonds of all Nations: seeking by those and by their runnagate Iesuits to winne parts, and haue by that meane ruined many Noble houses and others in this lande, and haue extinguished both their liues and families. What good, honour, or fortune euer man yet by them atchieued, is yet vnheard of, or vnwritten. And if our English Papists doe but looke into Portugall, against which they haue no pretense of Religion, how the Nobilitie are put to death, imprisoned, their rich men made a praye, and all sorts of people captiued; they shall finde that the obedience euen of the Turke is easie and a libertie, in respect of the slauerie and tyrannie of Spaine. What haue they done in Sicill, in Naples, Millaine, and in the Low countreis; who hath there bene spared for Religion at all: And it commeth to my remembrance of a certaine Burger of Antwerpe, whose house being entred by a company of Spanish souldiers, when they first sacked the Citie, hee besought them to spare him and his goods, being a good Catholique, and one of their owne partie and faction. The Spaniards answered, that they knew him to be of a good conscience for himselfe, but his money, plate, iewels, and goods were all hereticall, and therefore good prize. So they abused and tormented the foolish Fleming, who hoped that an Agnus Dei had bene a sufficient target against all force of that holy and charitable nation. Neither haue they at any time as they protest inuaded the kingdomes of the Indies and Peru, and elsewhere, but onely led thereunto, rather to reduce the people to Christianitie, then for either gold or Emperie. When as in one onely Island called Hispaniola, they haue wasted thirtie hundred thousand of the naturall people, besides many millions else in other places of the Indies: a poore and harmelesse people created of God, and might haue bene wonne to his knowledge, as many of them were, and almost as many as euer were perswaded thereunto. The storie whereof is at large written by a Bishop of their owne nation called Bartholomew de las Casas, and translated into

English and many other languages, intituled The Spanish cruelties. Who would therefore repose trust in such a nation of ravenous strangers, and especially in those Spaniards which more greedily thirst after English blood, then after the liues of any other people of Europe, for the many ouerthrowes and dishonours they haue receiued at our hands, whose weakeness wee haue discouered to the world, and whose forces at home, abroad, in Europe, in India, by sea and land, wee haue euen with handfulles of men and shippes, ouerthrowen and dishonoured. Let not therefore any English man, of what religion soeuer, haue other opinion of the Spaniards, but that those whom hee seeketh to winne of our Nation, he esteemeth base and trayterous, vnworthy persons, or vnconstant fooles: and that he vseth his pretense of religion, for no other purpose but to bewitch vs from the obedience of our naturall Prince, thereby hoping in time to bring vs to slauery and subiection, and then none shall be vnto them so odious, and disdayned as the traitours themselues, who haue solde their Countrey to a stranger, and forsaken their faith and obedience contrarie to nature and religion; and contrarie to that humane and generall honour, not onely of Christians, but of heathen and irreligious nations, who haue always sustayned what labour soeuer, and embraced euen death it selfe, for their countrey, Prince, or common wealth. To conclude, it hath euer to this day pleased God to prosper and defend her Maiestie, to breake the purposes of malicious enemies, of forsworne traytors, and of iniust practises and inuasions. She hath euer beene honoured of the worthiest kings, serued by faithfull subiects, and shall by the fauour of God, resist, repell, and confound all whatsoeuer attempts against her sacred person or kingdome. In the meane time let the Spaniard and traytour vaunt of their successe, and wee her true and obedient vassals guided by the shining light of her virtues, shall alwayes loue her, serue her, and obey her to the end of our liues. [Footnote: The most complete collection of contemporary documents relating to this interesting episode, is to be found in "*The Last Fight of the Revenge*", privately printed, Edinburgh, 1886 (GOLDSMID'S BIBLIOTHECA CURIOSA.)]

* * * * *

A particular note of the Indian fleet, expected to haue come into Spaine this present yeere of 1591. with the number of shippes that are perished of the same: according to the examination of certaine Spaniards lately taken and brought into England by the ships of London.

The fleete of Noua Hispania, at their first gathering together and setting foorth, were two and fiftie sailes. The Admirall was of six hundred tunnes, and the Vice Admirall of the same burthen. Foure or fiue of the shippes were of nine hundred and 1000 tunnes a piece, some fiue hundred, and some foure hundred and the least of two hundred tuns. Of this fleet 19 were cast away, and in them 2600 men by estimation, which was done along the coast of Noua Hispania, so that of the same fleet there came to the Hauana but 33 sailes.

The fleete of Terra Firma were, at their first departure from Spaine, fiftie sailes, which were bound for Nombre de Dios, where they did discharge their lading, and thence returned to Cartagena, for their healths sake, vntill the time the treasure was readie they should take in, at the said Nombre de Dios. But before this fleete departed, some were gone by one or two at a time, so that onely 23 sayles of this fieete arriued in the Hauana.

At the Hauana there met

33 sailes of Noua Hispania. 23 sailes of Terra Firma. 12 sailes of San Domingo. 9 sailes of the Hunduras.

The whole 77 shippes, ioyned and set sailes all together at the Hauana, the 17 of Iuly, according to our account, and kept together vntill they came into the height of thirtie fiue degrees, which was about the tenth of August, where they found the winde at Southwest chaunged suddenly to the North, so that the sea comming out of the Southwest, and the wind very violent at North, they were put all into great extremitie, and then first lost the Generall of their fleete, with 500 men in her; and within three or foure dayes after, an other storme rising, there were fiue or sixe other of the biggest shippes cast away with all their men, together with their Vice-Admirall.

And in the height of 38. degrees, about the end of August, grew another great storme, in which all the fleet sauing 48. sailes were cast away: which 48. sailes kept together, vntill they came in sight of the Ilands of Coruo and Flores, about the fift or sixt of September, at which time a great storme separated them: of which number fifteene or sixteene were after seene by these Spanyards to ride at anchor vnder the Tercera; and twelue or foureteene more to beare with the Island of S. Michael; what became of them after that these Spaniards were taken cannot yet be certified; their opinion as, that very few of thee fleet are escaped, but are either drowned or taken. And it is other waies of late certified, that of this whole fleete that should haue come into Spaine this yeere, being one hundred twentie and three sayle, there are arriued as yet but fiue and twentie. This note was taken out of the examination of certaine Spaniardes, that were brought into England by sixe of the ships of London, which tooke seuen of the aboue named Indian Fleete, neere the Islands of the Açores.

* * * * *

A report of Master Robert Flicke directed to Master Thomas Bromley, Master

Richard Staper, and Master Cordall concerning the successe of a part of the London supplies sent to my Lord Thomas Howard to the Isles of the Azores, 1591.

Worshipfull, my heartie commendations vnto you premised: By my last of the twelfth of August from this place I aduertised you particularly of the accidents of our Fleete vntill then. It remayneth now to relate our endeuours in accomplishing the order receiued for the ioyning with my Lorde Thomas Howard, together with the successe wee haue had. Our departure from hence was the seuenteenth of August, the winde not seruing before. The next day following I caused a Flagge of Counsell to be put foorth, whereupon the Captaines and Masters of euery shippe came aboord, and I acquainted them with my Commission, firmed by the Right honourable the Lordes of her Maiesties Counsell, and with all the aduertisements of Sir Edward Denny, of my Lordes determination to remaine threescore leagues to the West of Fayal, spreading North and South betwixt thirtie seuen and a halfe or thirty eight and a halfe degrees. And not finding him in this heighth to repaire to the Isles of Flores and Coruo, where a Pinnesse of purpose should stay our comming vntill the last of August, with intent after that day to repaire to the coast of Spaine, about the heigth of The Rocke, some twentte or thirtie leagues off the shoare. The which being aduisedly considered of hauing regard vnto the shortnesse of time, by reason of our long abode in this place, and the vncertainety of the weather to fauour vs, it was generally holden for the best and securest way to meete with my Lorde, to beare with the heigth of The Rocke, without making any stay vpon the coast, and so directly for the Islands which was accordingly fully agreed and performed. The 28 day wee had sight of the Burlings, and the 29 being thwart of Peniche, the winde seruing vs, without any stay we directed our course West for the Islands. The 30 day we met with Captaine Royden in the Red-Rose, sometime called the Golden Dragon, separated from my Lorde of Cumberland in a storme: who certified vs of 50 sayles of the Spanish kings Armadas to be gone for the Ilands, but could not informe vs any newes of my Lord Thomas Howard, otherwise then vpon presumption to remaine about the Islandes, and so wee continued our course the winde standing with vs.

The 4 of September we recouered Tercera, and ranged along all the Islands, both on the South and North sides the space of foure dayes: during which time it was not our hap to meete with any shipping, whereby either to vnderstand of my Lord, or of the Indian Fleete: hereupon we directed our course to the West from Fayal, according to the instructions of Sir Edward Denny. The 11 day in the plying to the Westwards we descried a sayle out of our maine toppe, and in the afternoone betweene two and three of the clocke hauing raysed her hull, the weather became calme, so that the ship could not fetch her. I sent off my Skiffe throughly manned, furnished with shot and swords, The Cherubin, and the Margaret and Iohn doing the like. Vpon this the sayle stood off againe, and the night approching, our boates lost her and so returned. In this our pursute after the sayle the Centurion being left a sterne, the next morning wee missed her, and spent that day in plying vp and down seeking her. And for as much as euery of the ships had receiued order, that, if by extremity of weather or any other mischance they should be seuered from our Fleete, they should meete and ioyne at Flores, we, according to the instructions of Sir Edward Denny, proceeded to the finding of my Lord Thomas Howard, being in the heigth appointed and not able to holde the same by reason of extreme tempestes which forced vs to the Isles of Flores and Coruo, which we made the 14 day in the morning, and there also ioyned againe with the Centurion, whose company before we had lost: who declared vnto vs that the 12 day, being the same day they lost vs, they met with fiue and forty sailes of the Indian Fleete. The same night, vpon these newes we came to an anker betweene Flores and Coruo, and the morow following at the breake of day, a flagge of Counsell being put out, the Captaines and Masters came abord me: where, for the desire to vnderstand some tidings of my Lord, as also the supplying of our want of water, it was thought good to send our boats furnished on shore, vnder the conduct of Captaine Brothus, and then it was also ordered after our departure thence to range along the Southsides of the Islands to the end we might either vnderstand of my Lord, or else light on the Indian fleete; and in the missing of our purpose to direct our course for Cape Sant Vincente.

The boates, according to the foresayd determination, being sent on shoare, it chaunced that the Costely ryding vttermost in the roade, did weigh to bring her selfe more neere among vs for the succour of the boates sent off, and in opening the land discouered two sayles, which we in the roade could not perceiue: whereupon shee gaue vs a warning piece, which caused vs to waue off our boates backe, and before they could recouer our shippes, the discryed ships appeared vnto vs, towardes the which we made with all haste, and in a very happie hour, as it pleased God. [Sidenote: A violent storm.] In that wee had not so soone cleared the lande, and spoken with one of them, which was a Barke of Bristoll, who had also sought my Lorde in the heigths appointed and could not finde him, but a violent storme arose, in such manner, as if we had remained in the roade, we had beene in daunger of perishing: and the same extremely continued during the space of threescore houres. In which storme I was separated from our Fleete, except the Cherubin and the Costely, which kept company with mee. And so sayling among the Ilands, I viewed the roade of Fayal, and finding no Roaders there, went directly for the Isle Tercera.

The nineteenth day in the morning comming vnto the same with intent to edge into the Road, a tempest arose and scanted the winde, that we could not sease it: from the which being driuen we fell among certaine of the Indian Fleete, which the sayde storme dispersed, and put them from the road: whereupon my selfe with the other two ships in companie gaue seuerall chases, and thereby lost the company each of other.

[Sidenote: A Portugall Prize taken.] In following our chase aboue noone we made her to strike and yeelde, being a Portugall, laden with hides, salsaperilla and Anile. At this very instant we espied another, and taking our Prise with vs followed her, and somewhat before night obtayned her, named the Conception, Francisco Spinola being Captaine, which was laden with hides, Cochonillio, and certaine raw silke. And for that the seas were so growen, as neither with boate nor shippe they were to bee boorded, we kept them till fit opportunitie. [Sidenote: A rich West-Indian Prize taken.] The same night a litle before day there happened another into our company, supposing vs by our two prizes to be of their Fleete, which we vntill the morning dissembled.

The 20 day in the morning, the sayle being shot somewhat a head of vs, hauing a speciall care for the safe keeping of the two former, we purposed to cause our Prizes to put out more sayle thereby to keep them neere in giuing chase to the other: vnto the which the Master would not hearken nor be perswaded, but that they would follow vs: by the which his wilfulnesse by such time as we had caused the other to yeelde, and sent men aboord, the Conception, Francisco Spinola Captaine being brought a sterne, and hauing gotten the winde of vs, stood off with all her sayles bearing, so as we were forced to make a new chase of her: and had not the winde enlarged vpon vs we had lost her. In the pursute before we recouered her and brought our selues againe in company of our other Prizes, the whole day was spent, and by this meanes we lost the oportunitie of that day, the weather fitly seruing to boord the Portugall Prize, which was in great distresse, and made request to take them being readie to sinke, and, as we well perceiued, they ceased not to pumpe day and night: the which ship to all our iudgements the same night perished in the sea.

The one and twentie day the Conception, whereof Francisco Spinola was Captaine, being also in a leake, and the same still increasing notwithstanding the continuall pumping, in such sort as not to be kept along aboue water, I tooke and discharged out of her two and forty chestes of Cochonillio and silkes, and so left her with 11 foote water in holde and her furniture and 4700 hides, vnto the seas.

The other prize which we haue brought into the harborough is named Nostra Sennora de los remedios, whereof Francisco Aluares is Captaine, laden with 16 chests of Cochonillio, certaine fardels of raw silke, and about 4000 hides. Vpon the discharge of the goods your worships shall be particularly aduertised thereof.

In the boording of the prizes the disorder of the company was such, as that they letted not presently besides the rifling of the Spaniards to breake open the chests and to purloyne such money as was in them: notwithstanding that it was ordered at convenient leasure to haue gone on boord my selfe, and therein the presence of three or foure witnesses to haue taken a iust account thereof, and the same to haue put in safe keeping, according to the effects of articles receiued in this behalfe.

And whereas there were also certaine summes of money taken from the company which they had thus purloyned and embeseled, and the same with some other parcels brought aboord my ship, amounting vnto 2129 pezoes and a halfe, the company as pillage due vnto them demanded to haue the same shared, which I refused, and openly at the maine maste read the articles firmed by my Lord Treasurer and my Lord Admirall, whereby we ought to be directed, and that it was not in mee any way to dispose thereof, vntill the same were finally determined at home. Hereupon they mutinied and at last grew into such furie, as that they would haue it or els breake downe the cabbine, which they were also readie to put into practise, whereby I was forced to yeeld, least the Spaniards which we had abord being many perceiuing the same, might haue had fit opportunitie to rise against vs, which, after their brawles were appeased, they sought to haue put into execution.

By the last aduise from Castile the Generall of the kings Armada which is lately come to sea hath receiued commaundement to ioyne his Fleete with those of the Indies, and for to stay altogether at Tercera vntill the 15 of October: for that 6 pataches with 7 or 8 millions of the kings treasure will come by that time, or els they stay their comming from Hauana vntill Ianuary next, or the kings further pleasure therein to be knowen. These pataches are said to be of 300 tuns the piece, and to cary 30 pieces of brasse, and also of saile reported to haue the aduantage of any shipping.

There perished of the Indies Fleete sunke in the sea before there comming to Flores 11 sailes, whereof the General was one, and not one man saued. And it is by the Spaniards themselues presupposed that the stormes which we had at Flores and at Tercera haue deuoured many more of them, whereof in part we were eye witnesses. And so what by the seas and our men of warre I presume that of 75 sailes that came from Hauana, halfe of them will neuer arriue in Spaine.

The 11 day of October at night we came to anker in the sound of Plimouth, and the next morning with our Prize came into Cattewater: for which God be thanked: for that a vehement storme arose, and with such fury increased, as that the Prize was forced to cut ouer her maine maste: otherwise with the violence of the storme, her ground tackle being bad, she had driuen on shore: which was the most cause that moued me to put in here; intending now here to discharge the goods without further aduenture, and haue certified thus much vnto my Lord Admirall, and therewith also desired to vnderstande the direction of the Lords of the Counsell together with yours, insomuch as my Lord Thomas Howard is not returned. How the rest of our consorts which were seperated from vs by weather haue sped, or what Prizes they haue taken, whereof there is much hope by reason of the scattering of the West Indian Fleete, as yet we are able to say nothing. And thus expecting your answere, and for all other matters referring me vnto the bearer Captaine Furtho, I end. Plymouth the 24 of October 1591.

Your worships louing friend

Robert Flicke.

∗ ∗ ∗ ∗ ∗

A large testimony of Iohn Huighen van Linschoten Hollander, concerning the worthy exploits atchieued by the right honourable the Earle of Cumberland, By Sir Martine Frobisher, Sir Richard Greenuile, and diuers other English Captaines, about the Isles of the Açores, and vpon the coasts of Spaine and Portugall, in the yeeres 1589, 1590, 1591, &c. recorded in his excellent discourse of voiages to the East and West Indies, cap. 96. 97. and 99.

The 22 of Iuly 1589 about Euening, being by the Ilands of Flores and Coruo, we perceiued 3 ships that made towards vs, which came from vnder the land, which put vs in great feare: for they came close by our Admirall, and shot diuers times at him, and at another ship of our companie, whereby we perceiued them to be Englishmen, for they bare an English flagge vpon their maine tops, but none of them shewed to be aboue 60 tunnes in greatnes. About Euening they followed after vs, and all night bore lanternes with candles burning in them at their sternes, although the Moone shined. The same night passing hard by the Island of Fayal, the next day being betweene the Island of S. George that lay on our right hand, and the small Island called Graciosa on our left hand, we espied the 3 English ships still following vs that tooke counsell together, whereof one sailed backwards, thinking that some other ship had come after vs without company, and for a time was out of sight, but it was not long before it came again to the other two, wherwith they tooke counsel and came all, 3 together against our ship, because we lay in the lee of al our ships, and had the Island of S. George on the one side in stead of a sconce, thinking to deale so with vs, that in the end we should be constrained to run vpon the shore, whereof we wanted not much, and in that manner with their flagges openly displayed, came lustily towardes vs, sounding their Trumpets, and sayled at the least three times about vs, beating vs with Musket and Caliuer, and some great pieces, and did vs no hurt in the body of our shippe, but spoyled all our sayles and ropes, and to conclude, wee were so plagued by them, that no man durst put foorth his head, and when wee shot off a peece, wee had at the least an houres worke to lade it againe, whereby we had so great a noise and crie in the shippe, as if we had all bene cast away, whereat the English men themselues beganne to mocke vs, and with a thousand iesting words called vnto vs. In the meane time the other shippes hoised all their sayles, and did the best they could to saile to the Island of Tercera, not looking once behinde them to helpe vs, doubting they should come too late thither, not caring for vs, but thinking themselues to haue done sufficiently so they saued their owne stakes, whereby it may easily be seene what company they keepe one with the other, and what order is among them. In the ende the English men perceiuing small aduantage against vs, (little knowing in what case and feare we were, as also because wee were not farre from Tercera) left vs, which made vs not a litle to reioyce, as thinking our selues to bee risen from death to life, although wee were not well assured, neyther yet voyde of feare till we lay in the road before Tercera, and vnder the safetie of the Portingales fort, and that we might get thither in good time wee made all the sailes we could: on the other side we were in great doubt, because we knew not what they did in the Island, nor whether they were our friends or enemies, and we doubted so much the more, because we found no men of warre nor any Caruels of aduise from Portingal, as wee made our accounts to doe, that might conuoy vs from thence, or giue vs aduise, as in that countrey ordinarily they vse to do: and because the English men had bene so victorious in those parts, it made vs suspect that it went not well with Spaine: they of the Island of Tercera were in no lesse fear then we, for seeing our fleete, they thought vs to bee Englishmen, and that wee came to ouerrun the Island, because the 3. Englishmen had bound vp their flags, and came in company with vs: for the which cause the Iland sent out two Caruels that lay there with aduise from the king, for the Indians ships that should come thither. Those Caruels came to view vs, and perceiuing what we were, made after vs, whereupon the English ships left vs, and made towardes them, because the Caruels thought them to be friends, and shunned them not, as supposing them to bee of our company, but we shot foure or fiue times and made signes vnto them that they should make towards the Island, which they presently did. The Englishmen perceiuing that, did put forwards into the sea, and so the Caruels borded vs telling vs that the men of the Island were all in armes, as hauing receiued aduise from Portugall, that Sir Frances Drake was in readinesse, and would come vnto those Islands. They likewise brought vs newes of the ouerthrow of the Spanish fleet before England, and that the English men had bene before the gates of Lisbon; wereupon the king gaue vs commandement that we should put into the Island of Tercera, and there lie vnder the safety of the Castle vntill we receiued further aduise what we should do, or whether we should saile: for that they thought it too dangerous for vs to go to Lisbon. Those newes put our fleet in great feare, and made vs looke vpon eche other not knowing what to say, as being dangerous for them to put into the road, because it lieth open to the sea: so that the Indian ships, although they had expresse commandement from the king, yet they durst not anker there, but onely vsed to come thither, and to lie to and fro, sending their boates on land to fetch such necessaries as they wanted, without ankering: but being by necessitie compelled thereunto, as also by the kings commandement, and for that we vnderstood the Erle of Cumberland not to bee farre from those Islands with certaine ships of warre, we made necessitie a vertue, and entring the road, ankered close vnder the Castle, staying for aduise and order from the king, to performe our voyage, it being then the 24. of Iuly, and S. Iames day.

The day before the Erle of Cumberland with 6. or 7. ships of war, sailed by the Island of Tercera, and to their great good fortune passed out of sight, so that they dispatched themselues in all haste, and for the more securitie, tooke with them 4. hundred Spaniards of those that lay in Garrison in the Island, and with them they sayled towards Lisbon, hauing a good wind: so that within 11 daies after they arriued in the riuer of Lisbon with great gladnes and triumph: for if they had stayed but one day longer before they had entred the riuer, they had all beene taken by Captaine Drake, who with 40 ships came before Cascais at the same time that the Indian ships cast anker in the riuer of Lisbon, being garded thither by diuers Gallies.

While I remained in Tercera, the Erle of Cumberland came to S. Marie, to take in fresh water, and some other victuals: but the inhabitants would not suffer him to haue it, but wounded both himselfe and diuers of his men, whereby they were forced to depart without hauing any thing there.

The Erle of Cumberland while I lay in Tercera, came vnto the Isle of Graciosa, where himselfe in person, with seuen or eight in his company went on land, asking certaine beasts, hens, and other victuals, with wine and fresh water, which they willingly gaue him, and therewith he departed from thence, without doing them any hurt: for the which the inhabitants thanked him, and commended him for his courtesie, and keeping of his promise.

The same time that the Erle of Cumberland was in the Island of Graciosa, he came likewise to Fayall, where at the first time that he came, they beganne to resist him, but by reason of some controuersie among them, they let him land, where he razed the Castle to the ground, and sunke all their Ordinance in the sea, taking with him certaine Carauels and ships that lay in the road, with prouision of all things that he wanted: and therewith departed againe to sea. Whereupon the king caused the principall actors therein to be punished, and sent a company of souldiers thither againe, which went out of Tercera, with all kinde of warlike munition, and great shot, making the fortresse vp againe, the better to defend the Island, trusting no more in the Portugales.

The 99 Chapter.

The ninth of October 1589. there arriued in Tercera fourteene ships that came from the Spanish Indies, laden with Cochinile, Hides, Golde, Siluer, Pearles, and other rich wares. They were fiftie in companie, when they departed out of the Hauen of Hauana, whereof, in their comming out of the Channell, eleuen sunke in the same Channell by foule weather, the rest by a storme were scattered and separated one from the other. The next day there came another ship of the same companie, that sailed close vnder the Island, so to get into the Roade: where she met with an English ship that had not aboue three cast peeces, and the Spaniards 12. They fought a long time together, which we being in the Island might stand and behold: wherevpon the Gouernour of Tercera sent two boates of Musketiers to helpe the shippe: but before they could come at her, the English ship had shot her vnder water, and we saw her sinke into the Sea with all her sayles vp, and not any thing seene of her aboue the water. The Englishmen with their boate saued the Captaine and about thirtie others with him, but not one penie-worth of the goods, and yet in the shippe there was at the least to the value of two hundred thousand Duckats in Golde, Siluer and Pearles, the rest of the men were drowned which might be about fiftie persons, among the which were some Fryers and women, which the Englishmen would not saue. Those that they had saued they set on land: and then they sayled away. The seuen and twentieth of the same moneth, the sayd foureteene ships hauing refreshed themselues in the Island departed from Tercera toward Siuill, and comming vpon the coast of Spaine they were taken by the English ships that lay there to watch for them, two onely excepted which escaped away, and the rest were wholly caried into England.

About the same time the Erle of Cumberland with one of the Queenes ships, and fiue or sixe more, kept about those Islands and came oftentimes so close vnder the Island, and to the Road of Angra, that the people on land might easily tell all his men that he had aboord, and knewe such as walked on the Hatches: they of the Island not once shooting at them, although they might easily haue done it, for they were within Musket shot both of the towne and fort. In these places he continued for the space of two moneths, and sayled round about the Islands, and landed in Graciosa and Fayal, as in the description of those Islands I haue alreadie declared.

Here he tooke diuers ships and Carauels, which he sent into England: so that those of the Island durst not once put foorth their heads. At the same time about three or foure dayes after the Erle of Cumberland had beene in the Island of Fayal, and was departed from thence, there arriued in the said Island of Fayal sixe Indian shippes, whose General was one Iuan Doriues: and there they discharged in the Iland 4 millions of golde and siluer. And hauing with all speede refreshed their ships, fearing the comming of the Englishmen they set sayle, and arriued safely in S. Lucar, not meeting with the enemie, to the great good lucke of the Spaniards and hard fortune of the Englishmen: for that within lesse then two dayes after the golde and siluer was laden againe into the Spanish ships, the Erle of Cumberland sayled againe by that Island: so that it appeared that God would not let them haue it, for if they had once had sight thereof, without doubt it had bene theirs, as the Spaniards themselues confessed.

In the moneth of Nouember there arriued in Tercera two great shippes, which were the Admirall and Viceadmirall of the Fleete laden with siluer, who with stormie weather were separated from the Fleete, and had beene in great torment and distresse, and readie to sinke: for they were forced to vse all their Pumps: so that they wished a thousand times to haue met with the Englishmen to whom they would willingly haue giuen their siluer and all that euer they brought with them onely to saue their liues. And although the Erle of Cumberland lay still about those Islands, yet they met not with him, so that after much paine and labour they got into the Road before Angra, where with all speede they vnladed and discharged aboue fiue millions of siluer, all in pieces of 8 or 10 pound great: so that the whole Kay lay couered with plates and chests of siluer, full of Ryales of eight, most wonderfull to behold, (each million being ten hundred thousand duckats,) besides pearles, gold and other stones, which were not registred. The Admirall and chiefe commander of those ships and Fleete called Aluaro Flores de Quiniones was sicke of the Neapolitan disease, and was brought to land, whereof not long after he died in Siuillia. He brought with him the Kings broad seale and full authoritie to be Generall and chiefe commander vpon the Seas, and of all Fleetes or ships, and of all places and Islands, or lands wheresoeuer he came: wherevpon the Gouernour of Tercera did him great honour, and betweene them it was concluded, perceiuing the weaknesse of their ships, and the danger of the Englishmen, that they would send the shippes, emptie with souldiers to conuey them, either to Siuill or Lisbon, where they could first arriue, with aduise vnto his Maiestie of all that had passed, and that he would giue order to fetch the siluer with good and safe conuoy. Wherevpon the said Aluero Flores stayed there, vnder colour of keeping the siluer, but specially because of his disease, and for that they were affraide of the Englishmen. This Aluaro Flores had alone for his owne part aboue 50000 Duckats in pearles which he shewed vnto vs, and sought to sell them or barter them with vs for spices or bils of exchange. The said two ships set saile with 3 or 4 hundred men, as well souldiers as others that came with them out of India, and being at sea had a storme, wherewith the Admirall burst and sunke in the sea, and not one man saued. The Vice-Admirall cut downe her mast, and ranne the ship on ground hard by Setuuel, where it burst in pieces, some of the men sauing them selues by swimming, that brought the newes, but the rest were drowned.

In the same moneth there came two great ships out of the Spanish Indies, and being within halfe a mile of the Road of Tercera, they met with an English ship, which, after they had fought long together, tooke them both. About 7 or 8 moneths before, there had beene an English shippe in Tercera, that vnder the name of a Frenchman came to traffike in the Island, there to lade woad, and being discouered was both ship and goods confiscated to the kings vse, and all the men kept prisoners: yet went they vp and downe the streetes to get their liuings, by labouring like slaues, being in deede as safe in that Island, as if they had beene in prison. But in the ende vpon a Sunday, all the Saylers went downe behinde the hils called Bresil: where they found a Fisher-boat, whereinto they got and rowed into the sea to the Erle of Cumberlands shippes, which to their great fortune chanced at that time to come by the Island, and ankered with his ships about halfe a mile from the Road of Angra, hard by two small Islands, which lie about a bases shot from the Island and are full of Goats, Deere and Sheepe, belonging to the inhabitants of the Island of Tercera. Those Saylers knew it well, and thereupon they rowed vnto them with their boates, and lying at anker that day, they fetched as many Goates and sheepe as they had neede of: which those of the towne and of the Island well saw and beheld, yet durst not once goe foorth: so there remained no more on land but the Master and the Marchant of the said English ship. This Master had a brother in lawe dwelling in England, who hauing newes of his brothers imprisonment in Tercera, got licence of the Queene of England to set forth a ship, therewith to see if he could recouer his losses of the Spaniards by taking some of them, and so to redeeme his brother that lay prisoner in Tercera, and he it was that tooke the two Spanish ships before the Towne, the Master of the ship aforesaid standing on the shore by me, and looking vpon them, for he was my great acquaintance. The ships being taken that were worth 300 thousand duckats, he sent al the men on land sauing onely two of the principall Gentlemen, which he kept aboord thereby to ransome his brother: and sent the Pilot of one of the Indian ships that were taken, with a letter to the Gouernor of Tercera; wherein he wrote that he should deliuer him his brother, and he would send the 2 Gentlemen on land: if not, he would saile with them into England, as indeed he did, because the Gouernour would not doe it, saying that the

Gentlemen might make that suite to the king of Spaine himselfe. This Spanish Pilot we bid to supper with vs, and the Englishmen likewise, where he shewed vs all the manner of their fight, much commending the order and maner of the Englishmens fighting, as also their courteous vsing of him: but in the end the English Pilot likewise stole away in a French ship, without paying any ransome as yet.

In the moneth of Ianuarie 1590 there arriued one ship alone in Tercera, that came from the Spanish Indies, and brought newes that there was a Fleete of a hundred shippes which put out from the Firme land of the Spanish Indies, and by a storme were driuen vpon the coast called Florida, where they were all cast away, she hauing onely escaped, wherein there were great riches, and many men lost, as it may well be thought: so that they made their account, that of 220 ships that for certaine were knowen to haue put out of Noua Spagna, S. Domingo, Hauana, Capo verde, Brasilia, Guinea, &c. in the yeere 1589. to saile for Spaine and Portugall, there were not aboue 14 or 15 of them arriued there in safetie, all the rest being either drowned, burst or taken.

In the same moneth of Ianuarie there arriued in Tercera 15 or 16 ships that came from Siuil, which were most Flieboats of the Low countries, and some Britons that were arrested in Spaine: these came full of souldiers, and well appointed with munition, to lade the siluer that lay in Tercera, and to fetch Aluares de Flores by the kings commandement into Spaine. And because that time of the yeere there are alwayes stormes about those Ilands, therefore they durst not enter into the road of Tercera, for that as then it blew so great a storme that some of their ships that had ankred were forced to cut downe their mastes, and were in danger to be lost: and among the rest a ship of Biscaie ran against the land and was striken in pieces, but all the men saued themselues. The other ships were forced to keepe the sea and seperate themselues one from the other, where wind and weather would driue them vntill the 15 of March for that in all that time they could not haue one day of faire weather to anker in, whereby they endured much miserie, cursing both the siluer and the Iland. This storme being past, they chanced to meet with a small English ship of about 40 tunnes in bignesse, which by reason of the great wind could not beare all her sailes: so they set vpon her and tooke her, and with the English flag in their Admirals sterne, they came as proudly into the hauen as if they had conquered all the realme of England: but as the Admirall that bare the English flag vpon her sterne was entring into the road, there came by chance two English ships by the Iland that paied her so well for her paines, that they were forced to cry Misericordia, and without all doubt had taken her, if she had bene but a mile further in sea: but because she got vnder the Fortresse, which also began to shoot at the Englishmen, they were forced to leaue her, and to put further into the sea, hauing slaine fiue or sixe of the Spaniards. The Englishmen that were taken in the small shippe were put vnder hatches, and coupled in bolts, and after they had bene prisoners 3 or 4 dayes, there was a Spanish Ensigne bearer in the ship that had a brother slaine in the Fleet that came for England, who as then minding to reuenge his death, and withall to shew his manhood on the English captiues that were in the English ship, which they had taken, as is aforesayd, tooke a poiniard in his hand and went downe vnder the hatches, where finding the poore Englishmen sitting in boltes, with the same poiniard he stabbed sixe of them to the heart: which two others of them perceiuing, clasped each other about the middle, because they would not be murthered by him, and threw themselues into the sea and there were drowned. This acte was of all the Spaniards much disliked and very ill taken, so that they caried the Spaniard prisoner vnto Lisbon, where being arriued, the king of Spaine willed he should be sent into England, that the Queene of England might vse him as she thought good: which sentence his friends by intreatie got to be reuersed, notwithstanding he commanded he should without all fauour be beheaded: but vpon a good Friday the Cardinall going to masse, all the captaines and Commanders made so great intreaty for him, that in the end they got his pardon. This I thought good to note, that men might vnderstand the bloody and dishonest minds of the Spaniards when they haue men vnder their subiection.

The same two English ships which folowed the Spanish Admirall till he had got the Fort of Tercera, as I sayd before, put into the sea, where they met with another Spanish ship being of the same Fleet, that had likewise bene scattred by the storme and was onely missing, for the rest lay in the road. This small ship the Englishmen tooke, and sent all the men on shore, not hurting any of them: but if they had knowen what had bene done vnto the foresayd English captiues I belieue they would soone haue reuenged themselues, as afterward many an innocent soule paied for it. This ship thus taken by the Englishmen, was the same that was taken and confiscated in the Iland of Tercera by the Englishmen that got out of the Iland in a fisher boat (as I said before) and was sold vnto the Spaniards that as then came from the Indies, wherewith they sayled to S. Lucar, where it was also arrested by the duke, and appointed to go in company to fetch the siluer in Tercera, because it was a ship that sailed well, but among the Spaniards Fleet it was the meanest of the company. By this means it was taken from the Spaniards and caried into England, and the owners had it againe when they least thought of it.

The 19 of March the aforesayd ships being 19 in number, set saile, hauing laden the kings siluer, and receiued in Aluaro Flores de Quiniones, with his company and good prouision of necessaries, munition and souldiers that were fully resolued (as they made shew) to fight valiantly to the last man before they would yeeld or lose their riches: and although they set their course for S. Lucar, the wind draue them vnto Lisbon, which (as it seemed) was willing by his force to helpe them, and to bring them thither in safetie, although Aluaro de Flores, both against the wind and weather would perforce haue sailed to Saint Lucar, but being constrained by the wind and importunitie of the sailers that protested they would require their losses and damages of him, he was content to saile to Lisbon: from whence the siluer was by land caried vnto Siuil. At Cape S. Vincent there lay a Fleet of 20 English ships to watch for the Armada, so that if they had put into S. Lucar, they had fallen right into their hands, which if the wind had serued they had done. And therefore they may say that the wind hath lent them a happy voiage: for if the Englishmen had met with them, they had surely bene in great danger, and possibly but few of them had escaped, by reason of the feare wherewith they were possessed, because fortune of rather God was wholy against them: which is a sufficient cause to make the Spaniards out of heart, and to the contrary to giue the Englishmen more courage, and to make them bolder for that they are victorious, stout and valiant: and seeing all their enterprises do take so good effect, that thereby they are become lords and masters of the sea, and need care for no man, as it wel appeareth by this briefe discourse.

The 7 of August 1590. a nauie of English ships was seene before Tercera, being 20 in number, and 5 of them the Queenes ships: their Generall was one Martin Frobisher, as we after had intelligence. They came purposely to watch for the Fleet of the Spanish Indies, and for the Indian ships, and the ships of the countreys in the West: which put the Ilanders in great feare, specially those of Fayal, for that the Englishmen sent a trumpet to the Gouernour to aske certaine wine, flesh, and other victuals for their money and good friendship. They of Fayal did not onely refuse to giue eare vnto them, but with a shot killed their messenger or trumpeter: which the Englishmen tooke in euil part, sending them word that they were best to looke to themselues and stand vpon their guard, for they ment to come and visite them whether they would or no. The Gouernour made them answere that he was there in the behalfe of his maiestie of Spaine, and that he would doe his best to keepe them out, as he was bound: but nothing was done, although they of Fayal were in no little feare, sending to Tercera for aide, from whence they had certaine barkes with ponder and munition for warre, with some bisket and other necessary prouision.

The 30 of August we receiued very certaine newes out of Portugal, that there were 80 ships put out of the Groine laden with victuals, munition, money and souldiers, to goe for Britaine to aide the Catholiques and Leaguers of France against the king of Nauarre. At the same time two

Netherland hulkes comming out of Portugall to Tercera being halfe the Seas ouer, met with 4 of the Queenes ships, their Generall being sir Iohn Hawkins, that staied them, but let them go againe without doing them any harme. The Netherlanders reported, that each of the Queenes ships had 80 pieces of Ordinance, and that captaine Drake lay with 40 ships in the English chanell watching for the armie of the Groine: and likewise that there lay at the Cape S. Vincent ten other English ships, that if any ships escaped from the Ilands, they might take them. These tidings put the Ilanders in great feare, least if they failed of the Spanish fleete and got nothing by them, that then they would fall vpon the Ilands, because they would not returne emptie home, whereupon they held streit watch, sending aduise vnto the king what newes they heard.

The first of September there came to the Iland of S. Michael a Portugall ship out of the hauen of Phernambuck in Brasile, which brought newes that the Admirall of the Portugall Fleet that came from India, hauing missed the Iland of S. Helena, was of necessitie constrained to put into Phernambuck, although the king had expresly vnder a great penaltie forbidden him so to doe, because of the wormes that there doe spoile the ships. The same shippe wherein Bernardin Ribero was Admirall the yeere before 1589. sailed out of Lisbon into the Indies, with 5 ships in her company, whereof but 4 got into India, the 5 was neuer heard of, so that it was thought to be cast away: the other foure returned safe againe into Portugall, though the Admiral was much spoiled, because he met with two English ships that fought long with him, and slew many of his men, but yet he escaped from them.

The 5 of the same moneth there arriued in Tercera a caruel of the Iland of Coruo, and brought with her 50 men that had bin spoiled by the Englishmen who had set them on shore in the Iland of Coruo, being taken out of a ship that came from the Spanish Indies, they brought tidings that the Englishmen had taken 4 more of the Indian ships, and a caruel with the king of Spaines letters of aduise for the ships comming out of the Portugal Indies, and that with those which they had taken, they were at the least 40 English ships together, so that not one bark escaped them, but fel into their hands, and that therefore the Portugall ships comming out of India durst not put into the Ilands, but tooke their course vnder 40 and 42 degrees, and from thence sailed to Lisbon, shunning likewise the cape S. Vincent, otherwise they could not haue had a prosperous iourney of it, for that as then the sea was ful of English ships. [Sidenote: Great hauock of Spaniards.] Whereupon the king aduised the fleete lying in Hauana in the Spanish Indies ready to come for Spaine, that they should stay there all that yeere till the next yeere, because of the great danger they might fal into by the Englishmen, which was no smal charge, and hinderance to the fleet, for that the ships that lie there do consume themselues, and in a manner eat vp one another, by reason of the great number of people, together with the scarcitie of al things, so that many ships chose rather one by one to aduenture themselues alone to get home, then to stay there: all which fell into the Englishmen hands, whereof diuers of the men were brought into Tercera, for that a whole day we could see nothing els, but spoiled men set on shore, some out of one ship, some out of another, that pitie it was to see all of them cursing the Englishmen and their owne fortunes, with those that had bene the causes to prouoke the Englishmen to fight, and complaining of the small remedie and order taken therein by the king of Spaines officers.

The 19 of the same moneth there came to Tercera a Carauel of Lisbon, with one of the kings officers, to cause the goods that were saued out of the ship which came from Malacca (for the which we staied there) to be laden and sent to Lisbon. And at the same time there put out of the Groine one Don Alonso de Baçan, with 40 great ships of warre to come vnto the Ilands, there to watch for the fleet of the Spanish and Portugall Indies, and the goods of the Malacca ship being laden, they were to convoy them all together into the riuer of Lisbon: but being certaine daies at sea, alwaies hauing a contrary wind, they could not get vnto the Ilands, onely two of them that were scattred from the fleet, arriued at Tercera, and not finding the fleet, they presently returned to seeke them: in the meane time the king changed his mind, and caused the fleet to stay in India, as I said before: and therefore hee sent worde vnto Don Alonso de Bassan, that hee should returne againe to the Groine, which he presently did (without doing any thing, nor once approching neer the Ilands, sauing onely the two foresayd ships, for he well knew that the Englishmen lay by the Iland of Coruo, but he would not visit them): and so he returned to the hauen the Groine, whereby our goods that came from Malacca were yet to ship, and trussed vp againe, and forced to stay a more fortunate time with patience perforce.

The 23 of October there arriued in Tercera a Carauel with aduise out of Portugall, that of 5 ships which in the yere 1590 were laden in Lisbon for the Indies, 4 of them were turned againe to Portin. After they had bene 4 moneths abroad, and that the Admirall, wherein the Viceroy called Mathias d'Albukerk sailed, had onely gotten to India, as afterward newes thereof was brought ouer-land, hauing bin at the least 11 moneths at sea and neuer saw land, and came in great misery to Malacca. In this ship there died by the way 280 men, according to a note by himselfe made, and sent to the Cardinal at Lisbon, with the names and surnames of euery man, together with a description of his voiage, and the misery they had endured, which was onely done, because he would not lose the gouernment of India: and for that cause he had sworne either to lose his life, or to arriue in India, as in, deed he did afterwards, but to the great danger, losse and hinderance of his companie, that were forced to buy it with their liues, and onely for want of prouision, as it may wel be thought: for he knew full well that if he had returned backe againe into Portugal as the other ships did, he should haue bin cassiered from his Indian regiment, because the people began already to murmure at him for his proud and lofty mind. And among other things that shewed his pride the more, behind aboue the gallery of his ship he caused Fortune to be painted, and his own picture with a staffe standing by her, as it were threatning Fortune, with this posie, Quero que vencas, that is, I wil haue thee to ouercome: which being read by the Cardinal and other gentlemen (that to honor him brought him aboord his ship) it was thought to be a point of exceeding folly: but it is no strange matter among the Portugals: for they aboue all others must of force let the foole peepe out of their sleeues, specially when they are in authority, for that I knew the said Mathias d'Albukerk in India, being a souldier and a captaine, where he was esteemed and accounted for one of the best of them, and much honoured, and beloued of all men, as behauing himselfe curteously to euery man, whereby they all desired that he might be Viceroy. But when he once had receiued his patent with full power and authoritie from the king to be Viceroy, he changed so much from his former behauiour, that by reason of his pride, they all began to feare and curse him, and that before hee departed out of Lisbon, as it is often seene in many men that are aduanced vnto state and dignitie.

The 20 of Ianuarie 1591. there was newes brought out of Portugall into Tercera, that the Englishmen had taken a ship that the king had sent into the Portugall Indies, with aduise to the Viceroy for the returning againe of the 4 ships that should haue gone to India, and because the ships were come backe againe, that ship was stuffed and laded as full of goods as possible it might be, hauing likewise in ready money 500 thousand duckets in roials of 8, besides other wares. It departed from Lisbon in the moneth of Nouember 1590. and met with the Englishmen, with whom for a time it fought, but in the end it was taken and caried into England with men and all, yet when they came there, the men were set at libertie, and returned into Lisbon, where the captaine was committed prisoner; but he excused himselfe and was released, with whom I spake my selfe, and he made this report vnto me. At the same time also they tooke a ship that came from the Mine laden with gold, and 2 ships laden with pepper and spices that were to saile into Italy, the pepper onely that was in them, being worth 170 thousand duckets: all these ships were caried into England, and made good prise.

In the moneth of Iuly 1591. there hapned an earthquake in the Iland of S. Michael, which continued from the 26 of Iuly, to the 12 of August, in which time no man durst stay within his house but fled into the fields, fasting and praying with great sorow, for that many of their houses fel down, and a towne called Villa Franca, was almost cleane razed to the ground, all the cloisters and houses shaken to the earth, and therein some people slaine. The land in some places rose vp, and the cliffs remooued from one place to another, and some hils were defaced and made euen with the ground. The earthquake was so strong, that the ships which lay in the road and on the sea, shaked as if the world would haue turned round: there sprang also a fountaine out of the earth, for whence for the space of 4 daies, there flowed a most cleare water, and after that it ceased. At the same time they heard such thunder and noise vnder the earth, as if all the deuils in hell had bin assembled together in that place, wherewith many died for feare. The Iland of Tercera shooke 4 times together, so that it seemed to turne about, but there hapned no misfortune vnto it. Earthquakes are common in those Ilands, for about 20 yeres past there hapned another earthquake, wherein a high hill that lieth by the same towne of Villa Franca, fell halfe downe, and couered all the towne with earth, and killed many men. The 25 of August the kings Armada comming out of Ferol arriued in Tercera being in all 30 ships, Biskaines, Portugals and Spaniards, and 10 Dutch flieboats that were arrested in Lisbon to serue the king, besides other small ships and pataxos, that came to serue as messengers from place to place, and to discouer the seas. This nauie came to stay for, and conuoy the ships that should come from the Spanish Indies, and the flieboats were appointed in their returne home, to take in the goods that were saued in the lost ship that came from Malacca, and to conuoy them to Lisbon.

The 13 of September the said Armada arriued at the Iland of Coruo, where the Englishmen with about 16 ships as then lay, staying for the Spanish fleet, whereof some or the most part were come, and there the English were in good hope to haue taken them. But when they perceiued the kings army to be strong, the Admiral being the lord Thomas Howard, commanded his Fleet not to fal vpon them, nor any of them once to separate their ships from him, vnlesse he gaue commission so to do: notwithstanding the viceadmirall sir Richard Greenuil being in the ship called the Reuenge, went into the Spanish fleet, and shot among them doing them great hurt, and thinking the rest of the company would haue folowed, which they did not, but left him there, and sailed away: the cause why could not be knowen. Which the Spaniards perceiuing, with 7 or 8 ships they boorded her, but she withstood them all, fighting with them at the least 12 houres together and sunke two of them, one being a new double Flieboat of 600 tunnes, and Admiral of the Flieboats, the other a Biscain; but in the end by reason of the number that came vpon her, she was taken, but to their great losse: for they had lost in fighting and by drowning aboue 400 men, and of the English were slaine about 100, Sir Richard Greenuil himselfe being wounded in his braine, whereof afterwards he died. He was caried into the ship called S. Paul, wherein was the Admirall of the fleet Don Alonso de Baçan: there his wounds were drest by the Spanish surgeons, but Don Alonso himselfe would neither see him nor speake with him: all the rest of the Captaines and gentlemen went to visite him, and to comfort him in his hard fortune wondering at his courage and stout heart, for that he shewed not any signe of faintnes nor changing of colour; but feeling the houre of death to approch, he spake these words in Spanish, and said: Here die I Richard Greenuil with a ioyful and quiet mind, for that I haue ended my life as a true souldier ought to do, that hath fought for his countrey, Queene, religion and honor, whereby my soule most ioyfull departeth out of this body, and shal alwayes leaue behind it an euerlasting fame of a valiant and true souldier that hath done his dutie as he was bound to doe. When he had finished these or such other like words, he gaue vp the Ghost, with great and stout courage, and no man could perceiue any true signe of heauines in him.

This sir Rich. Greenuil was a great and a rich gentleman in England, and had great yeerely reuenues of his owne inheritance, but he was a man very vnquiet in his mind, and greatly affected to war; insomuch as of his owne priuate motion he offred his seruice to the Queene: he had performed many valiant acts, and was greatly feared in these Ilands, and knowen of euery man, but of nature very seuere, so that his owne people hated him for his fiercenesse, and spake very hardly of him: for when they first entred into the fleet or Armada, they had their great saile in a readinesse, and might possibly enough haue sailed away, for it was one of the best ships for saile in England, and the master perceiuing that the other ships had left them, and folowed not after, commanded the great saile to be cut that they might make away: but sir Rich. Greenuil threatned both him and al the rest that were in the ship, that if any man laid hand vpon it, he would cause him to be hanged, and so by that occasion they were compelled to fight and in the end were taken. He was of so hard a complexion, that as he continued among the Spanish captains while they were at dinner or supper with him, he would carouse 3 or 4 glasses of wine, and in a brauerie take the glasses betweene his teeth and crash them in pieces and swalow them downe, so that oftentimes the blood ran out of his mouth without any harme at all vnto him: and this was told me by diuers credible persons that many times stood and beheld him. The Englishmen that were left in the ship, as the captaine of the souldiers, the master and others were dispersed into diuers of the Spanish ships that had taken them, where there had almost a new fight arisen between the Biscains and the Portugals: while each of them would haue the honour to haue first boorded her, so that there grew a great noise and quarel among them, one taking the chiefe ensigne, and the other the flag, and the captaine and euery one held his owne. The ships that had boorded her were altogether out of order, and broken, and many of their men hurt, whereby they were compelled to come into the Island of Tercera, there to repaire themselues: where being arriued, I and my chamberfelow, to heare some newes, went aboord one of the ships being a great Biscain, and one of the 12 Apostles, whose captaine was called Bartandono, that had bin General of the Biscains in the fleet that went for England. He seeing vs called vs up into the gallery, where with great curtesie he receiued vs, being as then set at dinner with the English captaine that sate by him, and had on a sute of blacke veluet, but he could not tell vs any thing, for that he could speake no other language but English and Latine, which Bartandano also could a litle speake. The English captaine got licence of the gouernour that he might come on land with his weapon by his side, and was in our lodging with the Englishman that was kept prisoner in the Iland, being of that ship whereof the sailers got away, as I said before. The gouernour of Tercera bade him to dinner, and shewed him great curtesie. The master likewise with licence of Bartandono came on land and was in our lodging, and had at the least 10 or 12 wounds, as well in his head as on his body, whereof after that being at sea betweene Lisbon and the Ilands he died. The captaine wrote a letter, wherein he declared all the maner of the fight, and left it with the English marchant that lay in our lodging, to send it to the lord Admiral of England. This English captaine comming vnto Lisbon, was there wel receiued and not any hurt done vnto him, but with good conuoy sent vnto Setuuel, and from thence sailed into England with all the rest of the Englishmen that were taken prisoners.

The Spanish armie staied at the Iland of Coruo til the last of September, to assemble the rest of the fleet together, which in the ende were to the number of 140 sailes of ships partly comming from India, and partly of the army, and being altogether readie to saile to Tercera in good company, there suddenly rose so hard and cruell a storme, that those of the Ilands did affirme, that in mans memorie there was neuer any such seen or heard off before: for it seemed the sea would haue swalowed vp the Ilands, the water mounting higher then the cliffs, which are so high that it amaseth a man to behold them: but the sea reached aboue them, and liuing fishes were throwen vpon the land. This storme continued not only a day or two with one wind, but 7 or 8 dayes continually, the wind turning round about in al places of the compasse, at the lest twise or thrise during that time, and all alike, with a continuall storme and tempest most terrible to behold, euen to vs that were on shore, much more then to such as were at sea: so that onely on the coasts and cliffes of the Iland of Tercera, there were aboue 12 ships cast away, and not onely vpon the one side, but round about it in euery corner, whereby nothing els was heard but complaining, crying, lamenting and telling, here is a ship broken in pieces against the cliffes, and there another, and all the men drowned: so that for the space of 20 dayes after the storme, they did nothing els but fish for dead men that continually came driuing on the shore. [Sidenote: The wracke of the Reuenge.] Among the rest was the English ship called the Reuenge, that was cast away vpon a cliffe neere to the Iland of Tercera, where it brake in an hundred pieces and sunke to the ground, hauing in her 70 men Galegos, Biscains, and others, with some of the captiue Englishmen, whereof but one was saued that got vp vpon the cliffes aliue, and had his body and head all wounded, and he being on shore brought vs the newes desiring to be shriuen, and thereupon presently died. The Reuenge had in her diuers faire brasse pieces that were all sunke in the sea, which they of the Iland were in good hope to waigh vp againe the next Sommer after. Among these ships that were cast away about Tercera, was likewise a Flie-boat, one of those that had bin arrested in Portugall to serue the king, called the white Doue, the master of her was one Cornelius Martenson of Schiedam in Holland, and there were in her 100 souldiers, as in euery one of the rest there were. He being ouer-ruled by the captaine that he could not be master of his owne, sayling here and there at the mercy of God, as the storme droue him, in the end came within the sight of the Iland of Tercera, which the Spaniards perceiuing thought all their safety onely to consist in putting into the road, compelling the Master and the Pilot to make towards the Iland, although the master refused to doe it, saying, that they were most sure there to be cast away and vtterly spoyled: but the captaine called him drunkard and Heretique, and striking him with a staffe, commaunded him to doe as he would haue him. The Master, seeing this and being compelled to doe it, sayd: well then my Masters, seeing that it is the desire of you all to bee cast away, I can but lose one life, and therewith desperately he sayled towards the shore, and was on that side of the Iland, where there was nothing els but hard stones and rocks, as high as mountaines, most terrible to beholde, where some of the inhabitants stood with long ropes and corke bound at the ende thereof, to throw them downe, vnto the men, that they might lay holde vpon them and saue their liues: but few of them got so neere, most of them being cast away, and smitten in pieces before they could get to the wall. The ship sailing in this maner (as I sayd before) towards the Iland, and approching to the shore, the master being an olde man, and full of yeeres, called his sonne that was in the ship with him, and hauing imbraced one another, and taken their last farewell, the good olde father willed his sonne not to take care for him, but seeke to saue himselfe; for (sayd he) sonne thou art yong, and mayest haue some hope to saue thy life, but as for me it is no great matter (I am olde) what become of me, and therewith ech of these shedding many teares, as euery louing father and kinde childe may well consider, the ship fell vpon the cliffes, and brake in pieces, the father on the one side, the sonne on the other side falling into the sea, ech laying holde vpon that which came next to hand, but to no purpose; for the sea was so high and furious, that they were all drowned, and onely foureteene or fifteene saued themselues by swimming, with their legs and armes halfe broken and out of ioynt, among which was the Masters sonne, and foure other Dutch boyes: the rest of the Spaniards and Sailers, with the Captaine and Master, were drowned. Whose heart would not melt with teares to beholde so grieuous a sight, specially considering with himselfe that the greatest cause thereof was the beastliness and insolency of the Spaniards, as in this onely example may well be seene? Whereby may be considered how the other shippes sped, as we ourselues did in part beholde, and by the men that were saued did heare more at large, as also some others of our countreymen that as then were in the like danger can well witnesse.

On the other Ilands the losse was no lesse then in Tercera: for on the Iland of Saint George there were two ships cast away: on the Iland of Pico two ships: on the Iland of Gratiosa three ships: and besides those there came euery where round about diuers pieces of broken ships, and other things fleeting towards the Ilands, wherewith the sea was all couered most pitifull to beholde. On the Iland of S. Michael there were foure ships cast away, and betweene Tercera and S. Michael three more were sunke, which were seene and heard to cry out; whereof not one man was saued. [Sidenote: About 100 Spanish and Portugall ships drowned.] The rest put into the sea without masts, all torne and rent: so that of the whole fleet and armada, being 140 ships in all, there were but 32 or 33 arriued in Spaine and Portugall, yea, and those few with so great misery, paine and labour, that not two of them arriued there together, but this day one, and tomorrow another, next day the third, and so one after the other to the number aforesayd. All the rest were cast away vpon the Ilands, and ouerwhelmed in the Sea, whereby may be considered what great losse and hindrance they receiued at that time: for by many mens iudgments it was esteemed to be much more then was lost by their army that came for England: and it may well be thought, and presumed, that it was no other but a iust plague purposely sent by God vpon the Spaniards, and that it might truely be sayd, the taking of the Reuenge was iustly reuenged vpon them, and not by the might or force of man, but by the power of God, as some of them openly sayd in the Ile of Tercera, that they beleeued verily God would consume them, and that he tooke part with the Lutherans and heretiks: saying further that so soone as they had throwen the dead body of the Viceadmirall Sir Richard Greenfield ouerboord, they verily thought that as he had a diuellish faith and religion, and therefore the diuels loued him, so he presently sunke into the bottome of the sea, and downe into hell, where he raised vp all the diuels to the reuenge of his death: and that they brought so great stormes and torments vpon the Spaniards, because they onely maintained the Catholike and Romish religion. Such and the like blasphemies against God, they ceased not openly to vtter, without being reprooued of any man therein, nor for their false opinions: but the most part of them rather sayd and affirmed, that of trueth it must needs be so.

As one of those Indian fleets put out of Noua Spagna, there were 35 of them by storme and tempest cast away and drowned in the Sea, being 50 in all; so that but 15 escaped. Of the fleet that came from Santo Domingo there were 14 cast away, comming out of the chanell of Hauana, whereof the Admirall and Viceadmirall were two of them: and from Terra Firma in India there came two ships laden with golde and siluer, that were taken by the Englishmen: and before the Spanish army came to Coruo, the Englishmen at times had taken at the least 20 ships, that came from S. Domingo, India, Brasilia, &c. and were all sent into England.

* * * * *

The miraculous victory atchieved by the English Fleete, under the discreet and happy conduct of the right honourable, right prudent, and valiant lord, the L. Charles Howard, L. high Admirall of England, &c. Vpon the Spanish huge Armada sent in the yeere 1588. for the invasion of England, together with the wofull and miserable success of the said Armada afterward, upon the Coasts of Norway, of the Scottish Westerne Isles, of Ireland, Spain, France, and of England, &c. Recorded in Latine by Emanuel van Meteran, in the 15. Booke of his history of the Low Countreys.

Hauing in part declared the strange and wonderfull euents of the yeere eightie eight, which hath bene so long time foretold by ancient prophesies; we will now make relation of the most notable and great enterprise of all others which were in the foresaid yeere atchieued, in order as it was done. Which exploit (although in very deed it was not performed in any part of the low Countreys) was intended for their ruine and destruction. And it was the expedition which the Spanish king, hauing a long time determined the same in his minde, and hauing consulted thereabout with the Pope, set foorth and vndertooke against England and the low Countreys. To the end that he might subdue the Realme of England, and reduce it vnto his catholique Religion, and by that meanes might be sufficiently reuenged for the disgrace, contempt and dishonour, which hee (hauing 34. yeeres before enforced them to the Popes obedience) had endured of the English nation, and for diuers other iniuries which had taken deepe impression in his thoughts. And also for that hee deemed this to bee the most readie and direct course, whereby hee might recouer his heredetarie possession of the lowe Countreys, hauing restrained the inhabitants from sayling vpon the coast of England. Which verily, vpon most weighty arguments and euident reasons, was thought would vndoubtedly haue come to passe, considering the great aboundance and store of all things necessary wherewith those men were furnished, which had the managing of that action committed vnto them. But now let vs describe the matter more particularly.

[Sidenote: The preparation of the Spanish King to subdue England and the lowe Countreys.] The Spanish King hauing with small fruite and commoditie, for aboue twentie yeeres together, waged warre against the Netherlanders, after deliberation with his counsellers thereabout, thought it most conuenient to assault them once againe by Sea, which had bene attempted sundry times heretofore, but not with forces sufficient. Vnto the which expedition it stoode him nowe in hand to ioyne great puissance, as hauing the English people his professed enemies; whose Island is so situate, that it may either greatly helpe or hinder all such as saile into those parts. For which cause hee thought good first of all to inuade England, being perswaded by his Secretary Escouedo, and by diuers other well experienced Spaniards and Dutchmen, and by many English fugitiues, that the conquest of that Island was lesse difficult then the conquest of Holland and Zeland. Moreouer the Spaniards were of opinion, that it would bee farre more behouefull for their King to conquere England and the lowe Countreys all at once, then to be constrained continually to maintaine a warlike Nauie to defend his East and West Indie Fleetes, from the English Drake, and from such like valiant enemies.

And for the same purpose the king Catholique had giuen commandement long before in Italie and Spaine, that a great quantitie of timber should be felled for the building of shippes; and had besides made great preparation of things and furniture requisite for such an expedition; as namely in founding of brasen Ordinance, in storing vp of corne and victuals, in trayning of men to vse warlike weapons, in leauying and mustering of souldiers: insomuch that about the beginning of the yeere 1588. he had finished such a mightie Nauie, and brought it into Lisbon hauen, as neuer the like had before that time sailed vpon the Ocean sea.

A very large and particular description of this Nauie was put in print and published by the Spaniards; wherein were set downe the number, names, and burthens of the shippes, the number of Mariners and souldiers throughout the whole Fleete; likewise the quantitie of their Ordinance, of their armour, of bullets, of match, of gun-poulder, of victuals, and of all their Nauall furniture was in the saide description particularized. Vnto all these were added the names of the Gouernours, Captaines, Noblemen and gentlemen voluntaries, of whom there was so great a multitude, that scarce was there any family of accompt, or any one principall man throughout all Spaine, that had not a brother, sonne or kinseman in that Fleete: who all of them were in good hope to purchase vnto themselues in that Nauie (as they termed it) inuincible endlesse glory and renowne, and to possesse themselues of great Seigniories and riches in England, and in the lowe

Countreys. But because the said description was translated and published out of Spanish into diuers other languages, we will here onely make an abridgment or briefe rehearsall thereof.

[Sidenote: The number and qualitie of the ships in the Spanish Fleete, with the souldiers, Mariners, and pieces of Ordinance.] Portugal furnished and set foorth vnder the conduct of the duke of Medina Sidonia generall of the Fleete, ten Galeons, two Zabraes, 1300. Mariners, 3300. souldiers, 300. great pieces, with all requisite furniture.

Biscay, vnder the conduct of Iohn Martines de Ricalde Admiral of the whole Fleetee, set forth tenne Galeons, 4. Pataches, 700. mariners, 2000. souldiers, 250. great pieces, &c.

Guipusco, vnder the conduct of Michael de Oquendo, tenne Galeons, 4 Pataches, 700. mariners, 2000. souldiers, 310. great pieces.

Italy with the Leuant Islands, vnder Martine de Vertendona, 10. Galeons, 800. mariners, 2000. souldiers, 310. great pieces, &c.

Castile, vnder Diego Flores de Valdez, 14. Galeons, two Pataches, 1700. mariners, 2400. souldiers, and 380. great pieces, &c.

Andaluzia, vnder the conduct of Petro de Valdez, 10. Galeons, one Patache, 800. mariners, 2400. souldiers, 280. great pieces, &c.

Item, vnder the conduct of Iohn Lopez de Medina, 23. great Flemish hulkes, with 700. mariners, 3200. souldiers, and 400. great pieces.

Item, vnder Hugo de Moncada, foure Galliasses containing 1200. gally-slaues, 460. mariners, 870. souldiers, 200. great pieces, &c.

Item, vnder Diego de Mandrana, foure Gallies of Portugall, with 888. gally-slaues, 360. mariners, 20 great pieces, and other requisite furniture.

Item, vnder Anthonie de Mendoza, 22. Pataches and Zabraes, with 574. mariners, 488. souldiers, and 193. great pieces.

Besides, the ships aforementioned there were 20 carauels rowed with oares, being appointed to performe necessary seruices vnto the greater ships: insomuch that all the ships appertayning to this Nauie amounted vnto the summe of 150. eche one being sufficiently prouided of furniture and victuals,

The number of mariners in the saide Fleete were aboue 8000. of slaues 2088. of souldiers 20000. (besides noblemen and gentlemen voluntaries) of great cast pieces 2650. The foresaid ships were of an huge and incredible capacitie and receipt. For the whole Fleete was large ynough to containe the burthen of 60 thousand tunnes.

[Sidenote: A description of the Galeons.] The Galeons were 64. in number, being of an huge bignesse, and very stately built, being of marueilous force also, and so high that they resembled great castles, most fit to defend themselues and to withstand any assault, but in giuing any other ships the encounter farre inferiour vnto the English and Dutch ships, which can with great dexteritie wield and turn themselues at all assayes. The vpperworke of the said Galeons was of thicknesse and strength sufficient to beare off musket-shot. The lower worke and the timbers thereof were out of measure strong, being framed of plankes and ribs foure or fiue foote in thicknesse, insomuch that no bullets could pierce them, but such as were discharged hard at hand: which afterward prooued true, for a great number of bullets were founde to sticke fast within the massie substance of those thicke plankes. Great and well pitched Cables were twined about the masts of their shippes, to strengthen them against the battery of shot.

[Sidenote: A description of the Galliasses.] The Galliasses were of such bignesse, that they contained within them chambers, chapels, turrets, pulpits, and other commodities of great houses. The Galliasses were rowed with great oares, there being in eche one of them 300. slaues for the same purpose, and were able to do great seruice with the force of their Ordinance. All these together with the residue aforenamed were furnished and beautified with trumpets, streamers, banners, warlike ensignes, and other such like ornaments.

[Sidenote: The great Ordinance, bullets, gunpoulder, and other furniture.] Their pieces of brasen ordinance were 1600. and of yron a 1000.

The bullets thereto belonging were 120. thousand.

Item of gun-poulder 5600. quintals. Of matche 1200. quintals.

Of muskets and kaleiuers 7000. Of haleberts and partisans 10000.

Moreouer they had great store of canons, double-canons, culuerings and field-pieces for land seruices.

[Sidenote: Their prouision of victuals and other things necessary.] Likewise they were prouided of all instruments necessary on land to conueigh and transport their furniture from place to place; as namely of carts, wheeles, wagons, &C. Also they had spades, mattocks and baskets to set pioners on worke. They had in like sort great store of mules and horses, and whatsoeuer else was requisite for a land-armie. They were so well stored of biscuit, that for the space of halfe a yeere, they might allow eche person in the whole Fleete half a quintall euery moneth; whereof the whole summe amounteth vnto an hundred thousand quintals.

Likewise of wine they had 147. thousand pipes, sufficient also for halfe a yeeres expedition. Of bacon 6500. quintals. Of cheese three thousand quintals. Besides fish, rise, beanes, pease, oile, vineger, &c.

Moreouer they had 12000. pipes of fresh water, and all other necessary prouision, as namely candles, lanternes, lampes, sailes, hempe, ox-hides and lead to stop holes that should be made with the battery of gunshot. To be short, they brought all things expedient either for a Fleete by sea, or for an armie by land.

This Nauie (as Diego Pimentelli afterward confessed) was esteemed by the King himselfe to containe 32000. persons, and to cost him euery day 30. thousand ducates.

[Sidenote: A Spanish terza consisteth of 3200. souldiers.] There were in the said Nauie fiue terzaes of Spaniards, (which terzaes the Frenchmen call Regiments) vnder the commaund of fiue gouernours termed by the Spaniards, Masters of the field, and amongst the rest there were many olde and expert souldiers chosen out of the garisons of Sicilie, Naples, and Terçera. Their Captaines or Colonels were Diego Pimentelli, Don Francisco de Toledo, Don Alonço de Luçon, Don Nicolas de Isla, Don Augustin de Mexia; who had eche of them 32. companies vnder their conduct. Besides the which companies there were many bands also of Castilians and Portugals, euery one of which had their peculiar gouernours, captaines, officers, colours and weapons.

It was not lawfull for any man, vnder grieuous penaltie, to cary any women or harlots in the Fleete: for which cause the women hired certaine shippes, wherein they sailed after the Nauie: some of the which being driuen by tempest arriued vpon the coast of France.

The generall of this mightie Nauie, was Don Alonso Perez de Guzman duke of Medina Sidonia, Lord of S. Lucar, and knight of the golden Fleece: by reason that the Marques of santa Cruz appointed for the same dignitie, deceased before the time.

Iohn Martines de Ricalde was Admirall of the Fleete.

Francis Bouadilla was chiefe Marshall: who all of them had their officers fit and requisite for the guiding and managing of such a multitude. Likewise Martin Alorcon was appointed Vicar generall of the Inquisition, being accompanied with more then a hundreth Monkes, to wit, Iesuites, Capuchines, and friers mendicant. Besides whom also there were Phisitians, Chirurgians, Apothecaries, and whatsoever else perteined vnto the hospitall.

Ouer and besides the forenamed gouernours and officers being men of chiefe note, there were 124. very noble and worthy Gentlemen, which went voluntarily of their owne costs and charges, to the ende they might see fashions, learne experience, and attaine vnto glory. Amongst whom was the prince of Ascoli, Alonzo de Leiua, the marques de Pennafiel, the marques de Ganes, the marques de Barlango, count de Paredes, count de Yeluas, and diuers other marqueses and earles of the honourable families of Mendoza, of Toledo, of Pachieco, of Cordoua, of Guzman, of Manricques, and a great number of others.

[Sidenote: The preparation of the Duke of Parma to aide the Spaniards.] While the Spaniards were furnishing this their Nauuie, the Duke of Parma, at the direction of king Philip, made great preparation in the low Countreys, to giue ayd and assistance vnto the Spaniards; building ships for the same purpose, and sending for Pilots and shipwrights out of Italy.

In Flanders hee caused certaine deepe chanels to be made, and among the rest the chanell of Yper commonly called Yper-lee, employing some thousands of workemen about that seruice: to the end that by the said chanel he might transport ships from Antwerp and Ghendt to Bruges, where hee had assembled aboue a hundreth small ships called hoyes being well stored with victuals, which hoyes hee was determined to haue brought into the sea by the way of Sluys, or else to haue conueyed them by the saide Yper-lee being now of greater depth, into any port of Flanders whatsoeuer.

In the riuer of Waten he caused 70. ships with flat bottomes to be built, euery one of which should serue to cary 30. horses, hauing eche of them bridges likewise for the horses to come on boord, or to goe foorth on land. Of the same fashion he had prouided 200. other vessels at Nieuport, but not so great. And at Dunkerk hee procured 28. ships of warre, such as were there to be had, and caused a sufficient number of Mariners to be leuied at Hamburgh, Breme, Emden, and at other places. Hee put in the ballast of the said ships, great store of beames of thicke plankes, being hollow and beset with yron pikes beneath, but on eche side full of claspes and hookes, to ioyne them together.

Hee had likewise at Greueling prouided 20. thousand of caske, which in a short space might be compact and ioyned together with nailes and cords, and reduced into the forme of a bridge. To be short, whatsoeuer things were requisite for the making of bridges, and for the barring and stopping vp of hauens mouthes with stakes, posts, and other meanes, he commanded to be made ready. Moreouer not farre from Neiuport hauen, he had caused a great pile of wooden fagots to be layd, and other furniture to be brought for the rearing vp of a mount. The most part of his ships conteined two ouens a piece to bake bread in, with a great number of sadles, bridles, and such other like apparell for horses. They had horses likewise, which after their landing should serue to conuey, and draw engines, field-pieces, and other warlike prouisions.

Neere vnto Neiuport he had assembled an armie, ouer the which he had ordained Camillo de Monte to be Camp-master. This army consisted of 30. bands or ensignes of Italians, of tenne bands of Wallons, eight of Scots, and eight of Burgundians, all which together amount vnto 56. bands, euery band containing a hundreth persons. Neare vnto Dixmund there were mustered 80. bands of Dutch men, sixtie of Spaniards, sixe of high Germans, and seuen bands of English fugitiues, vnder the conduct of sir William Stanley an English knight.

In the suburbes of Cortreight there were 4000. horsemen together with their horses in a readinesse: and at Waten 900. horses, with the troupe of the Marques Del Gwasto Captaine generall of the horsemen.

Vnto this famous expedition and presupposed victorie, many potentates, princes, and honourable personages hied themselues: out of Spaine the prince of Melito called the duke of Pastrana and taken to be the sonne of one Ruygomes de Silua, but in very deed accompted among the number of king Philips base sonnes. Also the Marques of Burgraue, one of the sonnes of Archiduke Ferdinand and Philippa Welsera. Vespasian Gonsaga of the family of Mantua, being for chiualry a man of great renowne, and heretofore Vice-roy in Spaine. Item Iohn Medices base sonne vnto the duke of Florence. And Amadas of Sauoy, the duke of Sauoy his base sonne, with many others of inferiour degrees.

[Sidenote: The Popes furtherance to the conquest of England, and of the low countries.] Likewise Pope Sixtus quintus for the setting forth of the foresaid expedition, as they vse to do against Turkes and infidels, published a Cruzado, with most ample indulgences which were printed in great numbers. These vaine buls the English and Dutchmen deriding, sayd that the deuill at all passages lay in ambush like a thiefe, no whit regarding such letters of safe conduct. Some there be which affirme that the Pope had bestowed the realme of England with the title of Defensor fidei, vpon the king of Spaine, giuing him charge to inuade it vpon this condition, that he should enioy the conquered realm, as a vassal and tributarie, in that regard, vnto the sea of Rome. To this purpose the said Pope proffered a million of gold, the one halfe thereof to be paied in readie money, and the other halfe when the realme of England or any famous port thereof were subdued. And for the greater furtherance of the whole businesse, he dispatched one D. Allen an English man (whom he had made Cardinall for the same ende and purpose) into the Low countries, vnto whom he committed the administration of all matters ecclesiasticall throughout England. This Allen being enraged against his owne natiue countrey, caused the Popes bull to be translated into English, meaning vpon the arriual of the Spanish fleete to haue it so published in England. By which Bull the excommunications of the two former Popes were confirmed, and the Queenes most sacred Maiestie was by them most vniustly depriued of all princely titles and dignities, her subjects being enioyned to performe obedience vnto the duke of Parma, and vnto the Popes Legate.

But that all matters might be performed with greater secrecie, and that the whole expedition might seeme rather to be intended against the Low countries, then against England, and that the English people might be perswaded that all was but bare words and threatnings, and that nought would come to effect, there was a solemne meeting appointed at Borborch in Flanders for a treatie of peace betweene her matestie and the Spanish king.

[Sidenote: A treatie of peace, to the end that Englad and the vnited prouinces might be secure of inuasion.] Against which treatie the vnited prouinces making open protestation, vsed all meanes possible to hinder it, alleaging that it was more requisite to consult how the enemie now pressing vpon them might be repelled from off their frontiers. Howbeit some there were in England that greatly vrged and prosecuted this league, saying, that it would be very commodious vnto the state of the realme, as well in regard of traffique and nauigation, as for the auoiding of great expenses to maintaine the warres, affirming also, that at the same time peace might easily and vpon reasonable conditions be obtained of the Spaniard. Others thought by this meanes to diuert some other way, or to keepe backe the nauy now comming vpon them, and so to escape the danger of that tempest. Howsoeuer it was, the duke of Parma by these wiles enchanted and dazeled the eyes of many English and Dutch men that were desirous of peace: whereupon it came to passe, that England and the vnited prouinces prepared in deed some defence to withstand that dreadfull expedition and huge Armada, but nothing in comparison of the great danger which was to be feared, albeit the constant report of the whole expedition had continued rife among them for a long time before. Howbeit they gaue eare vnto the relation of certaine that sayd, that this nauie was prouided to conduct and waft ouer the Indian Fleets: which seemed the more probable because the Spaniards were deemed not to be men of so small discretion as to aduenture those huge and monstrous ships vpon the shallow and dangerous chanel of England.

[Sidenote: Her maiesties warlike preparation by sea.] At length when as the French king about the end of May signified vnto her Maiestie in plaine termes that she should stand vpon her guard, because he was now most certainly enformed, that there was so dangerous an inuasion imminent vpon her realme, that he feared much least all her land and sea-forces would be sufficient to withstand it, &c. then began the Queens Maiestie more carefully to gather her forces together, and to furnish her own ships of warre, and the principall ships of her subiects with souldiers, weapons, and other necessary prouision. The greatest and strongest ships of the whole nauy she sent vnto Plimmouth vnder the conduct of the right honorable Lord Charles Howard, lord high Admirall of England, &c. Vnder whom the renoumed Knight Sir Francis Drake was appointed Vice-admiral. The number of these ships was about an hundreth. The lesser ships being 30. or 40. in number, and vnder the conduct of the lord Henry Seimer were commanded to lie between Douer and Caleis.

[Sidenote: Her Maiesties land-forces.] On land likewise throughout the whole realme, souldiers were mustered and trained in all places, and were committed vnto the most resolute and faithfull captaines. And whereas it was commonly giuen out that the Spaniard hauing once vnited himselfe vnto the duke of Parma, meant to inuade by the riuer of Thames, there was at Tilburie in Essex ouer-against Grauesend, a mightie army encamped, and on both sides of the riuer fortifications were erected, according to the prescription of Frederike Genebelli, an Italian enginier. Likewise there were certaine ships brought to make a bridge, though it were very late first. Vnto the sayd army came in proper person the Queens most roiall Maiestie, representing Tomyris that Scythian warlike princesse, or rather diuine Pallas her selfe. Also there were other such armies leuied in England.

The principall catholique Recussants (least they should stirre vp any tumult in the time of the Spanish inuasion) were sent to remaine at certaine conuenient places, as namely in the Isle of Ely and at Wisbich. And some of them were sent vnto other places, to wit, vnto sundry bishops and noblemen, where they were kept from endangering the state of the common wealth, and of her sacred Maiestie, who of her most gracious clemencie gaue expresse commandement that they should be intreated with all humanity and friendship.

[Sidenote: The preparation of the united prouinces.] The Prouinces of Holland and Zeland, &c. giuing credite vnto their intelligence out of Spain, made preparation to defend themselues: but because the Spanish ships were described vnto them to be so huge, they relied partly vpon the shallow and dangerous seas all along their costs. Wherfore they stood most in doubt of the duke of Parma his small and flat-bottomed ships. Howbeit they had all their ships of warre to the number of 90. and aboue, in a readinesse for all assayes: the greater part whereof were of a small burthen, as being more meete to saile vpon their riuers and shallow seas: and with these ships they besieged all the hauens in Flanders, beginning at the mouth of Scheld, or from the towne of Lillo, and holding on to Greueling and almost vnto Caleis, and fortified all their sea-townes with strong garrisons.

Against the Spanish fleets arriual, they had provided 25. or 30. good ships, committing the gouernment of them vnto Admirall Lonck, whom they commanded to ioine himselfe vnto the lord Henry Seymer, lying betweene Douer and Cales. And when as the foresaid ships (whereof the greater part besieged the hauen of Dunkerke) were driuen by tempest into Zeland, Iustin, of Nassau the Admiral of Zeland supplied that squadron with 35. ships being of no great burthen, but excellently furnished with gunnes, mariners and souldiers in great abundance, and especially with 1200. braue Musquetiers, hauing bene accustomed vnto seafights, and being chosen out of all their companies for the same purpose: and so the said Iustin of Nassau kept such diligent ward in that Station that the duke of Parma could not issue foorth with his nauy into the sea but of any part of Flanders.

[Sidenote: The Spanish fleete set saile vpon the 19. of May.] In the meaane while the Spanish Armada set saile out of the hauen of Lisbon vpon the 19. of May, An. Dom. 1588 vnder the conduct of the duke of Medina Sidonia, directing their course for the Baie of Corunna, alias the Groine in Gallicia, where they tooke in souldiers and warlike prouision, this port being in Spaine the neerest vnto England. As they were sailing along, there arose such a mightie tempest, that the whole Fleete was dispersed, so that when the duke was returned vnto his company, he could not escry aboue 80. ships in all, whereunto the residue by litle and litle ioyned themselues, except eight which had their mastes blowen ouer-boord. One of the foure gallies of Portingal escaped very hardly, retiring her selfe, into the hauen. The other three were vpon the coast of Baion in France, by the assistance and courage of one Dauid Gwin an English captiue (whom the French and Turkish slaues aided in the same enterprise) vtterly disabled and vanquished: one of the three being first ouercome, which conquered the two other, with the slaughter of their gouernours and souldiers, and among the rest of Don Diego de Mandrana with sundry others: and so these slaues arriuing in France with the three Gallies, set themselues at liberty.

[Sidenote: They set saile from the Groine vpon the 11. of Iuly. The Spaniards come within kenning of England. Captain Fleming.] The nauy hauing refreshed themselues at the Groine, and receiuing daily commandement from the king to hasten their iourney, hoised vp sailes the 11. day of July, and so holding on their course, till the 19. of the same moneth, they came then vnto the mouth of the narow seas or English chanel. From whence (striking their sailes in the meane season) they dispatched certaine of their smal ships vnto the duke of Parma. At the same time the Spanish Fleete was escried by an English pinasse, captaine whereof was M. Thomas Fleming, after they had bene aduertised of the Spaniards expedition by their scoutes and espials, which hauing ranged along the coast of Spaine, were lately returned home into Plimmouth for a new supply of victuals and other necessaries, who considering the foresayd tempest, were of opinion that the nauy being of late dispersed and tossed vp and downe the maine Ocean, was by no means able to performe their intended voiage.

Moreouer, the L. Charles Howard L. high admiral of England had receiued letters from the court, signifying vnto him that her Maiestie was aduertised that the Spanish Fleete would not come foorth, nor was to be any longer expected for, and therefore, that vpon her Maiesties commandement he must send backe foure of her tallest and strongest ships vnto Chatham.

[Sidenote: The L. Admirals short warning upon the 19. of Iuly.] The lord high Admiral of England being thus on the sudden, namely vpon the 19. of July about foure of the clocke in the afternoone, enformed by the pinasse of captaine Fleming aforesaid, of the Spaniards approch, with all speed and diligence possible he warped his ships, and caused his mariners and souldiers (the greater part of whom was absent for the cause aforesayd) to come on boord, and that with great trouble and drfficultie, insomuch that the lord Admiral himselfe was faine to lie without in the road with sixe ships onely all that night, after the which many others came foorth of the hauen. [Sidenote: The 20. of Iuly.] The very next day being the 20. of Iuly about high noone, was the Spanish Fleete escried by the English, which with a Southwest wind came sailing along, and passed by Plimmouth: in which regard (according to the iudgement of many skilful nauigators) they greatly ouershot themselues, whereas it had bene more commodious for them to haue staied themselues there, considering that the Englishmen being as yet vnprouided, greatly relied vpon their owne forces, and knew not the estate of the Spanish nauy. Moreouer, this was the most conuenient port of all others, where they might with greater securitie haue bene aduertised of the English forces, and how the commons of the land stood affected, and might haue stirred vp some mutinie, so that hither they should haue bent all their puissance, and from hence the duke of Parma might more easily haue conueied his ships.

But this they were prohibited to doe by the king and his counsell, and were expressely commanded to vnite themselues vnto the souldiers and ships of the said duke of Parma, and so to bring their purpose to effect. Which was thought to be the most easie and direct course, for that they imagined that the English and Dutch men would be vtterly daunted and dismaied thereat, and would each man of them retire vnto his owne Prouince and Porte for the defence thereof, and transporting the armie of the duke vnder the protection of their huge nauy, they might inuade England.

It is reported that the chiefe commanders in the nauy, and those which were more skilfull in nauigation, to wit, Iohn Martines de Ricalde, Diego Flores de Valdez, and diuers others found fault that they were bound vnto so strict directions and instructions, because that in such a case many particular accidents ought to concurre and to be respected at one and the same instant, that is to say, the opportunitie of the wind, weather, time, tide, and ebbe, wherein they might saile from Flanders to England. Oftentimes also the darkenesse and light, the situation of places, the depths and shoulds were to be considered: all which especially depended vpon the conuenience of the windes, and were by so much the more dangerous.

But it seemeth that they were enioined by their commission to ancre neere vnto, or about Caleis, whither the duke of Parma with his ships and all his warrelike prouision was to resort, and while the English and Spanish great ships were in the midst of their conflict, to passe by, and to land his souldiers vpon the Downes.

The Spanish captiues reported that they were determined first to haue entred the riuer of Thames, and thereupon to haue passed with small ships vp to London, supposing that they might easily winne that rich and flourishing Citie being but meanely fortified and inhabited with Citizens not accustomed to the warres, who durst not withstand their first encounter, hoping moreouer to finde many rebels against her Maiestie and popish catholiques, or some fauourers of the Scottish queene (which was not long before most iustly beheaded) who might be instruments of sedition.

Thus often aduertising the duke of Parrna of their approch, the 20. of Iuly they passed by Plimmouth, which the English ships pursuing and getting the wind of them, gaue them the chase and the encounter, and so both Fleets frankly exchanged their bullets.

[Sidenote: The 21. of Iuly.] The day following which was the 21. of Iuly, the English ships approched within musquet shot of the Spanish: at what time the lorde Charles Howard most hotly and valiantly discharged his Ordinance vpon the Spanish Vice-admirall. The Spaniards then well perceiuing the nimblenesse of the English ships in discharging vpon the enimie on all sides, gathered themselues close into the forme of an halfe moone, and slackened their sailes, least they should outgoe any of their companie. And while they were proceeding on in this maner, one of their great Galliasses was so furiously battered with shot, that the whole nauy was faine to come vp rounder together for the safegard thereof: whereby it came to passe that the principall Galleon of Siuill (wherein Don Pedro de Valdez, Vasques de Silua, Alonzo de Sayas, and other noble men were embarqued) falling foule of another shippe, had her fore-mast broken, and by that meanes was not able to keepe way with the Spanish Fleete, neither would the sayde Fleete stay to succour it, but left the distressed Galeon behind. The lord Admirall of England when he saw this ship of Valdez, and thought she had bene voyd of Mariners and Souldiers, taking with him as many shippes as he could, passed by it, that he might not loose sight of the Spanish Fleet that night. For sir Francis Drake (who was notwithstanding appointed to beare out his lanterne that night) was giuing of chase vnto fiue great Hulkes which had separated themselues from the Spanish Fleete: but finding them to be Easterlings, he dismissed them. The lord Admirall all that night following the Spanish lanterne in stead of the English, found himselfe in the morning to be in the midst of his enimies Fleete, but when he perceiued it, he cleanly conueyed himselfe out of that great danger.

[Sidenote: The 22. of Iuly.] The day folowing, which was the two and twentie of Iuly, Sir Francis Drake espied Valdez his shippe, whereunto hee sent foorth his pinasse, and being aduertised that Valdez himselfe was there, and 450. persons with him, he sent him word that he should yeeld himselfe. Valdez for his honors sake caused certaine conditions to be propounded vnto Drake: who answered Valdez that he was not now at laisure to make any long parle, but if he would yeeld himselfe, he should find him friendly and tractable: howbeit if he had resolued to die in fight, he should prooue Drake to be no dastard.

[Sidenote: Don Pedro de Valdez with his ship and company taken.] Vpon which answere Valdez and his company vnderstanding that they were fallen into the hands of fortunate Drake, being mooued with the renoume and celebritie of his name, with one consent yeelded themselues, and found him very fauourable vnto them. Then Valdez with 40. or 50. noblemen and gentlemen pertaining vnto him, came on boord sir Francis Drakes ship. The residue of his ship were caried vnto Plimmouth, where they were detained a yere and an halfe for their ransome.

Valdez comming vnto Drake and humbly kissing his hand protested vnto him, that he and they had resolued to die in battell, had they not by good fortune fallen into his power, whom they knew to be right curteous and gentle, and whom they had heard by generall report to bee most favourable vnto his vanquished foe: insomuch that he sayd it was to bee doubted whether his enimies had more cause to admire and loue him for his great, valiant, and prosperous exploites, or to dread him for his singular felicitie and wisedom, which euer attended vpon him in the warres, and by the which hee had attained vnto so great honour. With that Drake embraced him and gaue him very honourable entertainement, feeding him at his owne table, and lodging him in his cabbin.

Here Valdez began to recount vnto Drake the forces of all the Spanish Fleet, and how foure mightie Gallies were separated by tempest from them, and also how they were determined first to haue put into Plimmouth hauen, not expecting to bee repelled thence by the English ships which they thought could by no meanes withstand their impregnable forces, perswading themselues that by means of their huge Fleete, they were become lords and commaunders of the maine Ocean. For which cause they marueled much how the English men in their small ships durst approch within musket shot of the Spaniards mightie wooden castles, gathering the wind of them with many other such like attempts.

Immediately after, Valdez and his company, being a man of principal authoritie in the Spanish Fleete, and being descended of one and the same familie with that Valdez, which in the yeere 1574 besieged Leiden in Holland, were sent captiues into England. There were in the sayd ship 55. thousand duckates in ready money of the Spanish kings gold, which the souldiers merily shared among themselues.

[Sidenote: A great Biscaine ship taken by the English.] The same day was set on fire one of their greatest shippes, being Admirall of the squadron of Guipusco, and being the shippe of Michael de Oquendo Vice-admirall of the whole Fleete, which contained great store of gunnepowder and other warrelike prouision. The vpper part onely of this shippe was burnt, and an the persons therein contained (except a very few) were consumed with fire. And thereupon it was taken by the English, and brought into England with a number of miserable burnt and skorched Spaniards. Howbeit the gunpowder (to the great admiration of all men) remained whole and vnconsumed.

In the meane season the lord Admirall of England in his ship called the Arke-royall, all that night pursued the Spaniards so neere, that in the morning hee was almost left alone in the enimies Fleete, and it was foure of the clocke at afternoone before the residue of the English Fleet could ouertake him.

At the same time Hugo de Moncada gouernour of the foure Galliasses, made humble sute vnto the Duke of Medina that he might be licenced to encounter the Admirall of England: which libertie the duke thought not good to permit vnto him, because hee was loth to exceed the limites of his commission and charge.

[Sidenote: The 23. of Iuly.] Vpon Tuesday which was the three and twentie of Iuly, the nauie being come ouer against Portland, the wind began to turne Northerly, insomuch that the Spaniards had a fortunate and fit gale to inuade the English. But the Englishmen hauing lesser and nimbler Ships, recouered againe the vantage of the winde from the Spaniards, whereat the Spaniards seemed to bee more incensed to fight then before. But when the English Fleete had continually and without intermission from morning to night, beaten and battered them with all their shot both great and small: the Spaniardes vniting themselues, gathered their whole Fleete close together into a roundell, so that it was apparant that they ment not as yet to inuade others, but onely to defend themselues and to make hast vnto the place prescribed vnto them, which was neere vnto Dunkerk, that they might ioine forces with the Duke of Parma, who was determined to haue proceeded secretly with his small shippes vnder the shadow and protection of the great ones, and so had intended circumspectly to performe the whole expedition.

This was the most furious and bloodie skirmish of all, in which the lord Admirall of England continued fighting amidst his enimies Fleete, and seeing one of his Captaines afarre off, hee spake vnto him in these wordes: Oh George what doest thou? Wilt thou nowe frustrate my hope and opinion conceiued of thee? Wilt thou forsake me nowe? With which wordes hee being enflamed, approched foorthwith, encountered the enemie, and did the part of a most valiant Captaine. His name was George Fenner, a man that had bene conuersant in many Sea-fights.

[Sidenote: A great Venetian ship and other small ships taken by the English.] In this conflict there was a certaine great Venetian ship with other small ships surprised and taken by the English.

The English nauie in the meane while increased, whereunto out of all Hauens of the Realme resorted ships and men: for they all with one accord came flocking thither as vnto a set field, where immortall fame and glory was to be attained, and faithfull seruice to bee performed vnto their prince and countrey.

In which number there were many great and honourable personages, as namely, the Erles of Oxford, of Northumberland, of Cumberland, &c. with many Knights and Gentlemen: to wit, Sir Thomas Cecill, Sir Robert Cecill, Sir Walter Raleigh, Sir William Hatton, Sir Horatio Palauacini, Sir Henry Brooke, Sir Robert Carew, Sir Charles Blunt, Master Ambrose Willoughbie, Master Henry Nowell, Master Thomas Gerard, Master Henry Dudley, Master Edward Darcie, Master Arthur Gorge, Master Thomas Woodhouse, Master William Haruie, &c. And so it came to passe that the number of the English shippes amounted vnto an hundreth: which when they were come before Douer, were increased to an hundred and thirtie, being notwithstanding of no proportionable bignesse to encounter with the Spaniards, except two or three and twentie of the Queehes greater shippes, which onely, by reason of their presence, bred an opinion in the Spaniardes mindes concerning the power of the English Fleet: the mariners and souldiers whereof were esteemed to be twelue thousand.

[Sidenote: The 24 of Iuly.] The foure and twentie of Iuly when as the sea was calme, and no winde stirring, the fight was onely betweene the foure great Galleasses and the English shippes, which being rowed with Oares, had great vauntage of the sayd English shippes, which notwithstanding for all that would not bee forced to yeeld, but discharged their chaine-shot to cut assunder the Cables and Cordage of the Galliasses, with many other such Stratagemes. They were nowe constrained to send their men on land for a newe supplie of Gunne-powder, whereof they were in great skarcitie, by reason they had so frankely spent the greater part in the former conflicts.

The same day, a Counsell being assembled, it was decreed that the English Fleete should be diuided into foure squadrons: the principall whereof was committed vnto the lord Admirall: the second to Sir Francis Drake: the third, to Captaine Hawkins: the fourth, to Captaine Frobisher.

The Spaniards in their sailing obserued very diligent and good order, sayling three and foure, and sometimes more ships in a ranke, and folowing close vp one after another, and the stronger and greater ships protecting the lesser.

[Sidenote: The 25. of Iuly.] The fiue and twenty of Iuly when the Spaniardes were come ouer-gainst the Isle of Wight, the lord Admirall of England being accompanied with his best ships, (namely the Lion, Captaine whereof was the lord Thomas Howard: The Elizabeth Ionas vnder the commandement of Sir Robert Southwel sonne in lawe vnto the lord Admirall: the Beare vnder the lord Sheffield nephew vnto the lord Admirall: the Victorie vnder Captaine Barker: and the Galeon Leicester vnder the forenamed Captaine George Fenner) with great valour and dreadfull thundering of shot, encountered the Spanish Admirall being in the very midst of all his Fleete. Which when the Spaniard perceiued, being assisted with his strongest ships, he came foorth and entered a terrible combate with the English: for they bestowed each on other the broad sides, and mutually discharged all their Ordinance, being within one hundred, or an hundred and twentie yards one of another.

At length the Spaniardes hoised vp their sayles, and againe gathered themselues vp close into the forme of a roundel. In the meane while Captaine Frobisher had engaged himselfe into a most dangerous conflict. Whereupon the lord Admirall comming to succour him, found that hee had valiantly and discreetly behaued himselfe, and that hee had wisely and in good time giuen ouer the fight, because that after so great a batterie he had sustained no damage.

[Sidenote: The 26. of Iuly.] For which cause the day following, being the sixe and twentie of Iuly, the lord Admirall rewarded him with the order of knighthood, together with the lord Thomas Howard, the lord Sheffield, M. Iohn Hawkins and others.

The same day the lord Admirall receiued intelligence from Newhauen in France, by certaine of his Pinasses, that all things were quiet in France, and that there was no preparation of sending aide vnto the Spaniards, which was greatly feared from the Guisian faction, and from the Leaguers: but there was a false rumour spread all about, that the Spaniards had conquered England.

[Sidenote: The 27. of Iuly. The Spaniards ancre before Caleis.] The seven and twentie of Iuly, the Spaniards about the sunne-setting were come ouer-against Douer, and rode at ancre within the sight of Caleis, intending to hold on for Dunkerk, expecting there to ioyne with the Duke of Parma his, forces, without which they were able to doe litle or nothing.

Likewise the English Fleete following vp hard vpon them, ancred iust by them within culuering-shot. And here the lord Henry Seymer vnited himselfe vnto the lord Admiral with his fleete of 30. ships which road before the mouth of Thames.

As the Spanish nauie therefore lay at ancre, the Duke of Medina sent certaine messengers vnto the duke of Parma, with whom vpon that occasion many Noblemen and Gentleman went to refresh themselues on land: and amongst the rest the prince of Ascoli, being accounted the kings base sonne, and a very proper and towardly yong gentleman, to his great good, went on shore, who was by so much the more fortunate, in that hee had not opportunitie to returne on boord the same ship, out of which he was departed, because that in returning home it was cast away vpon the Irish coast, with all the persons contained therein.

The duke of Parma being aduertised of the Spanish Fleetes arriual vpon the coast of England, made all the haste hee could to bee present himselfe in this expedition for the performance of his charge: vainely perswading himselfe that nowe by the meanes of Cardinall Allen, hee should be crowned king of England, and for that cause hee had resigned the government of the Lowe countries vnto Count Mansfeld the elder. [Sidenote: The 28. of Iuly.] And having made his vowes vnto S. Mary of Hall in Henault (whom he went to visite for his blind deuotions sake) he returned toward Bruges the 28. of Iuly.

[Sidenote: The 29. of Iuly.] The next day trauelling to Dunkerk hee heard the thundering Ordinance of either Fleet: and the same euening being come to Dixmud, hee was giuen to vnderstand the hard successe of the Spanish Fleete.

[Sidenote: The 30. of Iuly.] Vpon Tuesday which was the thirtieth of Iuly, about high noone, hee came to Dunkerk, when as all the Spanish Fleete was now passed by: neither durst any of his ships in the meane space come foorth to assist the sayd Spanish Fleete for feare of fiue and thirtie warrelike ships of Holland and Zeland, which there kept watch and warde vnder the conduct of the Admirall Iustin of Nassau.

The foresayd fiue and thirtie shippes were furnished with most cunning mariners and olde expert souldiers, amongst the which were twelue hundred Musketiers, whom the States had chosen out of all their garisons, and whom they knew to haue bene heretofore experienced in sea-fights.

This nauie was giuen especially in charge not to suffer any shippe to come out of the Hauen, not to permit any Zabraes, Pataches, or other small vessels of the Spanish Fleete (which were more likely to aide the Dunkerkers) to enter thereinto, for the greater ships were not to be feared by reason of the shallow sea in that place. Howbeit the prince of Parma his forces being as yet vnreadie, were not come on boord his shippes, onely the English Fugitiues being seuen hundred in number vnder the conduct of Sir William Stanley, came in fit time to haue bene embarked, because they hoped to giue the first assault against England. The residue shewed themselues vnwilling and loath to depart, because they sawe but a few mariners, who were by constraint drawne into this expedition, and also because they had very bare prouision of bread, drinke, and other necessary victuals.

Moreouer, the shippes of Holland and Zeland stood continually in their sight, threatening shot and powder, and many inconueniences vnto them: for feare of which shippes the Mariners and Sea-men secretly withdrew themselues both day and night, lest that the duke of Parma his souldiers should compell them, by maine force to goe on boord, and to breake through the Hollanders Fleete, which all of them iudged to bee impossible by reason of the straightnesse of the Hauen.

[Sidenote: The Spaniards vaine opinion concerning their own fleet.] But it seemeth that the Duke of Parma and the Spaniards grounded vpon a vaine and presumptuous expectation, that all the ships of England and of the Low countreys would at the first sight of the Spanish and Dunkerk Nauie haue betaken themselues to flight, yeelding them sea roome, and endeuouring only to defend themselues, their hauens, and sea coasts from inuasion. Wherefore their intent and purpose was, that the Duke of Parma in his small and flat-bottomed shippes, should as it were vnder the shadow and wings of the Spanish fleet, conuey ouer all his troupes, armour, and warlike prouision, and with their forces so vnited, should inuade England; or while the English fleet were busied in fight against the Spanish, should enter vpon any part of the coast, which he thought to be most conuenient. Which inuasion (as the captiues afterward confessed) the Duke of Parma thought first to haue attempted by the riuer of Thames; vpon the bankes whereof hauing at his first arriuall landed twenty or thirty thousand of his principall souldiers, he supposed that he might easily haue woonne the Citie of London; both because his small shippes should haue followed and assisted his land-forces, and also for that the Citie it-selfe was but meanely fortified and easie to ouercome, by reason of the Citizens delicacie and discontinuance from the warres, who with continuall and constant labour might be vanquished, if they yeelded not at the first assault. They were in good hope also to haue mette with some rebels against her Maiestie, and such as were discontented with the present state, as Papists and others. Likewise they looked for ayde from the fauorers of the Scottish Queene, who was not long before put to death; all which they thought would haue stirred vp seditions and factions.

Whenas therefore the Spanish fleet rode at anker before Caleis, to the end they might consult with the Duke of Parma what was best to be done according to the Kings commandement, and the present estate of their affairs, and had now (as we will afterward declare) purposed vpon the second of August being Friday, with one power and consent to haue put their intended businesse in practise; the L. Admirall of England being admonished by her Maiesties letters from the Court, thought it most expedient either to driue the Spanish fleet from that place, or at leastwise to giue them the encounter: [Sidenote: The 28 of Iuly.] and for that cause (according to her Maiesties prescription) he tooke forthwith eight of his woorst and basest ships which came next to hand, and disburthening them of all things which seemed to be of any value, filled them with gun-powder, pitch, brimstone, and with other combustible and firy matter; and charging all their ordinance with powder, bullets, and stones, he sent the sayd ships vpon the 28 of Iuly being Sunday, about two of the clocke after midnight, with the winde and tide against the Spanish fleet: which when they had proceeded a good space, being forsaken of the Pilots, and set on fire, were, directly carried vpon the King of Spaines Nauie: which fire in the dead of the night put the Spaniards into such a perplexity and horrour (for they feared lest they were like vnto those terrible ships, which Frederick Ienebelli three yeeres before, at the siege of Antwerpe, had furnished with gun-powder, stones, and dreadfull engines, for the dissolution of the Duke of Parma his bridge, built vpon the riuer of Scheld) that cutting their cables whereon their ankers were fastened, and hoising vp their sailes, they betooke themselues very confusedly vnto the maine sea.

[Sidenote: The galliasse of Hugo de Moncado cast vpon the showlds before Caleis.] In this sudden confusion, the principall and greatest of the foure galliasses falling fowle of another ship, lost her rudder: for which cause when she conld not be guided any longer, she was by the force of the tide cast into a certaine showld vpon the shore of Caleis, where she was immediately assaulted by diuers English pinasses, hoyes, and drumblers.

[Sidenote: M. Amias Preston valiantly boordeth the galliasse.] And as they lay battering of her with their ordinance, and durst not boord her, the L. Admirall sent thither his long boat with an hundreth choise souldiers vnder the command of Captaine Amias Preston. Vpon whose approch their fellowes being more emboldened, did offer to boord the galliasse: against whom the gouernour thereof and Captaine of all the foure galliasses, Hugo de Moncada, stoutly opposed himselfe, fighting by so much the more valiantly, in that he hoped presently to be succoured by the Duke of Parma. In the meane season, Moncada, after he had endured the conflict a good while, being hitte on the head with a bullet, fell downe starke dead, and a great number of Spaniards also were slaine in his company. The greater part of the residue leaping ouer-boord into the sea, to saue themselues by swimming, were most of them drowned. Howbeit there escaped among others Don Anthonio de Manriques, a principall officer in the Spanish fleet (called by them their Veador generall) together with a few Spaniards besides: which Anthonio was the first man that carried certaine newes of the successe of their fleet into Spaine.

This huge and monstrous galliasse, wherein were contained three hundred slaues to lug at the oares, and foure hundred souldiers, was in the space of three houres rifled in the same place; and there were found amongst diuers other commodities 50000 ducats of the Spanish kings treasure. At length when the slaues were released out of the fetters, the English men would haue set the sayd ship on fire, which Monsieur Gourdon the gouernor of Caleis, for feare of the damage which might thereupon ensue to the Towne and Hauen, would not permit them to do, but draue them from thence with his great ordinance.

[Sidenote: The great fight before Greueling the 29 of Iuly.] Vpon the 29 of Iuly in the morning, the Spanish Fleet after the foresayd tumult, hauing arranged themselues againe into order, were, within sight of Greueling, most brauely and furiously encountered by the English; where they once againe got the winde of the Spaniards: who suffered themselues to be depriued of the commodity of the place in Calais rode, and of the aduantage of the winde neere vnto Dunkerk, rather then they would change their array or separate their forces now conioyned and vnited together, standing onely vpon their defence.

And albeit there were many excellent and warlike ships in the English fleet, yet scarse were there 22 or 23 among them all which matched 90 of the Spanish ships in bignesse, or could conueniently assault them. Wherefore the English shippes vsing their prerogatiue of nimble stirrage, whereby they could turne and wield themselues with the winde which way they listed, came often times very neere vpon the Spaniards, and charged them so sore, that now and then they were but a pikes length asunder: and so continually giuing them one broad side after another, they discharged all their shot both great and small vpon them, spending one whole day from morning till night in that violent kinde of conflict, vntill such time as powder and bullets failed them. In regard of which want they thought it conuenient not to pursue the Spaniards any longer, because they had many great vantages of the English, namely for the extraordinary bignesse of their ships, and also for that they were so neerely conioyned, and kept in so good array, that they could by no meanes be fought withall one to one. The English thought therefore, that they had right well acquited themselues, in chasing the Spaniards first from Caleis, and then from Dunkerk, and by that meanes to haue hindered them from ioyning with the Duke of Parma his forces, and getting the winde of them, to haue driuen them from their owne coasts.

The Spaniards that day sustained great losse and damage hauing many of their shippes shot thorow and thorow, and they discharged likewise great store of ordinance against the English; who indeed sustained some hinderance, but not comparable to the Spaniards losse: for they lost not any one shippe or person of account. For very diligent inquisition being made, the English men all that time wherein the Spanish Nauie sayled vpon their seas, are not found to haue wanted aboue one hundreth of their people: albeit Sir Francis Drakes shippe was pierced with shot aboue forty times, and his very cabben was twise shot thorow, and about the conclusion of the fight, the bedde of a certaine gentleman lying weary thereupon, was taken quite from vnder him with the force of a bullet. Likewise, as the Earle of Northumberland and Sir Charles Blunt were at dinner vpon a time, the bullet of a demi-culuering brake thorow the middest of their cabbin, touched their feet, and strooke downe two of the standers by, with many such accidents befalling the English shippes, which it were tedious to rehearse. Whereupon it is most apparant, that God miraculously preserued the English nation. For the L. Admirall wrote vnto her Maiestie that in all humane reason, and according to the iudgement of all men (euery circumstance being duly considered) the English men were not of any such force, whereby they might, without a miracle, dare once to approch within sight of the Spanish Fleet: insomuch that they freely ascribed all the honour of their victory vnto God, who had confounded the enemy, and had brought his counsels to none effect.

[Sidenote: Three Spanish shippes suncke in the fight.] The same day the Spanish ships were so battered with English shot, that that very night and the day following, two or three of them suncke right downe: and among the rest a certaine great ship of Biscay, which Captaine Crosse assaulted, which perished euen in the time of the conflict, so that very few therein escaped drowning; who reported that the gouernours of the same shippe slew one another vpon the occasion following: one of them which would haue yeelded the shippe was suddenly slaine; the brother of the slaine party in reuenge of his death slew the murtherer, and in the meane while the ship suncke.

[Sidenote: Two galeons taken and caried into Zealand.] The same night two Portugall galeons of the burthen of seuen or eight hundreth tunnes a piece, to wit the Saint Philip and the Saint Matthew, were forsaken of the Spanish Fleet, for they were so torne with shotte that the water entered into them on all sides. In the galeon of Saint Philip was Francis de Toledo, brother vnto the Count de Orgas, being Colonell ouer two and thirty bands: besides other gentlemen; who seeing their mast broken with shotte, they shaped their course, as well as they could, for the coast of Flanders: whither when they could not attaine, the principall men in the ship committing themseluds to their skiffe, arriued at the next towne, which was Ostend; and the ship it selfe being left behinde with the residue of their company, was taken by the Vlishingers.

In the other galeon, called the S. Matthew, was embarked Don Diego Pimentelli another camp-master and colonell of 32 bands, being brother vnto the marques of Tamnares, with many other gentlemen and captaines. Their ship was not very great, but exceeding strong, for of a great number of bullets which had batterd her, there were scarse 20 wherewith she was pierced or hurt: her vpper worke was of force sufficient to beare off a musket shot: this shippe was shot thorow and pierced in the fight before Greueling; insomuch that the leakage of the water could not be stopped: whereupon the duke of Medina sent his great skiffe vnto the gouernour thereof, that he might saue himselfe and the principal persons that were in his ship: which he, vpon a hault courage, refused to do: wherefore the Duke charged him to saile next vnto himselfe: which the night following he could not performe, by reason of the great abundance of water which entered his ship on all sides; for the auoiding wherof, and to saue his ship from sincking, he caused 50 men continually to labor at the pumpe, though it were to small purpose. And seeing himselfe thus forsaken and separated from his admirall, he endeuored what he could to attaine vnto the coast of Flanders: where, being espied by 4 or 5 men of warre, which had their station assigned them vpon the same coast, he was admonished to yeeld himselfe vnto them. Which he refusing to do, was strongly assaulted by them altogether, and his ship being pierced with many bullets, was brought into farre worse case then before, and 40 of his souldiers were slaine. By which extremity he was enforced at length to yeeld himselfe vnto Peter Banderduess and other captaines, which brought him and his ship into Zeland; and that other ship also last before mentioned: which both of them, immediatly after the greater and better part of their goods were vnladen, suncke right downe.

For the memory of this exploit, the fbresayd captaine Banderduess caused the banner of one of these shippes to be set vp in the great Church of

Leiden in Holland, which is of so great a length, that being fastened to the very roofe, it reached downe to the ground.

[Sidenote: A small shippe cast away about Blankenberg.] About the same time another small ship being by necessity dtiuen vpon the coast of Flanders, about Blankenberg, was cast away vpon the sands, the people therein being saued. Thus almighty God would haue the Spaniards huge ships to be presented, not onely to the view of the English, but also of the Zelanders; that at the sight of them they might acknowledge of what small ability they had beene to resist such impregnable forces, had not God endued them with courage, prouidence, and fortitude, yea, and fought for them in many places with his owne arme.

The 29. of Iuly the Spanish fleet being encountered by the English (as is aforesayd) and lying close together vnder their fighting sailes, with a Southwest winde sailed past Dunkerk, the English ships still following the chase. [Sidenote: The dishonourable flight of the Spanish nauy; and the prudent aduice of the L. Admirall.] Of whom the day following when the Spaniards had got sea roome, they cut their maine sailes; whereby they sufficiently declared that they meant no longer to fight but to flie. For which cause the L. Admirall of England dispatched the L. Henrie Seymer with his squadron of small ships vnto the coast of Flanders where, with the helpe of the Dutch ships, he might stop the prince of Parma his passage, if perhaps he should attempt to issue forth with his army. And he himselfe in the meane space pursued the Spanish fleet vntil the second of August, because he thought they had set saile for Scotland. And albeit he followed them very neere, yet did he not assault them any more, for want of powder and bullets. But vpon the fourth of August, the winde arising, when as the Spaniards had spread all their sailes, betaking themselues wholly to flight, and leauing Scotland on the left hand, trended toward Norway, (whereby they sufficiently declared that their whole intent was to saue themselnes by flight, attempting for that purpose, with their battered and crazed ships, the most dangerous nauigation of the Northren seas) the English seeing that they were now proceeded vnto the latitude of 57 degrees, and being vnwilling to participate that danger whereinto the Spaniards plunged themselues, and because they wanted things necessary, and especially powder and shot, returned backe for England; leauing behinde them certaine pinasses onely, which they enioyned to follow the Spaniards aloofe, and to obserue their course. [Sidenote: The English returne home from the pursute of the Spaniards the 4 of August.] And so it came to passe that the fourth of August with great danger and industry, the English arriued at Harwich: for they had bene tossed vp and downe with a mighty tempest for the space of two or three dayes together, which it is likely did great hurt vnto the Spanish fleet, being (as I sayd before) so maimed and battered.

The English now going on shore, prouided themselues foorthwith of victuals, gunnepowder, and other things expedient, that they might be ready at all assayes to entertaine the Spanish fleet, if it chanced any more to returne. But being afterward more certainely informed of the Spaniards course, they thought it best to leaue them vnto those boisterous and vncouth Northren seas, and not there to hunt after them.

[Sidenote: The Spaniards consult to saile round about Scotland and Ireland, and so to returne home.] The Spaniards seeing now that they wanted foure or fiue thousand of their people and hauing diuers maimed and sicke persons, and likewise hauing lost 10 or 12 of their principall ships, they consulted among themselues, what they were best to doe, being now escaped out of the hands of the English, because their victuals failed them in like sort, that they began also to want cables, cordage, ankers, masts, sailes, and other naual furniture, and vtterly despaired of the Duke of Parma his assistance (who verily hoping and vndoubtedly expecting the returne of the Spanish Fleet, was continually occupied about his great preparation, commanding abundance of ankers to be made, and other necessary furniture for a Nauy to be prouided) they thought it good at length, so soone as the winde should serue them, to fetch a compasse about Scotland and Ireland, and so to returne for Spaine.

For they well vnderstood, that commandement was giuen thorowout all Scotland, that they should not haue any succour or assistance there. Neither yet could they in Norway supply their wants. Wherefore, hauing taken certaine Scotish and other fisherboats, they brought the men on boord their ships, to the end they might be their guides and Pilots. Fearing also least their fresh water should faile them, they cast all their horses and mules ouerboord: and so touching no where vpon the coast of Scotland, but being carried with a fresh gale betweene the Orcades and Faar-Isles, they proceeded farre North, euen vnto 61 degrees of latitude, being distant from any land at the least 40. leagues. Heere the Duke of Medina generall of the Fleet commanded all his followers to shape their course for Biscay: and he himselfe with twenty or fiue and twenty of his ships which were best prouided of fresh water and other necessaries, holding on his course ouer the maine Ocean, returned safely home. The residue of his ships being about forty in number, and committed vnto his Vice-admirall, fell neerer with the coast of Ireland, intending their course for Cape Clare, because they hoped there to get fresh water, and to refresh themseiues on land. [Sidenote: The shippe-wracke of the Spaniardes vpon the Irish coast.] But after they were driuen with many contrary windes, at length, vpon the second of September, they were cast by a tempest arising from the Southwest vpon diuers parts of Ireland, where many of their ships perished. And amongst others, the shippe of Michael de Oquendo, which was one of the great Galliasses: and two great ships of Venice also, namely, la Raita and Belahzara, with other 36 or 38 ships more, which perished in sundry tempests, together with most of the persons contained in them.

Likewise some of the Spanish ships were the second time carried with a strong West winde into the channell of England, whereof some were taken by the English vpon their coast, and others by the men of Rochel vpon the coast of France.

Moreouer, there arriued at Neuhauen, in Normandy, being by tempest inforced so to doe, one of the foure great Galliasses, where they found the ships with the Spanish women which followed the Fleet at their setting forth. [Sidenote: Of 134 ships of the Spanish fleet, there returned home but 53.] Two ships also, were cast away vpon the coast of Norway, one of them being of a great burthen; howbeit all the persons in the sayd great ship were saued: insomuch that of 134 ships, which set saile out of Portugall, there returned home 53 onely small and great: namely of the foure galliasses but one, and but one of the foure gallies. Of the 91 great galleons and hulks there were missing 58. and 33 returned: of the pataches and zabraes 17 were missing, and 18 returned home. In briefe, there were missing 81 ships, in which number were galliasses, gallies, galeons, and other vessels, both great and small. And amongst the 53 ships remaining, those also are reckoned which returned home before they came into the English chanell. Two galeons of those which were returned, were by misfortune burnt as they rode in the hauen; and such like mishaps did many others vndergo. Of 30000 persons which went in this expedition, there perished (according to the number and proportion of the ships) the greater and better part; and many of them which came home, by reason of the toiles and inconueniences which they sustained in this voyage, died not long after their arriuall. The Duke of Medina immediatly vpon his returne was deposed from his authority, commanded to his priuate house, and forbidden to repaire vnto the Court; where he could hardly satisfie or yeeld a reason vnto his malicious enemies and backbiters. Many honourable personages and men of great renowne deceased soone after their returne; as namely Iohn Martines de Ricalde, with diuers others. A great part also of the Spanish Nobility and Gentry employed in this expedition perished either by fight, diseases, or drowning before their arriuall; and among the rest Thomas Perenot of Granduell a Dutchman, being earle of Cantebroi, and sonne vnto Cardinall Granduell his brother.

Vpon the coast of Zeland Don Diego de Pimentell, brother vnto the Marques de Tamnares, and kinseman vnto the earle of Beneuentum and Calua, and Colonell ouer 32 bands with many other in the same ship was taken and detained as prisoner in Zeland.

Into England (as we sayd before) Don Pedro de Valdez, a man of singular experience, and greatly honoured in his countrey, was led captiue, being accompanied with Don Vasquez de Silua, Don Alonzo de Sayas, and others.

Likewise vpon the Scottish Westerne Isles of Lewis, and Ila, and about Cape Cantyre vpon the maine land, there were cast away certaine Spanish shippes, out of which were saued diuers Captaines and Gentlemen, and almost foure hundred souldiers, who for the most part, after their shipwracke, were brought vnto Edenborough in Scotland, and being miserably needy and naked, were there clothed at the liberality of the King and the Marchants, and afterward were secretly shipped for Spaine; but the Scottish fleet wherein they passed touching at Yarmouth on the coast of Norfolke, were there stayed for a time vntill the Councels pleasure was knowen; who in regard of their manifolde miseries, though they were enemies, wincked at their passage.

Vpon the Irish coast many of their Noblemen and Gentlemen were drowned; and diuers slaine by the barbarous and wilde Irish. Howbeit there was brought prisoner out of Ireland, Don Alonzo de Luçon, Colonell of two and thirty bandes, commonly called a terza of Naples; together with Rodorigo de Lasso, and two others of the family of Cordoua, who were committed vnto the custodie of Sir Horatio Palauicini, that Monsieur de Teligny the sonne of Monsieur de Noüe (who being taken in fight neere Antwerpe, was detained prisoner in the Castle of Turney) might be ransomed for them by way of exchange. To conclude, there was no famous nor woorthy family in all Spaine, which in this expedition lost not a sonne, a brother, or a kinseman.

[Sidenote: New coines stamped for the memory of the Spaniards ouerthrow.] For the perpetuall memorie of this matter, the Zelanders caused newe coine of Siluer and brasse to be stamped: which on the one side contained the armes of Zeland, with this inscription: GLORY TO GOD ONELY: and on the other side, the pictures of certeine great ships, with these words: THE SPANISH FLEET: and in the circumference about the ships: IT CAME, WENT, AND WAS. Anno 1588. That is to say, the Spanish fleet came, went, and was vanquished this yere; for which, glory be giuen to God onely.

Likewise they coined another kinde of money; vpon the one side whereof was represented a ship fleeing and a ship sincking: on the other side foure men making prayers and giuing thanks vnto God vpon their knees; with this sentence: Man purposeth; God disposeth. 1588. Also, for the lasting memory of the same matter, they haue stamped in Holland diuers such like coines, according to the custome of the ancient Romans.

[Sidenote: The people of England and of the vnited prouinces, pray, fast, and giue thanks vnto God.] While this woonderfull and puissant Nauie was sayling along the English coastes, and all men did now plainely see and heare that which before they would not be perswaded of, all people thorowout England prostrated themselues with humble prayers and supplications vnto God: but especially the outlandish Churches (who had greatest cause to feare, and against whom by name, the Spaniards had threatened most grievous torments) enioyned to their people continuall fastings and supplications, that they might turne away Gods wrath and fury now imminent vpon them for their sinnes: knowing right well, that prayer was the onely refuge against all enemies, calamities, and necessities, and that it was the onely solace and reliefe for mankinde, being visited with affliction and misery. Likewise such solemne dayes of supplication were obserued thorowout the vnited Prouinces.

Also a while after the Spanish Fleet was departed, there was in England, by the commandement of her Maiestie, and in the vnited Prouinces, by the direction of the States, a solemne festiuall day publikely appointed, wherein all persons were enioyned to resort vnto the Church, and there to render thanks and praises vnto God: and the Preachers were commanded to exhort the people thereunto. The foresayd solemnity was obserued vpon the 29 of Nouember; which day was wholly spent in fasting, prayer, and giuing of thanks.

Likewise, the Queenes Maiestie herselfe, imitating the ancient Romans, rode into London in triumph, in regard of her owne and her subjects glorious deliuerance. For being attended vpon very solemnely by all the principall estates and officers of her Realme, she was carried thorow her sayd City of London in a tryumphant chariot, and in robes of triumph, from her Palace vnto the Cathedrall Church of Saint Paul, out of the which the ensignes and colours of the vanquished Spaniards hung displayed. And all the Citizens of London in their Liueries stood on either side the street, by their seuerall Companies, with their ensignes and banners: and the streets were hanged on both sides with Blew cloth, which, together with the foresayd banners, yeelded a very stately and gallant prospect. Her Maiestie being entered into the Church, together with her Clergie and Nobles gaue thanks vnto God, and caused a publike Sermon to be preached before her at Pauls crosse; wherein none other argument was handled, but that praise, honour, and glory might be rendered vnto God, and that Gods name might be extolled by thanksgiuing. And with her owne princely voice she most Christianly exhorted the people to doe the same: whereupon the people with a loud acclamation wished her a most long and happy life, to the confusion of her foes.

Thus the magnificent, huge, and mighty fleet of the Spaniards (which themselues termed in all places inuincible) such as sayled not vpon the Ocean see many hundreth yeeres before, in the yeere 1588 vanished into smoake; to the great confusion and discouragement of the authors thereof. In regard of which her Maiesties happy successe all her neighbours and friends congratulated with her, and many verses were penned to the honour of her Maiesty by learned men, whereof some which came to our hands we will here annexe.

* * * * *

AD SERENISSIMAM ELIZABETHAM ANGLIÆ REGINAM.

THEODOR. BEZA.

Strauerat innumeris Hispanus nauibus æquor,
  Regnis iuncturus sceptra Britanna suis.
Tanti huius, rogitas, quæ motus causa? superbos
  Impulit Ambitio, vexit Auaritia.
Quàm bene te ambitio mersit vanissima ventus?
  Et tumidos tumidæ vos superastis aquæ
Quàm bene totius raptores orbis auaros,
  Hausit inexhausti iusta vorago maris!
At tu, cui venti, cui totum militat æquor,
  Regina, ô mundi totius vna, decus,
Sic regnare Deo perge, ambitione remota,
  Prodiga sic opibus perge iuuare pios,
Vt te Angli longum, longum Anglis ipsa fruaris,
  Quàm dilecta bonis, tam metuenda malis.

The same in English.

The Spanish Fleet did flote in narrow Seas,
And bend her ships against the English shore,
With so great rage as nothing could appease,
And with such strength as neuer seene before:
  And all to ioyne the kingdome of that land
  Vnto the kingdomes that he had in hand.

Now if you aske what set this king on fire,
To practise warre when he of peace did treat,
It was his Pride, and neuer quencht desire,
To spoile that Islands wealth, by peace made great:
  His Pride which farre aboue the heauens did swell
  And his desire as vnsuffic'd as hell.

But well haue windes his proud blasts ouerblowen,
And swelling waues alayd his swelling heart,
Well hath the Sea with greedie gulfs vnknowen,
Deuoured the deuourer to his smart:
  And made his ships a pray vnto the sand,
  That meant to pray vpon anothers land.

And now, O Queene, aboue all others blest,
For whom both windes and waues are prest to fight,
So rule your owne, so succour friends opprest,
(As farre from pride, so ready to do right)

That England you, you England long enioy,
No lesse your friends delight, then foes annoy.

* * * * *

A briefe and true report of the Honorable voyage vnto Cadiz, 1596. of the ouerthrow of the kings Fleet, and of the winning, sacking, and burning of the Citie, with all other accidents of moment, thereunto appertaining.

After that the two most Noble and Renowmed Lords Generals: The L. Robert Earle of Essex, and the L. Charles Howard L. High Admirall of England, were come vnto Plymmouth (which was about the beginning of May last, 1596.) being there accompanied with diuers other Noble Peeres, as the Earle of Sussex, the L. Thomas Howard, the L. Harbert, the L. Warden Sir Walter Raleigh: the L. Marshall Sir Francis Vere: the L. Burk, Don Christopher young Prince of Portingall, young Count Lodouick of Nassaw, and the Admirall of the Hollanders, Sir Iohn Vanderfoord: besides many other most worthy Knights and Gentlemen of great woorth attending vpon this most honorable Action: It pleased them, there to make their abode for the time of that moneth, aswell for the new furnishing and reuictualing of her Maiesties Royall Nauie: as also for the expecting of some other ships, which were to come from diuers places of the Realme, and were as yet wanting: making that place as it should seeme the Rendezuous for all the whole Fleete, there to complete the full number of al such companies both for sea and land: as was in their noble and deepe wisedomes thought meete and agreed vpon.

All the time of this their abode there, there was a most zealous and diligent care had for the holy seruice of God dayly and reuerently to be frequented: and also for other good and ciuill orders of militarie discipline to be obserued, to the exceeding great comfort and reioycing of all the hearts of the godly and well disposed.

And for that it might the better appeare, that there was small hope of pardon to be expected of the offenders, if they did at any time neglect their duties, about due obseruation of matters of importance: Their orders, lawes, and decrees being once published: about the 8. or 9. of the same moneth, there were two offenders executed a little without the towne, in a very fayre pleasant greene, called the Ho: the one for beginning of a muteny in his company, the other for running away from his Colours.

And about the same time in the Dutch Regiment, an other for murthering of one of his companions, about a quarrell betweene themselues, rising as it was supposed, vpon their drinke, was by order of Martiall law, presently tyed to the partie so murthered, and foorthwith both of them so cast into the sea.

Moreouer, about the 28. of the same moneth, a certaine Lieutenant (whose name I will forbeare) was by sound of Drumme publikely in all the streetes disgraced, or rather after a sort disgraded, and cashierd for bearing any farther Office at that time, for the taking of money by way of corruption, of certaine prest souldiers in the Countrey, and for placing of others in their roomes, more vnfit for seruice, and of lesse sufficiency and abilitie. This seuere executing of iustice at the very first did breed such a deepe terror in the hearts of the whole armie, that it seemed to cut off all occasion of the like disorder for euer afterwards to be attempted.

And here before their departure from Plymmouth, it pleased their Lordships to publish in print, and make knowen to all the world, especially to such as whom it concerned, and that both in the Latine, French, Dutch, English and Spanish tongue, what were the true, iust and vrgent causes, that at this time prouoked her Maiestie, to vndertake the preparing and setting forth of this so great a Nauie, annexing thereunto a full declaration, what was good will and pleasure should be done and performed of all them that ment not to incurre their owne priuate present daungers, or else were willing to auoyde her Maiesties future indignation and displeasure.

Likewise now, at the same instant, their owne most prouident and godly decrees, which they had deuised for the honest cariage of euery particular person in their degrees and vocation, were made knowen to all men, and published in sundry writings, with diuers great punishments, set downe and appointed for the wilfull offenders and brekers of the same.

Thus then, all things being in very good order and well appointed, the most holy name of our Omnipotent God being most religiously and deuoutly called vpon, and his blessed and sacred Communion being diuers times most reuerently and publikely celebrated: These two most noble personages, with all their honorable Associats, and most famous worthy Knights, Gentlemen, Captaines, Leaders, and very willing and expert Souldiers, and Mariners, being furnished with 150. good sayle of shippe or thereabout: In the name of the most High and euerliuing God, and with all true and faithful obedience, to her sacred Maiesty, to the infinite good and tranquillitie of our Countrey, and to the perpetuall glory, and triumphant renowne of the eternall memory of their honorable names to all posterity, the first day of Iune embarked themselues, weighed Ancre, and hoysed vp sayle, and put to sea onward their iourney from the Sownds of Plymmouth.

The winde, at the first setting foorth, seemed very fauourable: but yet in the euening growing very scant, and all that night falling more and more against vs, and we hailing sayled no further then to a certaine place called Dodman Head: we were constrained the next day, to make our returne to the road of Plymmonth againe, and there in the Sownds to lie at ancre for that night.

About this time, and in this very place, by good fortune there came to my handes a prayer in English, touching this present Action, and made by her Maiestie, as it was voyced: The prayer seemed to me to be most excellent, aswell for the matter as also for the manner, and therefore for certaine diuers good motiues which then presently came to my minde, and whereof hereafter in his more conuenient time and place, I will make farther mention, I presumed at that very instant to translate it into Latine.

The Prayer is thus.

Most Omnipotent maker and guide of all our worlds masse, that onely searchest and fadomest the bottome of all our hearts conceits, and in them seest the true originals of all our actions intended: thou that by thy foresight doest truely discerne how no malice of Reuenge, nor quittance of iniury, nor desire of bloodshed, nor greedinesse of lucre hath bred the resolution of our now set out Army, but a heedfull care, and wary watch, that no neglect of foes, nor ouer-suretie of harme might breed either daunger to vs, or glory to them: these being the grounds wherewith thou doest enspire the mind, we humbly beseech thee with bended knees, prosper the worke, and with best forewindes guide the iourney, speed the victory, and make the returne the aduancement of thy glory, the tryumph of their fame, and surety to the Realme, with the least losse of the English blood. To these deuout petitions Lord giue thou thy blessed grant.

My homely translation, is thus.

Svmmè præpotens Deus, immensæ huius totius nostri mundi molis fabricator et Rector, qui solus perscrutaris intimos cordis nostri sensus, et ad fundum vsque nostrarum cogitationem explorando penetras, ac in eis, quid verè, et ex ammo cogitemus, et quæ sint actionum nostrarum rationes, ac fundamenta, cognoscis: Tu, qui ea, quæ in te est, ab omni æternitate præscientia, vides, quòd nec aliqua viciscendi malitiosa cupiditas, nec iniuriarum referendarum desiderium, nec sanguinis effundendi sitis, nec alicuius lucri, quæstusue auiditas ad istam classem præparandam, et emittendam nos commouerit: sed potiùs, quòd prouida quædam cura, solérsque vigilantia huc nos impulerit: ne vel inimicorum nostrorum neglectus, vel status nostri firmitaris nimium secura cogitatio, aut illis gloriam et honorem, aut nobis damnum et periculum pariat: Cum, inquam, hæc sint nostri, quicquid attentatur, negotii fundamenta: cumque tu hunc nobis animum, mentémque inieceris, vt istud aggrederemur: curuatis genibus a te humillimè petimus, vt velis hoc nostrum incoeptum secundissimè fortunare, totum iter prosperrimis flatibus dirigere, celerem et expeditiam victoriam nobis concedere, reditúmque talem nostris militibus elargiri, qualis et nomini tuo incrementum gloriæ, et illis famæ, laudisque triumphum, et Regno nostro firmam tranquillitatem possit apportare: idque cum minimo Anglorum sanguinis dispendio. His nostris religiosis petitionibus concede, Domine, sacrosanctum et annuentem voluntatem tuam.

After that we had anchored at Plymmouth that night, as I haue said, the third of Iune very early in the morning, hauing a reasonable fresh gale of winde, we set sayle, and kept our course againe, and the ninth of the same moneth comming something neere to the North cape, in a maner in the same altitude, or not much differing, which was about xliii. degrees, and something more, yet bearing so, as it was impossible to bee descried from the land: There it pleased the Lords to call a select Councell, which was always done by hanging out of a flagge of the armes of England, and shooting off of a great warning peece. On this select or priuie Councell were no moe than these: The two Lords Generall, the Lord Thomas Howard, the Lorde Warden Sir Walter Raleigh, the Lord Martiall Sir Francis Vere, Sir George Cary master of the Ordinance, Sir Coniers Clifford, and Sir Anthony Ashley, Clarke of the sayde Councell. And when it pleased the Lords Generall to call a common Counsell (as often times they did vpon weightie matters best knowen to their honours) then they would cause an other kinde of flagge to be hanged put, which was the Redcrosse of S. George, and was verie easie to be discerned from the other that appertained onely to the select Counsell, and so often as this flagge of Saint George was hanged out, then came all the Masters and Captaines of all the ships, whose opinions were to be demaunded, in such matters as appertayned vnto this sayd select Counsell: It was presently concluded, that our course in sayling should foorthwith be altered, and that we should beare more into the West, for some purposes to them best knowen.

At that very instant many letters of instructions were addressed and sent to euery particular Master and Captaine of the Ships: What the contentes of those letters of instructions were it was not as yet knowne vnto any, neither was it held meet to be enquired or knowen of any of vs. But vnder the titles and superscriptions of euery mans particuler letter these wordes were endorsed. Open not these letters on pain of your liues, vnles we chance to be scattered by tempest, and in that case open them, and execute the contents thereof: but if by mishap you fall into your enemies hand, then in any case cast them into the sea, sealed as they are. It should seeme that these letters did conteine in them the principall place and meaning of this entended action, which was hitherto by their deepe foresights kept so secret, as no man to my knowledge either did, or coulde so much as suspect it, more then themselues, who had the onely managing thereof. A conceite in my iudgement of greatest moment in the world, to effect any matter of importance. I meane, to entertaine those two vertues, Fidem, et Taciturnitatem: so much commended by the old writers. And if there was euer any great designement, in this our age, and memorie, discreetly, faithfully, and closely caried, I assure my selfe it was this, and though it were but in respect to that poynt onely: yet for such faithfull secrecie, it deserueth immortall praise.

All this while, our ships, God be thanked, kept in a most excellent good order, being diuided into fiue squadrons: that is to say, The Earle of Essex, the Lord Admirall, the Lord Thomas Howard, the Lord Warden Sir Walter Raleigh, and the Admirall of the Hollanders. All which squadrons, albeit they did euery day separate themselues of purpose, by the distance of certaine leagues, as well to looke out for such shippes as were happily vnder sayle, as also for the better procuring of sea-roome: yet alwayes commonly eyther that day, or the next day, towarde euening, they came all together, with friendly salutations and gratulations one to an other: which they terme by the name of Hayling: a ceremonie done solemnly, and in very good order, with sound of Trumpets and noyse of cheerefull voyces: and in such sort performed as was no small encouragement one to the other, beside a true report of all such accidents, as had happened in their squadrons.

Hitherto, as I sayde, our iourney was most prosperous, and all our shippes in very good plight, more then that the Mary Rose, by some mischance, either sprang or spent her fore-yarde, and two dayes after Sir Robert Crosse had in a maner the like mischance.

Nowe being thus betweene the North cape, and cape S. Vincent, and yet keeping, such a course a loofe, that by no meanes, those from the shoare might be able to descrie vs: The tenth of Iune, a French Barke, and a Fleming comming from the coast of Barbarie were brought in by some of our companie: but they were both of them very honourably and well vsed by the Lords Generall: and so after a fewe dayes tarrying, were peaceably sent away, after that they had conferred with them about such matters, as was thought good in their honorable wisedomes.

The twelfth of the same moneth, Sir Richard Leuison Knight, assisted with Sir Christopher Blunt, fought with three Hamburgers, and in that fight slewe two of them, and hurt eleuen, and in the end brought them all three in: and this was the very first hansell and maydenhead (as it were) of any matter of importance, or exployt worthy obseruation that was done in the way outward of this honorable voyage, and was so well perfourmed of those most worthy Gentlemen, as euery man highly commended them for their great valure, and discretion, and no lesse reioyced at this their fortunate succcsse.

The next day after, Sir Richard Weston meeting with a Flemming, who refused to vale his foretoppe, with the like good courage and resolution, attempted to bring him in. The fight continued very hot betweene them, for a good space: in the end the Swan, wherein the sayd Sir Richard was, had her forebeake strooken off: and having spent before in fight the one side of her tire of Ordinance, while she prepared to cast about, and to bestow on him the other side, in the meane time the Fleming taking this opportunity, did get almost halfe a league from him: and so for that time made his escape. And yet the next day after, the sayd Flemming being in a maner got to the very mouth of the Riuer vp to Lisbone, was taken, and brought in by M. Dorrell, being Captaine of the Iohn and Francis of London. Thus by diuiding their squadrons, and spreading the whole sea ouer a mighty way, there could not so much as the least pinke passe but she was espied and brought in.

The 13. 14. and 15. dayes, certaine littte stragling Carauels were taken by certaine of the Fleete, and in one of them a young beggarly Fryer vtterly vnlearned, with a great packet of letters for Lisbon: the poore wretches were maruellously well vsed by the Lords Generall, and that Carauel, and the like still as they were taken were commaunded to giue their attendance, and their Honours did vnderstand what they might of these poore men, of the estate of Spaine for that present.

About this time and in this place it was, that first in all my life time I did see the flying fishes, who when they are hardly pinched and chased by the Bonitoes and other great fishes, then to auoyde the daunger, they presently mount vp, and forsake the water, and betake themselues to the benefite of their winges and make their flight, which commonly is not aboue fiue or sixe score, or there about, and then they are constrayned to fall downe into the water againe, and it is the Mariners opinion that they can fly no longer then their wings be wet. The fish it selfe is about the bignesse of a Mackrell or a great white Hearing, and much of that colour and making, with two large wings shaped of nature very cunningly, and with great delight to behold, in all the world much like to our Gentlewomens dutch Fans, that, are made either of paper, parchment, or silke, or other stuffe, which will with certaine pleights easily runne and fold themselues together. One of these flying fishes was presented to my L. Admirall by a fisher man, and newly taken in his L. returne from Cadiz, and then I [had] good leisure and opportunitie to view it. ['had' missing in source text—KTH]

The 18. day early in the morning wee tooke an Irish man, and he came directly from Cadiz, hauing beene there but the day before at twelue of the clocke at high noone. This man being examined, told truely that there was now great store of shipping at Cadiz, and with them xviii. or xix. gallies in a readinesse, and that among those ships there were diuers of the kings best: and namely, that the Philip of Spaine was amongst them, but what their intent was, hee could not tell. This man was commanded also to giue his attendance.

The 20. of Iune being Sunday, we came before Cadiz very early in the morning, and in all this time as yet, the whole Nauy had not lost either by sicknesse or by any other maner of wayes sixe men to my knowledge: as for the Dutch company, I am not able precisely to say what happened there, for that they were no part of our charge to be looked vnto, but were a regiment entire of themselues, and by themselues to be prouided for, either for their diet, or for the preservation of their healths by phisicke.

Thus then I say, being all in good plight and strong, the 20. of Iune wee came to Cadiz, and there very earely in the morning presented our selues before the Towne, ryding about a league or something lesse, from it. The sea at that instant went maruelous high, and the winde was exceeding large. Notwithstanding, a Councell being called, our Lords Generall foorthwith attempted with all expedition to land some certaine companies of their men at the West side of the Towne, by certaine long boats, light horsemen, pynnesses, and barges made for the purpose, but could not compasse it, and in the attempting thereof; they chanced to sinke one of their Barges, with some foure score good souldiers well appointed in her, and yet by good hap and great care the men were all saued excepting viii. And therefore they were constrayned to put off their landing till an other more convenient time.

That morning very timely, there, lighted a very faire doue vpon the maine yard of the L. Admirals ship, and there she sate very quietly for the space of 3. or 4. houres, being nothing dismayed all that while, euery man gazed and looked much vpon her, and spake their minds and opinions, yet all concluding by no meanes to disquiet her: I for my part, tooke it for a very good omen and boading, as in trueth (God be thanked) there fell out nothing in the end to the contrary. And as at our very first comming to Cadiz this chanced, so likewise on the very last day of our departing from the same towne, another Doue presented her selfe in the selfe same order into the same ship, and presently grew wonderfull tame and familiar to vs all, and did so still keepe vs company, euen till our arriuall here in England.

We no sooner presented our selues, but presently a goodly sort of tall Spanish ships came out of the mouth of the Bay of Cadiz, the Gallies accompanying them in such good order, and so placed as all of them might well succour each other, and therewithall kept themselues very close to their towne, the castle, and the forts, for their better guard and defence, abiding there still, and expecting our farther determination. All that day passed, being very rough and boysterous, and litle or nothing could be done, more then that about the euening there passed some friendly and kinde salutations sent one from the other in warlike maner, by discharging certain great peeces, but to my knowledge no hurt done at all, or else very litle.

A carefull and diligent watch was had all that night thoroughout the whole armie, and on monday morning being the 21. day, the winde and weather being become moderate and fauourable, betweene fiue and sixe of the clocke in the morning, our ships in the name of almightie God, and in defence of the honour of England, without any farther delay, with all speed, courage, and alacritie, did set vpon the Spanish ships, being then vnder sayle, and making out of the mouth of the Bay of Cadiz, vp toward Puente de Suaço on Grenada side, being in number lix. tall ships, with xix. or xx. Gallies attending vpon them, sorted in such good order, and reasonable distance as they might still annoy vs, and alwayes relieue themselues interchangeably: hauing likewise the Castle, Forts, and Towne, continually to assist them and theirs, and alwayes readie to play vpon vs and ours.

In most mens opinions it seemed that the enemy had a wonderful aduantage of vs, all circumstances being well weighed, but especially the straightnesse of the place, and the naturall forme and situation of the Bay it selfe, being rightly considered. For albeit the very Bay it selfe is very large and exceeding beautifull, so that from Cadiz to Port S. Mary, is some vi. or vii. English miles ouer or there abouts, yet be there many rockes, shelues, sands and shallowes in it, so that the very chanell and place for sea roome, is not aboue 2. or 3. miles, yea and in some places not so much, for the ships of any great burthen, to make way in, but that they must either be set on ground or else constrained to run fowle one on another. All this notwithstanding, with great and inuincible courage, the Lords generall presently set vpon them, and sorting out some such conuenient ships, as to their honorable wisedomes seemed fittest for that times seruice, they were driuen to take some other course then before had beene by them entended. Wherefore vpon a graue consultation had by a select Counsell, what great dangers might ensue vpon so mightie a disaduantage as appeared in all probability, if it were not by good and sound iudgement preuented, and therewithall in their singular wisedomes foreseeing that some great stratageme might be practised by the enemy, either by fire-worke, or some other subtill politike deuise, for the hazarding of her Maiesties ships of honor in so narrow a place, thus with al expedition they concluded that the Viceadmirall, the L. Thomas Howard, that most noble L. Howard (whose exceeding great magnanimity, courage, and wisedome, ioyned with such an honorable kind of sweet courtesie, bountie, and liberalitie, as is not able by me and my weakenes to be expressed, hath wonne him all the faithfull louing hearts of as many as euer haue had any maner of dealing with him) This L. Thomas, I say, in the Non Pareille for that time, and the Reare Admirall Sir Walter Raleigh (a man of maruellous worth and regard, for many his exceeding singular great vertues, right fortitude and great resolutenes in all matters of importance) in the Warspight associated with diuers most famous worthy knights, namely, Sir Francis Vere the L. Martiall in the Rainbow, Sir George Cary M. of the Ordinance, in the Mary rose, Sir Robert Southwell in the Lyon, gentlemen for all laudable good vertues, and for perfect courage and discretion in all military actions, of as great praise and good desert as any gentlemen of their degree whosoeuer, hauing with them some of the shippes of London and some of the Dutch squadron of reasonable burthen, should leade the dance, and giue the onset, and that the two most noble Lords generall with some others of their companies, should in their conuenient time and order, second the maine battell. The fight being begunne and growen very hot, the L. Generall the Earle of Essex, (whose infinite princely vertues with triumphant fame deserue to be immortalized) being on Port S. Mary side, vpon a sudden and vnlooked for of others, thrust himselfe among the formost into the maine battell. The other most honorable L. Generall (whose singular vertues in all respects are of such an excellencie and perfection as neither can my praise in any part increase them, nor any mans enuy any whit blemish or diminish them) vnderstanding, the most noble Earle to be in fight among them, and perceiuing by the M. of his ship, the Arke Royall, that lacke of water, it was not possible, that he might put any neerer, without farther delay, called presently for his Pynnesse, and in the same Pynnesse put himselfe, and his honorable son L. William Howard that now is, aboord the Honor de la mer, and there remained in the fight till the battell was ended. The fight was very terrible, and most hideous to the beholder by the continuall discharging of those roaring thundering great peeces, on all sides, and so continued doubtful till about one or two of the clocke in the afternoone: about which time the Philip, whom in very truth, they had all most fancie vnto, began to yeeld and giue ouer, her men that remained aliue shifting for themselues as they were able, and swimming, and running a shoare with all the hast that they could possibly, and therewithall, at the very same instant themselues fired their ship, and so left her, and presently thereupon a great Argosie, with an other mighty great ship, fired themselues in the like maner. Immediately hereupon, the residue of the ships ran themselues on ground, as farre from vs as they could, and therby purchased their owne safety, or rather breathing space for the time. Of them all two faire ships only were boorded and taken by our men with most part of their furniture in them, the one called S. Matthy, a ship by estimation of some xii. hundred tunne, and the other S. Andrew, being a shippe of not much lesser burthen. The Gallies, seeing this suddaine great victorious ouerthrow, made all the hast they could toward the Bridge called Puente de Suaço, and there shrowded themselues in such sort as our shippes could not by any meanes possible come nigh them for lacke of water.

The Spanish ships in all were lix. and as is sayd, all tall ships and very richly furnished and well appointed, whereof some of them were bound for the Indies, and other freighted and furnished for Lisbon, as themselues affirme;

and had we not come that very time that we did, (which for my part, I do not attribute so much vnto meere chance, as to some secret deepe insight and foreknowledge of the two most worthy Lords generall, who no doubt spared for no cost or labour for true intelligence) we had certainely mist of them all.

Of what great wealth and riches these ships were, that I leaue to other mens iudgement and report, but sure I am that themselues offered two millions and a halfe of ducats for the redemption of the goods and riches that were in them: which offer of theirs, albeit it was accepted of the Lords Generall, and should haue beene receiued, yet we were defeated of it, as hereafter shall be more at large declared.

What maner of fight this was, and with what courage performed, and with what terror to the beholder continued, where so many thundering tearing peeces were for so long a time discharged, I leaue it to the Reader to thinke and imagine. Yet such was the great mercy and goodnes of our liuing God, that in all this cruell terrible fight, in the end, there were not either slaine or hurt by any maner of meanes (excepting one mischance that happened, wherof I will by and by make mention) many aboue the number of 100. of our men: notwithstanding diuers of our shippes were many times shot thorow and thorow: yea and some of them no lesse then two and twentie times, as I was enformed by credible report of the Captaines and Masters themselues. I knowe not of any other hurt done, sauing onely that Sir Robert Southwell, who alwayes shewed himselfe a most valiant resolute knight in all this action, making a litle too much haste with his Pinnesse to boord the Philip, had there his said Pinnesse burnt with the Philip at the same instant, and yet by good care and diligence his men were saued.

One other mischance (as I said) there happened, and it was thus: One of the Flemings flieboats, who had, in all the conflict before, caried himselfe very well and valiantly, about ten of the clocke while the fight continued sharpest, chanced by great negligence and misfortune, to be fired and blowen vp by his owne powder, who could not haue any fewer in him, then one hundred fighting men by all supposall, and so in the very twinckling of an eye, both shippe and men were all cast away, excepting vii. or viii. which by very good fortune, and great care and diligence of some of the other ships were saued.

Immediatly vpon this notable victory without any farther stay in all the world, the Lord generall the Earle of Essex put to shore and landed about 3000. shot, and pikemen: of the which number the one halfe was presently dispatched to the bridge Puente de Suaço, vnder the conduct of three most famous worth; knights. Sir Christopher Blunt, Sir Coniers Clifford, and Sir Thomas Gerard: with the other halfe, being about fifteene hundred, the most noble Earle of Essex himselfe, being accompanied with diuers other honorable Lords, namely the Earle of Sussex, the Lord Harbert, the Lord Burt, Count Lodouick of Nassaw, the Lord Martiall Sir Francis Vere, with many other worthy Knights, and men of great regard, who all in that dayes seruice did most valiantly behaue themselues, with all expedition possible marched on foote toward the towne of Cadiz, which was about three English miles march. That time of the day was very hot and faint and the way was all of dry deepe slyding sand in a maner, and beside that, very vneuen, and by that meanes so tiresome and painefull as might be. The enemie hauing reasonable companie both of horse and footemen, stoode in a readinesse some good distance without the towne to welcome vs, and to encounter the Lorde Generall. But the most famous Earle with his valiant Troupes, rather running in deede in good order, then marching, hastened on with such vnspeakeable courage and celeritie, as within one houres space and lesse, the horsemen were all discomfited and put to flight, their leader being strooken downe at the very first encounter, whereat the footemen being wonderfully dismayed and astonished at the vnexspected manner of the Englishmens kinde of such fierce and resolute fight retyred themselues with all the speede possible that they could, to recouer themselues into the Towne againe, which being done by them, with farre swifter legges then manly courage, our men were enforcd to skale the walles: which thing in very deede, although it was not without great danger and difficulty to be perfourmed: Yet such was the inuincible resolution, and the wonderfull dexterity of the English, that in one halfe houre or thereabout, the enemie was repulsed, and the towne wall possessed, by the noble Earle himselfe, being in all this action, either the uery first man or else in a maner ioyned with the first.

The towne walles being then possessed, and the English Ensigne being there displayed vpon them, with all speede possible they proceeded on to march through the towne, making still their waie with sworde and shot as well as they could, being still fought withall at euery turne.

Immediately vpon this most famous entrie, the noble Earle, (according to their resolutions, as I take it, put downe before) was seconded by the noble L. Admirall in person, who was accompanied, with the noble L. Thomas Howard, the most worthy gentleman his sonne, now L. Howard, Sir Robert Southwell, Sir Richard Leuison, and with diuers other gentlemen, his L. followers of good account: his colours being aduanced by that valiant resolute gentleman, (a man beautified with many excellent rare gifts, of good learning and vnderstanding) S. Edward Hobby Knight. And thus he likewise marching with al possible speede on foote, notwithstanding his L. many yeres, the Intolerable heate, for the time, and the ouertiring tedious deepe sands, with other many impediments: Yet in good time, ioyned himselfe with the Earle and his companies, and gaue them the strongest, and best assistance that he could.

Thus then the two Lords Generall with their companies being ioyned together, and proceeding so farre as the market place, there they were hotly encountered, where and at what time, that worthy famous knight Sir Iohn Winkfield, being sore wounded before on the thigh, at the very entry of the towne, and yet for all that no whit respecting himselfe being caried away, with the care he had to encourage and direct his company, was with the shot of a musket in the head, most vnfortunately slaine.

And thus before eight of the clocke that night were these two most noble Lords General, Masters of the market place, the forts, and the whole Towne and all, onely the Castle as yet holding out, and from time to time as they could, still annoying them, with seuen battering pieces. By this time night began to grow on, and a kind of peace or intermission was obtained by them of the Castle: to whome the Lords Generall had signified: that vnlesse before the next day in the morning they would absolutely render themselues, they should looke for no mercy, but should euery one be put to the sword: vpon which message they tooke deliberation that night: but in the morning before breake of day, they hanged out their flag of truce, and so without any further composition did yeeld themselues absolutely to their mercy, and deliuered vp the Castle.

And yet notwithstanding all this, in the night time while they had this respite to pause, and deliberate about the peacemaking, there were diuers great and suddaine alarms giuen: which did breed some great outrages and disorder in the towne. At euery which alarme, the two Lordes Generall shewed themselues maruelous ready and forward, insomuch that at the very first alarme, skant wel furnished with any more defence then their shirts, hose, and dublets, and those too altogether in a maner vntied, they were abroad in the streets themselues, to see the vttermost of it. But for that it is not as yet very well knowen (or at the least not well knowen vnto me) either wherfore, or by whom these alarmes were attempted: I am therefore to intreat, that a bare report, that such a thing was done, may suffice.

These things being done, and this surrender being made, present proclamation was published, that the fury now being past, all men should surcease from all maner of blood and cruell dealing, and that there should no kind of violence or hard vsage be offered to any, either man, woman or child, vpon paine of death: And so permitting the spoyle of so much of the towne as was by them thought meete, to the common souldiers for some certaine dayes, they were continually in counsell about other graue directions, best knowen to their honourable wisedomes.

This honourable and mercifull Edict I am sure was streightly and religiously obserued of the English: But how well it was kept by the Dutch, I will nether affirme, nor yet denie. For I perceiue betweene them and the Spaniards, there is in implicable hartburning, and therefore as soone as the Dutch squadron was espied in the fight, immediatly thereupon both they of Siuil and S. Lucar and also some, of some other places, did not onely arrest all such Dutch ships, as delt with them friendly by the way of traffick and Marchandise, and so confiscated their goods, but also imprisoned the Marchants and Owners of the same, and, as the report goeth, did intreat many of them with extreame cruelty thereupon.

In the meane while the very next day being the two and twenty day of Iune, all the Spanish shippes which were left on ground in the Bay of Cadiz, where the great ouerthrowe had beene but the day before, were by the Spaniards themselues there set on fire, and so from that time forward they neuer left burning of them, till euery one of them, goods and all, as farre as wee know were burnt and consumed. This their doing was much maruelled at of vs, and so much the more, for that, as I sayd before, there had bene made some offer for the redemption and sauing of the goods, and it was not to them vnknowen that this their offer was not misliked, but in all probabilitie should haue bene accepted. The common opinion was, that this was done either by the appointment of the Duke de Medina Sidonia, or els by expresse commandement from the higher powers.

Not long after the same time (three dayes as I remember) the gallies that were runne on ground, did quitte themselues also out of that place, and by the bridge of the Iland called Puente de Suaço, made their way round about the same Iland, and so by putting themselues to the maine sea, escaped to a towne called Rotta, not farre off, but something vp towards the Towne of Saint Lucars, and there purchased their safety by that meanes.

Thus was this notable victorie, as well by sea as by land, both begunne and in effect perfourmed, within the compasse, in a maner, of foureteene houres: A thing in trueth so strange and admirable, as in my iudgement will rather bee wondered at then beleeued of posteritie. And if euer any notable exploit in any age was comparable to Cæsars Veni, Vidi, Vici, certainely in my poore opinion it was this.

Here it is to be wished (and perchance of some too it is looked for) that euery mans particular worthy acte in this dayes seruice, with the parties names also, should be put downe, that thereby both they and their good deserts might be registered to all posteritie: and for my part I would it were so, and wish I were able to doe it. But for that I confesse it is a matter that passeth my power, yea, and for that I thinke it also a thing impossible to be precisely perfourmed by any other, I am to craue pardon for that I rather leaue it out altogether, then presume to doe it maymedly: and in this point I referre the Reader onely to the Mappe that is set foorth of this iourney, where it is in some parte conueniently touched and specified.

The Towne of it selfe was a very beautifull towne, and a large, as being the chiefe See of the Bishop there, and hauing a goodly Cathedrall Church in it, with a right goodly Abbey, a Nunnery, and an exceeding fine College of the Jesuites, and was by naturall situation, as also by very good fortification, very strong, and tenable enough in all mens opinions of the better judgement. Their building was all of a kind of hard stone, euen from the very foundation to the top, and euery house was in a manner a kinde of a fort or Castle, altogether flat-roofed in the toppe, after the Turkish manner, so that many men together, and that at ease, might walke thereon: hauing vpon the house top, great heapes of weighty stoanes piled vp in such good order, as they were ready to be throwen downe by euery woman most easily vpon such as passed by, and the streetes for the most part so exceeding narrow, (I thinke to auoide the intollerable great heat of the Sunne) as but two men or three at the most together, can in any reasonable sorte march thorough them, no streete being broader commonly then I suppose Watling streete in London to be.

The towne is altogether without glasse, excepting the Churches, yet with faire comely windowes, and with faire grates of iron to them, and haue very large folding leaues of wainscot or the like. It hath very fewe Chimnies in it, or almost none at all: it may be some one chimney in some one or other of the lower out roomes of lest account, seruing for some necessary vses, either to wash in, or the like, or els nowe and then perchance for the dressing of a dish of meate, hauing, as it should seeme vnto me, always a greater care and respect how to keepe themselues from all kind of great heat, then how to prouide for any store of great roste. It had in it by report of them that should best know it, some foure thousand and moe, of very good able fighting men, and six hundred horsemen at the least. No question but that they were well furnished of all things appertaining thereunto, especially so many good ships lying there, and being so well stored with all manner of munition, shot, and powder, as they were.

Whether they had knowledge of our comming or no, I can say nothing to it: Themselues giue it out that they vnderstood not of it, but onely by a Carauel the Friday at euening before we came. But whether they knew it or no, thus much I dare boldly affirme, that if the English had bene possessed of that or the like Towne, and had bene but halfe so well prouided as they were, they would haue defended it for one two moneths at the least, against any power whatsoeuer in at Christendome. But surely GOD is a mighty GOD, and hath a wonderfull secret stroke in all matters, especially of weight and moment. Whether their hearts were killed at the mighty ouerthrow by sea, or whether they were amased at the inuincible courage of the English, which was more then ordinary, caring no more for either small shot or great, then in a maner for so many hailestones, or whether the remorse of a guilty conscience toward the English nation, for their dishonourable and diuelish practices, against her Sacred Maiestie, and the Realme, (a matter that easily begetteth a faint heart in a guilty minde) or what other thing there was in it I know not, but be it spoken to their perpetuall shame and infamie, there was neuer thing more resolutely perfourmed, of the couragious English, nor more shamefully lost of the bragging Spaniard.

Of what wealth this towne should be, I am not able to resolue the asker: for I confesse that for mine owne part, I had not so much good lucke, as to be partaker so much as of one pennie, or penny worth. Howbeit my ill fortune maketh that towne neuer a whit the poorer. But as it should appear by the great pillage by the common souldiers, and some mariners too, and by the goodly furnitures; that were defaced by the baser people, and thereby vtterly lost and spoyled, as not woorth the carying away, and by the ouer great plenty of Wine, Oyle, Almonds, Oliues, Raisins, Spices, and other rich grocery wares, that by the intemperate disorder of some of the rasher sort were knockt out, and lay trampled vnder feete, in euery common high way, it should appeare that it was of some very mighty great wealth to the first owners, though perchance, not of any such great commoditie to the last subduers, for that I iudge that the better part was most ryotously and intemperately spent and consumed. A disorder in mine opinion very much to be lamented, and if it might be by any good meanes remedied, in my conceit, it were a most honourable deuice.

The Wednesday, Thursday, and Friday following, the Lords Generall spent in counsell, about the disposing of all matters, aswell touching the towne and prisoners, as also concerning all other matters, thought meete of them in their honourable wisedomes, and in all that meane while did shew such honourable bounty and mercy, as is not able to be expressed. For not onely the liues of euery one were spared, but also there was an especial care had, that al the Religious, as wel men as women, should be well and fauourably intreated, whom freely without any maner of ransome or other molestation, they caused to be safely transported ouer to Port Saint Marie, a towne in a maner as fayre as Cadiz: but at that time, as the case did stand, certainly knowen to be of no wealth in the world, and it was some sixe or seuen miles distant ouer against Cadiz, in a maner as Paules is against Southwarke, on the other side of the Bay, in a part of Andaluzia, subiect to the territory of the Duke de Medina Sidonio.

Moreouer, at the same instant they did appoint that worthy knight Sir Amias Preston, and some others in some conuenient Barkes, to transport ouer to the sayd Towne safely and in good order, a hundred or moe of the better sort of ancient gentlewomen, and marchants wiues, who were suffered to put vpon themselues, some of them two, yea, some three sutes of apparell, with some conuenient quantitie of many Iewels, Chaines, and other ornaments belonging to their estate and degree. Such was the heroicall liberality, and exceeding great clemencie of those most honourable Lords Generall, thereby, as it should seeme vnto mee, beating downe that false surmised opinion, which hath bene hitherto commonly spread abroad, and setled among the Spaniards: which is, That the English doe trouble them and their countries, more for their golde, riches and pearle &c. then for any other iust occasion. Whereas by these their honourable dealings it is manifest to all the world, that it is onely in respect of a iust reuenge for the manifolde iniuries, and most dishonourable practises that haue bene from time to time attempted by them against vs and our nation, and also in the defence of the true honour of England: which they haue sought, and daylie doe seeke, by so many sinister and reprochfull deuices, so much as in them lieth, to deface.

Vpon Saturday being the 26. Sir Iohn Winkfield knight was buried, in honourable and warlike manner, so farre foorth us the circumstances of that time and place could permit. At whose funerals the Nauie discharged a great part of their Ordinance, in such order, as was thought meete and conuenient by the Lords Generals commandement.

The twenty seuenth day being Sunday, in the Abbey the diuine seruice was had, and a learned Sermon was made there by one Master Hopkins, the right honourable Earle of Essex his Preacher, a man of good learning and sweete vtterance, and euen there the same day, something before the sermon was made, these worthie Gentlemen following were knighted by the Lords General. And here I am to signifie by the way that two of these were knighted three or foure dayes before, and some three or foure moe were knighted after that time, vpon certaine occasions: but yet I holde it beste (and I trust without offence) to recite their names in this place altogether.

The names of such noble men and gentlemen, as were knighted at Cadiz in Iune 1596 by the two most honourable Lordes Generall.

June 21. Sir Samuel Bagnol. Sir Alexander Clifford.
22. Sir Arthur Sauage. Sir Maurice Barkley.
27. The Earle of Sussex. Sir Charles Blunt
      The Lord Harbert. Sir George Gifford.
      The Lord Burk. Sir Robert Crosse.
      Count Ludowick. Sir Iames Escudamor.
      Sir William Howard. Sir Vrias Leigh.

Sir George D'Eureux. Sir Iohn Leigh, alias Lee.
Sir Henry Neuel. Sir Richard Weston.
Sir Edmund Rich. Sir Richard Wainman.
Sir Richard Leuen. Sir Iames Wootton.
Sir Peter Egomort. Sir Richard Ruddal.
Sir Anthonie Ashley. Sir Robert Mansfield.
Sir Henry Leonard. Sir William Mounson.
Sir Richard Leuison. Sir Iohn Bowles.
Sir Horatio Vere. Sir Edward Bowes.
Sir Arthur Throchmorton. Sir Humfrey Druel.
Sir Miles Corbet Sir Amias Preston.
Sir Edward Conway. Sir Robert Remington.
Sir Oliuer Lambert Sir Iohn Buck.
Sir Anthony Cooke. Sir Iohn Morgan.
Sir Iohn Townesend. Sir Iohn Aldridg.
Sir Christopher Heydon. Sir Iohn Asshindon.
Sir Francis Popham. Sir Matthew Browne.
Sir Philip Woodhouse. Sir Iohn Acton.
Sir Thomas Gates. Sir Iohn Gylbert.
Sir Gilly Mericke. Sir William Haruie.
Sir Thomas Smith. Sir Iohn Gray.
Sir William Pooley. Don Christ. prince of Portingall.
Sir Thomas Palmer. Sir Iohn Vanderfoord,
Sir Iohn Stafford. Admirall of the Hollanders.
Sir Robert Louel. Sir Robert Duley. 8. August.

[In the preceding List, the last name should undoubtedly be Sir Robert Dudey.]

I am not curious in placing these gentlemen, but put them downe at a venture. Only I haue obserued, as neere as I could, the iust day and time when they were created. And I trust where the place of it selfe is so worthy and equall, there the bare naming and placing of the parties, shal brede no offence, or make a disparity. The two gentlemen that were last knighted receiued their knighthood in the way of our returne from Cadiz: the one of them vpon the sea, not farre from the Bay of the Groyne, at what time our ships stood vpon their staies for a space while certaine Pinnasses were sent to descrie what shipping was at the Groine: The other at Plimmouth in the open streete, when the Lords Generall came from the Sermon. The one a man of long seruice, and good desert among the Dutch: the other of so many good parts of a worthy gentleman, as the like are seldome seene to concurre in any.

I spake in the beginning of her Majesties praier, which I presumed (though vnworthy) to translate into Latine: and nowe at this very time there was some opportunity offered, for to make some vse of that translation. For nowe being in Cadiz, attending vpon my most honourable good Lord, I talked with certaine of the Religious men, such as I found learned, whereof indeed there were some, though not very many. I talked also with the Bishop of Cusco there, a graue aged comely man, and being of late chosen to that Bishopricke, he was as then to have gone to the Indies had not we then taken him prisoner, and so stayed his iourney for that time. With these men euer as occasion did serue, I did seeke nowe and then to spende some speech, and to entertaine time withall, I would breake with them of this our victorie, and of the iniuries and bad dealings of their Prince and Countrey offered to her Maiestie, whereby shee was prouoked, and in a manner drawn to this action: though otherwise of her own most excellent princely good nature, she was altogether giuen to peace, and quietnes. And alwayes in some part of our conferences, I would shew them a copie of her Maiesties praier in Latine, which I had alwayes of purpose ready about me; whereby it might the better appeare vnto them, how vnwillingly, and vpon how great and vrgent occasions her Maiesty was, as it were enforced to vndertake this action: and therewithall I did vse now and then to bestow vpon them a copy of the same in writing. They seemed in all outward shew to allow of my speeches, and to praise her Maiesties good inclination; and earnestly to wish that there might be a firme concord and peace againe.

It pleased the Lords general to deale exceeding fauourably with this said Bishop of Cusco: for it was their good pleasure to giue him his free passage without any ransome, and therewithal to let him to vnderstand, that they came not to deale with Church-men, or vnarmed men, or with men of peace, weaklings and children, neither was it any part of their meaning to make such a voyage for gold, siluer, or any other their wealth and riches, &c. But that, their only comming was to meet with their dishonorable practises, and manifold iniuries, and to deale with men of warre and valour, for the defence of the true honour of England: and to let them to vnderstand, that whensoeuer they attempted any base-conceited and dishonorable practise to their soueraigne Queene, their Mistresse, that it should be reuenged to the vttermost, &c.

In this meane space, while the Lords general continued at Cadiz, there came to them certain poore wretched Turks, to the number of 38, that had bin a long time gally-slaues, and either at the very time of the fight by sea, or els immediately thereupon, taking the opportunity, did then make their escape, and did swim to land: yeelding themselues to the mercy of their most honorable Lordships. It pleased them with all speed to apparel them, and to furnish them with money, and all other necessaries, and to bestow on them a barke, and a Pilot, to see them freely and safely conueied into Barbary, willing them to let the countrey vnderstand what was done, and what they had seene. Whereby I doubt not, but as her Maiesty is a most admirable

Prince already, ouer all Europe, all Africk, and Asia, and throughout Christendome: so the whole worlde hereafter shall haue iust cause to admire her infinitely Princely vertues, and thereby bee prouoked to confesse, that as she hath bin mightily protected from time to time, by the powerful hand of the almighty, so vndoubtedly, that she is to be iudged and accounted of vs, to be his most sacred handmaide, and chosen vessel. And therefore, whatsoever wicked designement shalbe conspired and plotted against her Maiesty hereafter, shalbe thought to be conspired, plotted, and intended against the almighty himselfe: and for that cause, as I trust, shalbe by the infinite goodnes and mercy of that almighty, mightily frustrate and ouerthrowen.

The 28. day being Munday, the L. Admirall came aboord the Arke againe, minding there to remaine for a space, as indeed he did, and vpon the aduise of his Physition, to deale something in Physicke, for that his L. found his body something out of frame. At that time it pleased his L. to write certain letters to the Duke of Medina Sidonia, for the deliuerance of English captiues, who were remaining in the gallies. For by this time, it was reported, that the said Duke was come downe in person with some power, and that he was either at Port S. Mary, or els at Rotta, or thereabout. His L. did endite the letters himselfe, but his pleasure was, they should be turned into Latine by another: and so to be sent (as indeed they were) in the latine tongue vnto the Duke.

A copie of the Lord Admirals letters to the Duke of Medina Sidonia.

Illustrissimo Principi Duci de Medina Sidonia.

Illustrissime Princeps, ex nonnullis quibusdam Hispanis intelligimus, Excellentiam vestram iam nunc esse apud portam S. Mariæ. Et quoniam in anno Domini 1588. id nobis tunc muneris assignatum erat à sereniss. nostra Regina domina mea, vt contra vos, vestrásque copias, Ego solus pro eo tempore Generalis essem constitutus: Idcircò non opinamur vobis ignotum esse, quàm mite quoddam, et humanum bellandi genus, tum hîc iam in hoc ipso tempore, aduersus huius loci populum atque incolas vsurpauerimus: tum etiam sæpius antehac quàm humaniter, benignèque eos omnes tractauerimus, quos ex vestris iure belli captiuos acceperimus. Ex quorum numero quàm multa milia etiam gratis, nullo accepto pretio, libertate donauerimus, id putamus omnibus esse testatius, quàm vt à quoquam denegetur. Quocirca, neque vllo modo nobis in mentem venire potest, vt dubitemus, quin parem etiam in vobis humanitatem aduersus nostros captiuos simus reperturi. Cum igitur nobis compertum iam sit, habere vos in vestris galeris, ex Reginæ nostræ serenissimæ Dominæ meæ subditis vnum et quinquaginta captiuos: non equidem dubitamus, quin eos omnes sitis relaxaturi, et ad nos missuri: ea lege, ac conditione, vt totidem ex vestris hîc captíuis eiusdem loci atque ordinis, melioris etiam fortassis notæ, ac conditionis, homuncios, ad os vicissim remittamus. Id quod nos facturos data fide spondemus, quàm primùm nostros captiuos ex vestris manibus acceperimus. Hac in re si nostro desiderio ac voluntati parùm satisfactum erit, aliud profectò tunc posthac belli genus ingrediemur, aliúmque bellandi morem cogemur, etiam inuiti, et contra voluntatem prosequi. Ex Regia Anglicana classe apud Cadiz vltimo Iunij, stilo antiquo. 1596.

Carolus Howard.

These letters were sent by a Spaniard, and an answere was brought from the Duke with al conuenient speed, and as it should seeme by the L. Admirals next answere returned to him in writing, which immediately hereafter foloweth, the Duke de Medina Sidonia his letters were honorable, and with good regard.

A Copie of my L. Admirals second letter to the Duke of Medina Sidonia.

Illustrissimo Principi Duci de Medina Sidonia.

Illustrissime Princeps, literas ab excellentia vestra hodiè accepimus: quæ verò nostra sit ad illas responsio, nobiles isti viri, qui vestras literas ad nos pertulerunt: pleniùs declarabunt. Hoc interim cupimus esse penitùs persuasum Excellentiæ vestræ; nos sedulò operam daturos, vt in omni honorificæ benignitatis humanitatisque genere, expectationi vestræ omni ex parte respondeamus. Quod ad Anglicos nostros captiuos attinet, quos ab Excellentia vestra huc ad nos crastino die missum iri expectamus, in ea re pollicemur Excellentiæ vestræ, quòd plenius à nobis vestræ voluntati satisfactum erit: et quòd pro illis captiuis tales nos captiuos vobis remittemus, quales tum ab ipso Dom. Mendoza, tum ab alijs illustrib. viris, qui à Dom. Porta Carero in illorum ad nos fauorem mittebantur, communi cum consensu erant ab ipsis approbati. Si verò quis alius iam captiuus est vel posthac futurus erit in nostra potestate, pro cuius redemptione nondum plenè conuentum est et stipulatum de certo pretio persoluendo: concedimus Excellentiæ vestræ, vt in hoc etiam casu vos, vestro pro arbitrio, de illis quicquid velitis, imperetis. Ex Regia classe Anglicana, apud Cadiz, 3. die Iulij stylo antique. 1596.

Carolus Howard.

The next day after, being the 4. of Iuly, the L. L. generall caused the towne of Cadiz to be set on fire, and rased and defaced so much as they could, the faire cathedral Church, and the religious houses only being spared, and left vnblemished. And with the town al such prouision for shipping, and other things, as were seruiceable for the K. vse, and yet were not either so conuenient for vs to be caried away, or els such as we stood no whit at all in need of, were likewise at the same instant consumed with fire. And presently therupon, their Lordships, with as conuenient, speed as they could, and the whole army in such good order and leisure, as they thought best, came aboord.

The next day being the 5. of Iuly, the L. L. generall with all the armie being vnder saile and now making for England, and but as yet passing the very mouth of the Bay of Cadiz, a galley full of English prisoners, with a flag of truce, met vs from Rotta, sent by the D. of Medina Sidonia, and sent as it should seeme, one day later then his promise: but yet their flag being either not big enough, or not wel placed in the galley, or not wel discerned of our men, or by what other mischance I know not: but thus it was: by one of our smallest ships that sailed formost, assoone as the said galley came within gunshot, there was a great peece discharged vpon her, and at that instant there was one man slaine outright, and 2. other grieuously hurt. The error being espied and perceiued, our ship gaue ouer immediatly from any farther shooting. Assoone as the galley came neere vs, my L. Admirall caused a gracious salutation to be sounded with his trumpets, and willed the captains forthwith to come aboord his ship: which they did, and then he feasted them with a very fine and honorable banket, as the time and place might serue. And then by them vnderstanding of that unfortunate mischance that had hapned by the shot of the said ship, he was very sory for the same, and yet such was the merciful prouidence of almighty God, that euen in this mischance also, he did hold his holy hand ouer the English. And al the harme that was done did light onely vpon the poore Turk, and the Spaniard himselfe. When this Lorde had well banqueted them, hee presently called for his barge, and did accompany the said galley to the Lorde general the Earle of Essex, who then did ride with his ship a good distance off: and there they being in like maner most honorably receiued, and intertained, the Spanish gentlemen deliuered vp their prisoners the English captiues, of whom some had bin there 6 yere, some 8, or ten: yea, and some 22. yeere, and vpward, and some of them but lately taken in S. Francis Drakes last voiage to the Indies. The number of the prisoners deliuered were but 39, and no mo, and were brought in, and deliuered by Don Antonio de Corolla and his brother, and, by Don Pedro de Cordua, and certaine others. If you demaund why, of one and fiftie Captiues, there were no moe deliuered then was, I presuppose, (and I thinke it true to) that at that time the residue were farther off in some remote places of Spaine bestowed, and so by that meanes, not able at this time to bee in a readinesse, but yet like enough that there is some good order taken for them hereafter, to be redeemed, and sent ouer into England.

If any man presume here so farre, as to enquire how it chanced, that the Lords generall rested so long at Cadiz, and went no farther, and why Port S. Mary being so faire a towne, and so neere to them, was forborne? and why

Sheres aliàs Xeres? And why Rotta and the like? And why this or that was done? And why that or this left vndone? I will not answere him with our common English prouerbe, as I might, which is: That one foole may aske moe questions in one houre, then ten discrete men can wel answere in fiue dayes.

But that graue auncient writer, Cornelius Tacitus, hath a wise, briefe, pithy saying, and it is this: "Nemo tentauit inquirere in columnas Herculis, sanctiúsque ac reuerentius habitum est de factis Deorum credere, quàm scire." Which saying, in my fancy, fitteth marueilous well for this purpose: and so much the rather, for that this Cadiz is that very place, (at least by the common opinion) where those said pillers of Hercules were thought to be placed: and, as some say, remaine as yet not farre off to be seene. But to let that passe, the saying beareth this discrete meaning in it, albeit in a pretty kind of mystical maner vttered: That it befitteth not inferiour persons to be curious, or too inquisitiue after Princes actions, neither yet to be so sawcy and so malapert, as to seeke to diue into their secrets, but rather alwayes to haue a right reuerend conceite and opinion of them, and their doings: and thereon so resting our inward thoughts, to seek to go no further, but so to remaine ready alwaies to arme our selues with dutiful minds, and willing obedience, to perform and put in execution that which in their deepe insight and heroicall designements, they shall for our good, and the care of the common wealth determine vpon.

This, and much lesse to, might suffice to satisfie any honest minded man. But yet if any will needs desire to be a little farther satisfied, albeit it neede not, yet then, this much I dare say and affirme, that vpon my knowledge, the chiefest cause why Port Saint Mary, and the rest were left vntouched, was this: For that it was most certainly knowen, that they were townes not woorth the saluting of such a royal companie, in which there was no maner of wealth in the world left, more then bare houses of stone, and standing walles, and might well haue serued rather as a stale, perchance, to haue entrapped, then as a meanes to haue enriched. And it had bin more then a suspicion of follie, for such an army as this, to haue sought to fight with the aire, and to haue laboured with great paine and charges, yea, and with some euident danger too, to haue ouerthrowen that, which could very litle or nothing haue profited, being destroyed: and yet nowe, can doe as little harme being left, as it is, vntouched.

And thus much for our iourney to Cadiz: for the accidents that happened by the way, for the winning, spoiling, and burning of the saide towne, for the ouerthrowe of the Spanish Fleet there, and for al other by-matters that happened, as appendances to the same, both in the time of our abode there, as also at the very last houre of our comming from thence.

As for our returne home, and our entrance into a part of Portingal by the way, with the taking, spoyling, and burning of the towne of Faraon there, and marching into the Spanish confines therabouts, &c. I minde to leaue it to some other, whose chance was to be present at the action, as myselfe was not, and shalbe of more sufficient ability to performe it.

* * * * *

The Most Honourable Tragedie of Sir Richard Grinuile, Knight. 1595.
   [Footnote: At London, printed by I. Roberts, for Richard Smith, 1595.
   (Written by Gervase Markham—KTH).]

That time of yeare when the inamored Sunne
Clad in the richest roabes of liuing fiers,
Courted the Virgin signe, great Nature Nunne,
Which barrains earth of al what earth desires
Euen in the month that from *Augustus* wonne,
His sacred name which vnto heauen aspires,
   And on the last of his ten trebled days,
   When wearie labour new refresh assayes.

Then when the earth out-brau'd the beautious Morne,
Boasting his cornie Mantle stird with aire,
Which like a golden Ocean did adorne,
His cold drie carcasse, featurelesse, vnfaire,
Holding the naked shearers scithe in scorne,
Or ought that might his borrowed pride empaire,
   The soule of vertue seeing earth so ritch,
   With his deare presence gilds the sea as mitch.

The sea, which then was heauie, sad, and still,
Dull, vnapplyed to sportiue wantonnesse,
As if her first-borne *Venus* had beene ill,
Or *Neptune* seene the *Sonne* his loue possesse,
Or greater cares, that greatest comforts kill,
Had crowned with griefe, the worlds wet wildernesse,
   Such was the still-foot *Thetis* silent paine,
   Whose flowing teares, ebbing fell backe againe.

Thetis, the mother of the pleasant springs,
Grandam of all the Riuers in the world,
To whom earths veins their moistning tribut brings,
Now with a mad disturbed passion hurld,
About her caue (the worlds great treasure) flings:
And with wreath'd armes, and long wet hairs uncurld,

Within her selfe laments a losse vnlost,
  And mones her wrongs, before her ioyes be crost

Thus whilst churning sorrowe ceaz'd her hart,
Grinuile (ô melt my spyrit in that name,)
As sings the Swan her funerall depart,
And waues her wings the ensignes of her fame,
So he, with vertue sweetning bitter smart,
Which from the seas long toyling seruice came:
  For why, sixe Moones, and so oft times the Sunne
  Was past, and had one halfe the signes ore-runne,

Ere he the earth, our common Mother saw;
Now earlie greets black *Flores* banefull Ile,
(*Flores*, from whence afflictions selfe doth draw
The true memorialls of a weeping stile;)
And with *Caisters* Querristers[1] which straw
Descant, that might Death of his darts beguile,
  He tunes saluting notes, sweeter then long,
  All which are made his last liues funerall song.

Skillesse in deaths great Parliament he cals
His fellow mat's, and minions to his fame,
Shewes them long lookt for land, and how it brauls,
Repulsing backe the billowes as they came,
Much he triumphes, and passed griefe for-stals
With present ioy (sorrow lights pleasures flame:)
  And whilst his hopes of *Happy-Fortune* sings,
  Misfortune by, controls them with her wings.

Desir'd reliefe, and euer welcome rest,
The elements that forme the wearie man,
Began to hold a counsaile in his brest,
Painting his wants by sicknes pale and wan;
With other griefes, that others force opprest,
Aduising stay, (as what is but they can,)
  Whilst he that fate to come, and past, nere feard,
  Concludes to stay till strength decayd repaird.

Then casts he Anchor hulling on the maine,
And all his shyps poore Citizens recounts,
And hundred iust were free from sicknes paine,
Fourscore and ten death their redress accounts;
So that of all both sicke and sound vnslaine,
Vnto two hundred wanting ten amounts.

A slender armie for so great a guide,
  But vertue is vnknowne till it be tride.

Those whom their harts enabled to attempt,
He puts a shoare to make supplie for neede;
Those whom long sicknes taught of death contempt,
He visits, and from *Ioues* great Booke doth reede
The balme which mortall poysen doth exempt;
Those whom new breathing health like sucklings feed,
  Hie to the sands, and sporting on the same,
  Finde libertie, the liues best liuing flame.

Looke how a troope of Winter-prisoned Dames,
Pent in th' inclosure of the walled townes,
Welcoms the Spring, Vsher to Somer flames,
Making their Pastimes in the flowrie downes,
Whose beauteous Arras[2] wrought in natures frames,
Through eyes admire, the hart with wonder crownes,
  So the wood-walled citizens at sea,
  Welcome both Spring and Sommer in a day.

The warring byllowes, seas artillerie,
With long held siege, had bruz'd their beaten keele,
Which to repaire the most, most busied be,
Lab'ring to cure, what want in labours feele;
All pleas'd with toyle, clothing extremitie
In Hopes best robes, that hang on Fortunes wheele
  But men are men, in ignorance of Fate,
  To alter chaunce, exceedeth humaine state.

For when the Sun, towred in heauens head,
Downe from the siluer mountaine of the skye,
Bent his bright Chariot on the glassie bed,
Faire christall, guilded with his glorious eye,
Fearing some usurpation in his stead,
Or least his Loue should too-long daliance spy
  Tweene him and *Virgo*, whose attractiue face,
  Had newly made him leaue the *Lyons* chase.

In that same myd-daies hower came sayling in,
A thought-swift-flying Pynnase, taught by winde,
T' outstrip in flight Times euer flying wing;
And being come where vertue was inshrinde,
First vaild his plumes, and wheeling in a ring,
With Goat-like dauncing, stays where *Grinuile* shynd,

The whyle his great Commaunder calls the name,
Which is ador'd of all that speakes the same.

The great Commaunder of this little Barke,
Which like an Eglet armes the Eagles side,
Was *Midleton*, the ayme of Honors marke,
That more had prou'd then danger durst haue tride,
Now seeing all good fortunes sun-shine darke,
Thrise calls Sir *Richard*, who as oft replyde,
  Bidding him speake, and ring his newes aloude,
  Ill, not apald, nor good could make him proude.

O then (quoth Midleton) thou soule of all
What euer boasts in magnanimitie,
Thou, whom pure Vertue her best part doth call,
Better then valure, stronger then dietie,
Whom men adore, and all the gods exhall
Into the bookes of endlesse memorie,
  I bring thee tidings of a deadly fray,
  Begun in Heauen, to end vpon the Sea.

The glorious Senate of the Skyes was set,
And all the gods were royaliz'd in state,
When *Happy-fortune* and *Ill-fortune* met,
Striuing who first should enter Heauen's gate,
The one made mad the others fame to let,
Neither but stirr'd with rage to wonder at,
  Confusedly, as water floods doe passe
  Their common bounds, such their rude entrance was.

The gods disturb'd, admire their strange aproch,
Censuring their angers by their gloing eyes,
Ill-fortune was attended by *Reproch*,
Good-fortune, *Fame*, and *Vertue* stellesies;[3]
One sweares the other doth her right incroch,
Which is the elder house, none can deuise:
  The gods diuide, yct in the end agree
  The Fates shall iudge each others pedigree.

Good-Fortune, drawes from heauen her hye descent, Making hie *Ioue* the
roote of her large tree; She showes from him how many god-heads went,
Archangells, *Angells*, heauen's posteritie: From thence, she shows the glorious
thrid she lent, To *Monarks*, *Emperours*, and *Kyngs* in fee, Annexing as
Colatteralls to her line, *Honour*, *Vertue*, *Valure*, and *Endles-time*.

Naithlesse, *Ill-fortune* will be elder borne,
She saith, she springs from *Saturne, Ioues* wronged Sier,
And heauen, and earth, and hell her coate haue borne,
Fresh bleeding harts, within a field of fier;
All that the world admires, she makes her scorne,
Who farthest seemes, is to *Ill-fortune* nier,
  And that iust proofe may her great praise commend,
  All that *Best-chaunce* begins, *Ill-chaunce* doth ende.

Thus they, dispute, guilding their tongues report
With instances, and argumental sawes,
Ill-fortune, bids let all the worlde resort,
And show within their Chronicles and lawes,
The man whose liue-line neuer did consort,
With sharpe affliction, deaths first grounded cause,
  Then will she yeeld, else, is shee victor still.
  Worlds good is rare, perpetuall is their ill.

Euen as the racket takes the balls rebound;
So doth *Good-fortune* catch *Ill-fortunes* proofe,
Saying, she wil her in herselfe confound,
Making her darts, Agents for her behoofe;
Bow but thine eies (quoth she) whence ha'ts abound,
And I will show thee vnder heauens roofe
  Th' vnconquered man whom no mischance importunes.
  Crown of my kingdom, deaths man to misfortune.

At this, the casments of the skye broke ope,
Discouering all what's girdled in her frame,
Whilst *Happy-fortune* through her eyes large scope
Like a Cosmographer comments on the same;
Three parts with praise she past and future hope,
Then to the fourth, the Westerne world she came,
  And there, with her eyes festrawe paints a storie,
  Stranger than strange, more glorified than glorie.

See (sayd *Faire-fortune*, to her soule shapt *Foe*)
How on the scourge that beates against the Ile
Of *Flores*, whence they curst oblations growe,
A winde-taught capring ship which ayre beguiles,
(Making poore *Cephalus* for-lorne with woe,
Curse arte, which made arte framed saile such smiles)
  Richlie imbrodred with the Iems of warre,
  In thy dispight commaunds a lucky starrye.

In that faire vessel liues my garlands flower.
Grinuile, my harts immortall arterie;
Of him thy deitie had neuer power,
Nor hath hee had of griefe one simpathie;
Successe attends him, all good hap doth shower
A golden raine of perpetuitie
  Into his bossome, whete mine Empire stands,
  Murdring the Agents of thy blacke commands.

Say, and say true, (for what but thou wilt say,)
That euer *Grinuils* fortunes came before thee,
Of euer prostrate at thine Altars lay,
Or with one wreath of Cipresse did adore thee?
Proue one blacke storme in all his Sommers day,
Whose threatening clouds compeld him to implore thee.
  Then wil I staine my milkwhite vaile with weeping,
  And as thine handmaide dye in sorrowes keeping.

As wounds the lightning, yet preserues the skinne,
So did these words split *Lucklesse-fortunes* hart,
Her smiling *Superficies*, lockt within
A deepe exulcerated festring smart;
Heere shee perceiu'd her first disgrace begin,
And wordlesse from the heauens takes her depart.
  Yet as she flewe her wings in flying cri'd
  On *Grinuile* shall my fame and power be tride.

At her departure all the heauens were glad.
Triumphing in *Ill-fortunes* banishment,
Apollo set new *Anthems* as *Ioue* bad,
Which spheare tunes made more then most excellent;
No light in heauen but with new fier was clad,
Making next *Ioue, Good-fortune* president,
  Enrowling in the Bookes of destenie,
  This memorable famous victorie.

Only the *Fat's* su'd for her backe repeale,
(For they *Ill-fortune* lou'd exceeding well)
Many her deedes and Tropheis they reueale,
And all her liues blacke legend, weeping tell;
Yet all they speake, cannot in heauen preuaile,
Which seene, in spight they follow her to hell,
  And there inhoused with their mother *Night*,
  All foure deuise, how heauen and earth to spight.

Hence sprang the loues of *Ioue*, the *Sonnes* exile,
The shame of *Mars* and *Venus* in a net;
Iunos forsaken bed; Saturns compile
Of frantike discontentment, which beset
All heauen with armes; *Diana* hence had while
To court her sleeping boy; whilst *Thetis* let
  Phoebus imbrace her in her *Neptunes* stead,
  Who made complaints, breach of his bridall bed:

Yet not content with these disparagments,
Much greater mischiefes issues from their minds,
Grinuile, thy mountaine honour it augments
Within their breasts, a Meteor like the winds,
Which thrall'd in earth, a reeling issue rents
With violent motion; and their wills combinds
  To belch their hat's, vow'd murdrers of thy fame,
  Which to effect, thus they begin the same.

Fast to *Iberia* flies vntoward chaunce,
Iberia, which we vulgar Christen *Spaine*,
Vpon whose Sunne-burnt continent doth daunce
Westerne *Ducallidon*, the greatest maine,
Thither shee packs, *Error* doth their aduance
Her coale-blacke standerd in the hands of paine;
  And as escapt from rauishment or bale,
  With false teares, thus shee tunes a falser tale.

Great Empire (said shee) blessed in thy birth,
Beautious created for-head of this round,
That with thy smiles first lent to heauen mirth,
And bout thy temples all perfections woond,
Lodgd in th' immagin'd corners of the earth;
Thou whom our centers Monarchesse art crownd,
  Attend my suite, baptisd in mournefull teares,
  Who but ere while triumphed on the spheares.

Nor for my selfe more then thine owne decay
Which blindfold pleasure clouds as they arise,
Be gracious, and retort the domefull daye
Which thee and me to shame would sacrifice.
Loe, on the great west-walling boisterous sea,
Which doth imbrace thy gold-enclosing eyes,
  Of many sailes one man, of one poor Ile,
  That will my fame, and all thy faire defile.

His numberlesse great infinits of fame,
Haue shut against me heauens great christall dore,
The clouds, which once my feets dust had to name,
Hang ore my forhead, threatning euermore
Death to my praise; life to my infant shame,
Whilst I with sighes mediate a new restore.
  And in my selfe behold my pleasures past,
  Swimming amongst the ioyes I cannot tast.

Th' ambrosian Nectar-filled banqueting,
No more shall I communicate, or see,
Triumphes in heauen, *Ioues* masks, and reuelling,
Are cleene exempt, both from my ioyes and me.
The reason, for my loue to thee I bring,
Trimming the locks with Iems of dietie,
  Making the gods a dread a fatall day,
  Worse then the Giants warre or Centaurs fray.

Poore goddesse, rob'd of all eternall power,
Whose broken Statues, and down razed Fan's,
Neuer warm'd altars, euer forgotten hower
Where any memorie of praise is tane,
Witnes my fall from great *Olympus* tower;
Prostrate, implore blame for receiued bane,
  And dyre reuenge gainst heauens impietie,
  Which els in shame will make thee follow mee.

Behold these robes, maps of my fortunes world,
Torne, and distaind with eye-scornd beggerie;
These rags deuide the Zones, wherein is hurld
My liues distemprate, hote cold miserie;
These teares are points, the scale these hairs vncurld,
My hands the compasse, woe the emperie:
  And these my plaints, true and auriculer,
  Are to my Globe the perpendiculer.

Looke how I am, such art thou like to be
If armes preuent not heauens intendiment,
Grinuile, which now surfeits with dignitie,
Burd'ning the Sea with my disparagement;
Chiding the wanton winds if greedelie
They kisse his sailes; or els too slowlie vent,
  Like *Ioue*, which bad the day be and it was,
  So bids he Conquest warre; she brings to passe.

The sole incouragement he giues his power,
Is Prophet-like presaging of thy death,
Courage he cries, euen in the dying hower,
And with his words, recalls departing breath;
O (sayes he to his Mat's) you are my glories tower,
Impregnable, wall'd with vnuanquisht faith,
  You are the hands and agents of my trust,
  I but the hart reuoluing what we must.

Liue Saints, til we haue ript the wombe of *Spayne*,
And wounded *Error* in the armes of hell,
Crushing the triple Myter in disdaine,
Which on the seauenfold mounted Witch doth dwel,
Angells rewards for such dissignes remaine,
And on heauens face men shall your stories tell;
  At this they shoute; as eager of the pray,
  As Ants in winter of a sunne-shine day.

Thus like triumphant *Cæsar* drawne in Rome,
By winged *Valure*, and vnconquered *Chaunce*,
He plowes the Sea (ô were it made his tombe)
Whilst *Happy-fortune* pypes unto his daunce.
Yet may thy power alternat heauens doome,
So pleaseth thee thy forward will t'aduance,
  And cheare the sinews of thy mighty arme,
  Whose out-strecht force shall quell his proud alarme.

Then giue newe fuell to his honours fier,
Least slight regard wealth-winning *Error* slay,
And so old *Saturns* happie world retyer,
Making *Trueths* dungion brighter than the day;
Was neuer woe could wound thy kingdom nyer,
Or of thy borrowed beautie make display,
  Because this vow in heauens booke doth remaine,
  That *Errors* death shall consumate thy raigne.

Now, for my god-heads remnant liues in thee,
Whose lost successe breeds mine eternall end,
Take for thine ayde, afflicting *Miserie*,
Woe, mine attendant, and *Dispayre* my freend,
All three my greatest great *Triumuerie*,
Blood bath'd *Carnifici*, which will protend
  A murdring desolation to that will,
  Which me in thee, and thee in mee would kill.

Here, with her fixed Comet-blazing eyes,
The damned *Augurs* of vntimely death,
Shee ends her tale, whilst from her harts caue flyes
A storme of winds, no gentle sighing breath,
All which, like euill spirits in disguise,
Enter *Iberias* eares, and to her sayth,
  That all the substance of this damned storie,
  Was zealous true, coyned for her *Spanish* glorie.

Sworne to beleeue, for ill, in ill assies,
Spayne then enamour'd with the *Romane* trull,
Calls all her forces, more then Atomies,
And tells *Ill-fortunes* storie to the full;
Many Parenthises shee doth deuise,
And frost-relenting words doth choycely cull,
  Bewitching those whom oft shee had deceiued,
  With such like Hemlock as her selfe receiued.

The first and greatest one, commaunding all,
The soule of mischiefes old created mother,
Was *Don Alphonso Bassan*, proud in brall,
The Marques *Sancta Cruces* onely brother;
Him shee coniures by typ's emperiall,
And all that falshoods seeming trueth could couer,
  To vndertake this hie (she termed it) act,
  Which craues a curse of all that reads the fact.

Her selfe (shee said) and all the flowers of *Spayne*,
Should vnder his, as heauens Ensigne warre:
Thus from her harts foule dunghill flyes amaine
Grosse vapours, metamorphosd to a starre;
Her words in fumes like prodogies retaine
His hart, by her tongues witchcraft bound so farre,
  And what shee will, that will hee vnder-take,
  Be it to warre with heauen for her sake.

The seeming Nectar of her poysoning speech,
So well shee saw surprise his licoras sence,
That for to reare her ill beyonds ills reach,
With selfe-like tropes, decks self-like eloquence,
Making in *Britain Dona* such a breach,
That her arm'd wits, conqu'ring his best wits sence,
  He vowes with *Bassan* to defende the broile,
  Which men of praise, and earth of fame shal spoile.

To him shee giues the *Biscaynnoys* for guard,
Mechanicall Artificers for death,
And those which of affliction neuer hard,
She tempers with the hammer of her breath:
To euery act shee giues huge lyp-reward,
Lauish of oathes, as falshood of her faith;
  And for the ground of her pretended right,
  T'is hate, which enuies vertue in a Knight.

These two to her fast bound in vassailage,
Vnto the Marques *Arumburch* shee flyes,
Him shee prouokes, him shee finds apt to rage,
Imprisoning Pitties teares in flintie eyes;
To him the power of *Siuill* for a gage
Shee doth bequeath; bidding his prowesse ryse,
  And clense his Countries face from widowes tears,
  To which he posts, like lightning from the sphears.

Lastly, to make vp mischiefes perfect square,
To *Luis Cutino* shee takes her flight,
Him shee commaunds, he to her homage sware
To guide a Nauie to this damned fight,
Of Hulks and Fly-boats such as durst to dare.
Shee giues him soueraine rule, and publique right,
  And then vniting all foure powers in one,
  Sends them to sea, to calme *Misfortunes* mone.

And now behold (diuine for valiancie)
Like flying Castells sayle they to this strand,
Fiftie three saile, strong in artillarie;
Best men of warre knowne in the *Spanish* land;
Fifteene Armados, Kings of soueraigntie,
Which led the lesser with a mightie hand:
  And these in foure battalions hither flie,
  With whom three dayes I sailed in companie.

Then gentle *Grinuile, Thetis* parramoure,
Dearer than *Venus*, Daughter of the flood,
Set sailes to wind, let not neglect deuoure
Thy gracious fortunes and thine Angell goode,
Cut through the maine, compell thy keele to scoure,
No man his ill too timelie hath with-stoode
  And when *Best-chaunce* shal haue repaird thy fortune,
  Time for this flight may iust reuenge importune.

Here *Midelton* did end the passing peale
Which gaue the warning to a dismall end,
And as his words last knell began to faile,
This damned Nauie did a glimmering send,
By which *Sir Richard* might their power reueale,
Which seeming conquerlesse did conquests lend;
  At whose appearance *Midelton* did cry,
  See where they come, for fame and pitty flie.

This certaine story, of too certaine ill,
Did not extinguish, but gaue honour fier,
Th'amazing prodigie, (bane of my quill,)
Bred not astonishment, but a strong desier,
By which this heauen-adopted Knights strong will,
Then hiest height of Fame, flew much more hier:
  And from the boundlesse greatnes of his minde,
  Sends back this answer through his lyps refin'd.

Thanks hardie *Midelton* for thy dilate,
Perswasiue presage to auoyde my death,
But if thou wed my fortunes with my state,
This sauing health shall suffocate my breath,
To flye from them that holds my God in hate,
My Mistres, Countrey, me, and my sworne fayth,
  Were to pull of the load from *Typhons* back,
  And crush my selfe, with shame and seruille wrack.

Nor if my hart degenerate should yeeld,
To entertaine an amorus thought of life,
And so transport mine honour to the field,
Where seeming valure dies by cowards knife,
Yet zeale and conscience shall new forces build,
And others soules, with my soule holdeth strife;
  For halfe my men, and all that draw sound breath,
  Are gone on shore, for foode to conquer death.

If I forsake them, certaine is their end,
If I obtaine them, doubtfull is our fall,
Vpon my flight, shame and their sacks depend,
Vpon my stay, hope of good hap doth call,
Equall to me, the meanest I commend;
Nor will I loose, but by the losse of all:
  They are the sinewes of my life and fame,
  Dismembred bodies perish cripple-lame.

This sayd, he sends a cock-boate to the shore,
To summon backe his men vnto their ship,
Who com'd a board, began with some vprore
To way their Anchors, and with care to dip
Their hie reuolues in doubt, and euermore,
To paint deaths visage with a trembling lip,
  Till he that was all fearelesse, and feare slew,
  With Nectard words from them all dangers drew.

When *Midelton* saw *Grinuills* hie reuolue,
Past hope, past thought, past reach of all aspire,
Once more to moue him flie he doth resolue,
And to that purpose tips his tongue with fier;
Fier of sweete words, that easelie might dissolue
And moisten flint, though steeld in stiffe attire,
  Had not desier of wonder praise, and fame,
  Extinkt the sparks, and still keepe dead the flame.

Greater, and better then inarked he,
Which in the worlds huge deluge did suruiue,
O let thy wings of magnanimitie,
Not vainlie flatter, *Honour* to acchiue,
Gainst all conceit impossibilitie,
By which thou murderst *Vertue*, keepe aliue,
  Nor in thy seeking of diuinitie,
  Kill not heauens fame by base mortalitie.

O *Grinuile* thou hast red Philosophy
Nature and Arte hath made thee excellent,
And what thou read'st, hath grafted this in thee,
That to attempt hie dangers euident
Without constraint or neede, is infamie,
And honor turnes to rashhes in th'euent:
  And who so darrs, not caring how he darrs,
  Sells vertues name, to purchase foolish starrs.

Deere Knight, thou art not forst to hazard fame,
Heauens haue lent thee meanes to scape thine ill,
If thou abide, as true as is thy name,
So truly shall thy fault, thy death fulfill:
And as to loue the life for vertues flame,
Is the iust act of a true noble will,
  So to contemne it, and her helps exclude,
  Is baseness, rashness, and no *Fortitude*.

He that compard mans bodie to an hoast,
Sayd that the hands were scouts, discouering harmes,
The feete were horsemen, thundring on the coast,
The brest, and stomacke, footmen, huge in swarmes.
But for the head, in soueraigntie did boast,
It Captayne was, director of alarms,
　Whose rashness, if it hazarded an ill,
　Not hee alone but all the hoast did spill.

Rash *Isadas*, the *Lacedemon* Lord,
That naked fought against the *Theban* power,
Although they crown'd his valure by accord,
Yet was hee find for rashness in that hower:
And those which most his carelesse praise affoard,
Did most condemne what follie did deuoure;
　For in attempting, prowesse is not ment,
　But wiselie doing what we doe attempt.

Then sith t'is valure to abandon fight,
And base to darre, where no hope is to winne,
(Renowned man, of all renowne the light)
Hoyst vp thy sailes, delay attrackts thy sinne,
Flie from ill-boding starres with all thy might,
Vnto thy hart let praise and pittie in.
　This sayd, and more desirous much to crie,
　Sir *Richard* stayd him, with this rich replie.

Captayne, I praise thy warlike eloquence,
And sober Axioms of Philosophie,
But now's no time for schoole points difference,
When Deaths blacke Ensigne threatens miserie;
Yet for thy words sound of such consequence.
Making flight praise, and fight pale obloquie,
　Once ere I die, Ile clense my wits from rust,
　And proue my flying base, my stay most iust.

Whence shall I flie? from refuge of my fame,
From whom? euen from my Countreis mortall foe,
Whither? but to the dungeon of my shame,
Why shall I flie? for feare of happie woe,
What end of flight? to saue vile life by blame,
Who ist that flies? *Grinuile*? Captayne no,
　T'is *England* flies, faire Ile of happines,
　And true diuine *Elizas* holynes.

Shall then my life regard taynt that choice faire?
First will I perrish in this liquid round,
Neuer shall Sunne-burnt *Spanyards* tongue endeare
Iberian eares with what shall me confound,
The life I haue, I for my Mistris beare,
Curst were that life, should it her scepter wound,
  And trebble cursed be that damned thought,
  Which in my minde hath any fayntnes wrought.

Now, for Philosophie defends thy theame,
Euen selfe Philosophie shall arme my stile,
Rich buskin'd *Seneca*, that did declaime,
And first in *Rome* our tragicke pompe compile,
Saith, *Fortitude* is that which in extreme
And certaine hazard all base feares exile:
  It guides, saith he, the noble minde from farre,
  Through frost, and fier, to conquer honors warre.

Honie-tongd *Tullie*, Mermaid of our eares,
Affirmes no force, can force true *Fortitude*,
It with our bodies, no communion beares,
The soule and spyrit, sole doth it include;
It is that part of honestie which reares
The hart to heauen, and euer doth obtrude
  Faint feare, and doubt, still taking his delight
  In perrills, which exceed all perrills might.

Patience, Perseuerance, Greatnes, and *Strong Trust*, These pages are to *Fortitude* their King, *Patience* that suffers, and esteemeth iust, What euer woe, for vertue fortunes bring; *Perseuerance*, holds constant what we must, *Greatnes*, that still effects the greatest thing. And armed *Trust*, which neuer can dispaire, But hopes good hap; how euer fatall deare.

The Roman *Sergius*, hauing lost his hand,
Slew with one hand foure in a single fight,
A thing all reason euer did with-stand.
But that bright *Fortitude* spred forth her light
Pompey, by storme held from *th' Italyan* land,
And all his sailors quaking in his sight,
  First hoisted saile, and cry'd amidst the strife,
  There's neede I goe, no neede to saue my life.

Agis that guilt the *Lacedemon* streete,
Intending one day battaile with his foes,
By counsaile was repeld, as thing vnmeete,
The enemie beeing ten to one in shoes;

But he reply'd, Tis needful that his feete
Which many leads, should leade to many bloes:
  And one being good, an Armie is for ten
  Foes to religion, and known naughty men.

To him that told *Dienecus*, his foes
Couer'd the Sun with darts and armed speares,
Hee made reply, Thy newes is ioy in woes,
Wee'le in the shadow fight, and conquer feares.
And from the *Polands* words my humor floes,
I care for naught but falling of the Spheares.
  Thunder affrights the Infants in the schooles,
  And threatnings are the conquerors of fooles.

As these, my case is not so desperate,
And yet, then these, my darre shall be no lesse:
If this in them, for fame was wondred at,
Then this in mee, shall my desiers expresse;
Neuer shall *Greece*, nor *Rome*, nor Heathen state,
With shining honor, *Albions* shine depresse,
  Though their great circuits yeelds their acts large bounds,
  Yet shall they neuer darr for deeper wounds.

And thus resolu'd, deere *Midelton* depart,
Seeke for thy safetie in some better soyle,
Thy stay will be no succour in my smart,
Thy losse will make them boast of better spoyle.
And be assur'd before my last breath part,
Ile make the Sunne, for pittie backe recoyle.
  And clothe the sea within a scarlet pale,
  Iudge of their death which shall my life exhale.

This ship which now intombs my iealous soule,
Honestlie enuious of aspiring laude,
Is cald *Reuenge*, the scourge which doth controule,
The recreants that *Errors* right applaud,
Shall like her selfe, by name and fame enroule
My spyrits acts, by no *Misfortune* aw'd,
  Within eternall Bookes of happie deeds,
  Vpon whose notes, immortall Vertue reeds,

Say, if I perish, t'was mine honours will,
My Countries loue, religion, and my Queene,
And if that enuie glorie in mine ill,
Say that I dyed, conqu'ring, vnconquered seene.
Say fiftie three strong shyps could not fulfill,

Gainst one poore mayden vessell their foule teene,
  But that in spight of death, or miserie,
  She fought, and foyled, and scapt captiuitie.

Replie not *Midelton*, mine eares are clos'd,
Hie in heauen's for-head are my vowes ingrau'd,
I see the banefull Nauie nowt disclosed,
Begon betime, Fate hath thy fortune sau'd;
To me good starres were neuer yet opposed,
Glorie hath crownd me when I glorie crau'd,
  Farwel, and say how euer be my chaunce,
  My death at honours wedding learnt to daunce.

This sayd, away sailes Midelton with speede,
Sad, heauie, dull, and most disconsolate,
Shedding stout manlie teares at valures deed,
Greeuing the ruine of so great estate;
But *Grinuile*, whose hope euer did exceede,
Making all death in daungers fortunate,
  Gan to prouide to quell this great vprore,
  Then which the like was neuer heard before.

His fights set vp; and all things fit prepard,
Low on the ballast did he couch his sick,
Being fourscoore ten, in Deaths pale mantle snar'd,[4]
Whose want to war did most their strong harts prick.
The hundred, whose more sounder breaths declard,
Their soules to enter Deaths gates should not stick,
  Hee with diuine words of immortall glorie,
  Makes them the wondred actors of this storie.

Nothing he left vnsaid that tongue could say,
To breede contempt of death, or hate of thrall,
Honours reward, fame for a famous day,
Wonder of eares, that men halfe gods shall call:
And contrarie, a hopelesse certaine way,
Into a Tyrants damned fists to fall,
  Where all defame, base thoughts, and infamie,
  Shall crowne with shame their heads eternally.

In this great thunder of his valiant speech,
From whence the eares-eyes honors lightning felt,
The *Spanish* Nauie came within the reach
Of Cannon shot, which equallie was delt
On eyther side, each other to impeach;
Whose volleys made the pittying skyes to melt,

Yet with their noyse, in *Grinuiles* heart did frame,
Greater desier, to conquer greater fame.

And now the sunne was past his middle way,
Leaning more louely to his Lemans bed,
And the noones third hower had attacht the day,
When fiftie three gainst one were basely led;
All harts were fierd; and now the deadlie fray,
Began tumultuouslie to ouer-spread.
  The sea with fier, the Element with smoake
  Which gods, and monsters from their sleep awoake.

In foure great battailes marcht the *Spanish* hoast,
The first of *Siuill*, led in two great squares,
Both which with courage, more then can be most,
Sir *Richard* forst to giue him way with cares;
And as the Sea-men terme it in our coast,
They sprang their luffe, and vnder lee declares,
  Their manie forces feebled by this one,
  Whose thoughts, saue him, are rightly due to none.

And now he stands amidst the thickest throngs,
Walld round with wooden Castels on the waue,
Fiftie three Tygers greedie in their wrongs,
Besiedge the princelie Lion in his caue:
Nothing sees *Grinuile* which to hope belongs,
All things are fled that any hap could saue;
  Bright day is darkned by incurtaind night,
  And nothing visits them but Canons light.

Then vp to heauen he lifts his loftie hart,
And cryes, old *Salon*, I am happy made.
All earthlie thoughts cleane from his spirits part,
Vertue and *Valure* all his sences lade,
His foes too fewe, too strong he holds his part,
Now doth he wish for millions to inuade,
  For beeing conqueror he would conquer all,
  Or conquered, with immortall honour fall.

Neuer fell hayle thicker then bullets flew,
Neuer show'rd drops faster than showring blowes,
Liu'd all the *Woorthees*, all yet neuer knew
So great resolue in so great certaine woes;
Had *Fame* told *Cæsar* what of this was true,
His Senate-murdred spirite would haue rose,

And with faire honors enuie wondred then,
Cursing mortalitie in mightie men.

Whilst thus affliction turmoyld in this brall,
And *Grinuile* still imployed his Actor death,
The great *San-philip*, which all *Spayne* did call
Th' vnuanquisht ship, *Iberias* soule and faith,
Whose mountaine hugenes more was tearmed then tall,
Being twice a thousand tuns as rumour saith,
  Came rushing in, becalming *Grinuiles* sailes,
  Whose courage grew, the more his fortunes failes.

Hotlie on eyther side was lightning sent,
And steeled thunder bolts dinge men to hell,
Vnweldie *Phillip*, backt with millions lent,
Worse cracks of thunder then on *Phaeton* fell,
That with the dayes fier fiered the Element;
And why? because within her ribs did dwell,
  More store of shot and great artillarie,
  Then might haue seru'd the worlds great victorie.

Three tire of Cannon lodg'd on eyther side,
And in each tire, eleuen stronglie lay,
Eyght in her chase, that shot forth right did bide,
And in her sterne, twice eight that howerlie play;
Shee lesse great shot, in infinets did hide,
All which were Agents for a dismall day.
  But poore *Reuenge*, lesse rich, and not so great,
  Aunswered her cuffe for cuffe, and threat for threat.

Anon they graple eyther to the other,
And doth the ban-dogge with the Martins skinne;
And then the wombe of *Phillip* did vncouer,
Eight hundred Souldiers, which the fight beginne:
These board Sir *Richard*, and with thronging smother
The daye, the ayre, the time, and neuer linne,
  But by their entrance did instruct eight more,
  To doe the like, on each side foure and foure.

Thus in one moment was our Knight assaild,
With one huge *Argosie*, and eight great ships,
But all in vaine, their powers naught preuaild,
For the *Reuenge*, her Canon loud-dogs slips,
Whose bruzing teeth, so much the *Phillip* quaild,
That foundring in the greedie maine, he dips

His damned bodie in his watrie tombe,
Wrapt with dishonour in the Oceans wombe.

The other eight, fighting, were likewise foild,
And driuen perforce vnto a vile retraite,
None durst abide, but all with shame recoild,
Whilst *Valures* selfe, set *Grinuile* in her seate;
Onely *Don Luis Saint Iohn*, seeing spoild,
His Countries honour by this strange defaite,
  Single encountred *Grinuile* in the fight,
  Who quicklie sent his soule to endlesse night.

George de Prunaria, a Spanish Knight,
Euer held valiant in dispight of fate,
Seconded *Luis*, and with mortall might,
Writ on Sir *Richards* target souldiers hate,
Till *Grinuile* wakned with his loud rung fight,
Dispatcht his soules course vnto *Plutos* gate:
  And after these two, sent in post all those
  Which came within his mercie or his blowes.

By this, the sunne had spread his golden locks,
Vpon the pale green carpet of the sea,
And opned wide the scarlet dore which locks
The easefull euening from the labouring day;
Now Night began to leape from iron Rocks,
And whip her rustie wagon through the way,
  Whilst all the *Spanish* host stoode maz'd in sight,
  None darring to assayle a second fight.

When *Don Alfonso*, Generall of the warre,
Saw all his Nauie with one ship controld,
He toare his hayre, and loudlie cryd from farre,
For honour *Spanyards*, and for shame be bold;
Awaken Vertue, say her slumbers marre
Iberias auncient valure, and infold
  Her wondred puissance, and her glorious deeds,
  In cowards habit, and ignoble weeds.

Fie, that the spyrit of a single man,
Should contradict innumerable wills,
Fie, that infinitiues of forces can,
Nor may effect what one conceit fulfills;
Woe to the wombe, ceaselesse the teats I ban,
That cherrisht life, which all our liues ioyes kills;

Woe to our selues, our fortunes, and our minds,
  Agast and scarrd, with whistling of the winds.

See how he triumphes in dispight of death,
Promethean like, laden with liuing fier,
And in his glorie spits disdainfull breath,
Loathing the baseness of our backe retire;
Euen now me thinke in our disgrace he saith,
Foes to your fames, why make you Fate a lyer,
  When heauen and she haue giuen into your hand,
  What all the world can neuer back demand?

Say that the God of *Warre*, Father of Chiualrie,
The *Worthies*, *Heroes*, all fam'd Conquerours,
Centaurs, *Gyants*, victorious *Victorie*,
Were all this *Grinuils* hart-sworne paramours.
Yet should we fightlesse let our shyps force flie:
Well might we crush his keele with rocklike powers,
  And him with them ore-whelme into the maine,
  Courage then harts, fetch honour backe againe.

Heere shame, the fretting canker of the mind,
That fiers the face with fuell from the hart,
Fearing his weapons weakenes, eft assigned
To desperate hardines his confounding dart,
And now the *Spanyards* made through words stone blind,
Desperate by shame, ashamd dispaire should part,
  Like damned scritchowles, chimes to dead mens hours,
  Make vowes to fight, till fight all liues deuours.

And now the tragicke sceane of death begins,
Acts of the night, deeds of the ouglie darke,
When Furies brands gaue light to furious sins,
And gastlie silence gaping wounds did marke;
Sing sadlie then my Muse (teares pittie wins)
Yet mount thy wings beyond the mornings Larke,
  And wanting thunder, with thy lightnings might,
  Split cares that heares the dole of this sad night.

The fier of *Spaynes* pride, quencht by *Grinuils* sword,
Alfonso rekindles with his tong,
And sets a batelesse edge, ground by his word
Vpon their blunt harts feebled by the strong,
Loe animated now, they all accord,
To die, or ende deaths conflict held so long;

And thus resolud, too greedelie assay
His death, like hounds that hold the Hart at bay.

Blacker then night, more terrible then hell,
Louder then thunder, sharper then *Phoebus* steele,
Vnder whose wounds the ouglie *Python* fell,
Were bullets mantles, clowding the haplesse keele,
The slaughtered cryes, the words the cannons tell,
And those which make euen rocky Mountaines reele,
  And thicker then in sunne are Atomies,
  Flew bullets, fier, and slaughtered dead mens cries.

At this remorsles Dirgie for the dead,
The siluer Moone, dread Soueraigne of the Deepe,
That with the floods fills vp her horned head
And by her waine the wayning ebbs doth keepe:
Taught by the Fat's how destenie was led,
Bidds all the starres pull in their beames and weepe:
  For twas vnfit, chast hallowed eyes should see
  Honour confounded by impietie.

Then to the night she giues all soueraigne power,
Th'eternall mourner for the dayes diuorce,
Who drowned in her owne harts killing shower,
Viewes others torments with a sad remorse.
This flintie Princesse, ayme cryes to the hower,
On which to looke, kinde eies no force could force.
  And yet the sight her dull hart so offended,
  That from her sight a fogge dewe descended.

Now on our Knight, raines yron, sword, and fiers,
Iron wrapt in smoke, sword bath'd in smoking blood,
Fiers, furies king, in blood and smoke aspires
The consumation of all liuing good,
Yet *Grinuile*, with like Agents like expires
His foemen's darts, and euermore withstood
  Th'assaults of death, and ruins of the warre,
  Hoping the splendour of some luckie starre.

On eyther side him, still two *Gallions* lay,
Which with continuall boardings nurst the fight,
Two great *Armados*, howrelie ploy'd their way,
And by assaulte, made knowne repellesse might.
Those which could not come neere vnto the fray,
Aloose dicharg'd their volleys gainst our Knight.

And when that one shrunk back, beat with disgrace,
An other instantly supply'd the place.

So that their resting, restlesse him containd,
And theyr supplies, deny'd him to supply:
The *Hydra* of their mightines ordaind
New spoile for death, when old did wounded lie:
But hee, *Herculian*-like one state retaind,
One to triumph, or one for all to die.
  Heauen had onelie lent him but one hart,
  That hart one thought, that thought no feare of smart.

And now the night grew neere her middle line,
Youthfully lustie in her strongest age,
When one of *Spaynes* great *Gallions* did repine,
That one should many vnto death ingage,
And therefore with her force, halfe held diuine,
At once euaporates her mortall rage,
  Till powerfull *Grinuille*, yeelding power a toombe
  Splyt her, & sunck her in the salt waves wombe.

When *Cutino*, the Hulks great Admirall,
Saw that huge Vessel drencht within the surge,
Enuie and shame tyered vpon his gall,
And for reuenge a thousand meanes doth vrge;
But *Grinuile*, perfect in destructions fall,
His mischiefes with like miseries doth scourge,
  And renting with a shot his wooden tower,
  Made *Neptunes* liquid armes his all deuouer.

These two ore-whelm'd, *Siuills Ascension* came,
A famous ship, well man'd and strongly drest,
Vindicta from her Cannons mouthes doth flame,
And more then any, our dread Knight oppresst:
Much hurt shee did, many shee wounded lame,
And *Valurs* selfe, her valiant acts confest.
  Yet in the end, (for warre of none takes keepe)
  Grinuile sunck her within the watry deepe.

An other great *Armado*, brusd and beat,
Sunck neere *S. Michaels* road, with thought to scape,
And one that by her men more choicely set,
Beeing craz'd and widow'd of her comly shape,
Ran gainst the shore, to pay *Ill-chaunce* her debt,
Who desolate for desolations gape:

Yet these confounded, were not mist at all.
For new supplies made new the aged brall.

This while on *Grinuile* ceazed no amaze.
No wonder, dread, nor base astonishment,
But true resolue, and valurs sacred blaze,
The crowne of heauen, and starrie ornament
Deck't his diuine part, and from thence did raze
Affects of earth, or earth's intendiment.
  And in this broyle, as cheerefull was his fight,
  As *Ioues*, embracing *Danae* by night.

Looke how a wanton Bridegroome in the morne,
Busilie labours to make glad the day,
And at the noone, with wings of courage borne,
Recourts his bride with dauncing and with play,
Vntil the night which holds meane bliss in scorne,
By action kills imaginations sway,
  And then, euen then, gluts and confounds his thought,
  With all the sweets, conceit or Nature wrought,

Euen so our Knight the bridegroome vnto *Fame*,
Toild in his battailes morning with vnrest,
At noone triumph'd and daunst, and made his game,
That vertue by no death could be deprest;
But when the night of his loues longings came,
Euen then his intellectuall soule confest
  All other ioyes imaginarie were
  Honour vnconquerd, heauen and earth held deare.

The bellowing shotte which wakened dead mens swounds,
As *Dorian* musick, sweetned his cares,
Ryuers of blood, issuing from fountaine wounds,
Hee pytties, but augments not with his teares,
The flaming fier which mercilesse abounds,
Hee not so much as masking torches feares,
  The dolefull Eccho of the soules halfe dying,
  Quicken his courage in their banefull crying.

When foule *Misfortune* houering on a Rock,
(The stonie girdle of the *Florean* Ile,)
Had seene this conflict, and the fearfull shock,
Which all the *Spanish* mischiefes did compile,
And saw how conquest licklie was to mock
The hope of *Spayne*, and fauster her exile,

Immortall shee, came downe herselfe to fight,
And doe what else no mortall creature might.

And as she flew the midnights waking starre,
Sad *Cassiopea* with a heauie cheare,
Pusht forth her forehead, to make known from farre,
What time the dryrie dole of earth drew neare,
But when shee saw *Misfortune* arm'd in warre,
With teares she blinds her eyes, and clouds the ayre,
  And asks the Gods, why *Fortune* fights with man?
  They say, to doe, what else no creature can.

O why should such immortall enuie dwell,
In the enclosures of eternall mould?
Let Gods with Gods, and men with men retell,
Vnequall warres t'vnequall shame is sould;
But for this damned deede came shee from hell,
And *Ioue* is sworne, to doe what dest'nie would,
  Weepe then my pen, the tell-tale of our woe,
  And curse the fount from whence our sorrows flow.

Now, now, *Misfortune* fronts our Knight in armes,
And casts her venome through the *Spanysh* hoast,
Shee salues the dead, and all the lyuing warmes
With vitall enuie, brought from *Plutos* coast;
Yet all in vaine, all works not *Grinuils* harmes;
Which seene, shee smiles, and yet with rage imbost[5]
  Saith to her selfe, since men are all too weake,
  Behold a goddesse shall thy lifes twine breake.

With that shee takes a Musket in her hand,
Raft from a dying Souldiour newlie slaine,
And ayming where th' vnconquered Knight did stand,
Dischargd it through his bodie, and in twaine
Deuids the euer holie nuptiall band,
Which twixt his soule, and worlds part shold remaine,
  Had not his hart, stronger then *Fortunes* will,
  Held life perforce to scorne *Misfortunes* ill.

The bubling wound from whence his blood distild,
Mourn'd to let fall the hallowed drops to ground,
And like a iealous loue by riuall illd,
Sucks in the sacred moisture through the wound;
But he, which felt deaths fatall doome fulfilld,
Grew fiercer valiant, and did all confound,

Was not a *Spanyard* durst abord him rest,
  After he felt his deaths wound in his brest.

Hundreds on hundreds, dead on the maymed fall,
Maymed on sounde, sound in them selues lye slaine,
Blest was the first that to his ship could crall,
For wounded, he wounds multituds againe;
No sacrifice, but sacrifice of all,
Could stay his swords oblations vnto paine,
  Nor in *Phillipie*, fell for *Cæsars* death,
  Soules thicker then for *Grinuils* wasting breath.

The *Nemian* Lyon, *Aramanthian* Bore,
The *Hircanian* Tyger, nor the *Cholcean* Bulls,
Neuer extended rage with such vprore,
Nor in their brests mad monstrous furie lulls;
Now might they learne, that euer learnt before,
Wrath at our Knight, which all wrath disanulls,
  For slauish death, his hands commaunded more,
  Then Lyon, Tyger, Bull, or angrie Bore.

Had *Pompey* in *Pharsalia* held his thought, *Cæsar* had neuer wept vpon his head, Had *Anthonie* at *Actiome* like him fought, *Augustus* teares had neuer drowned him dead, Had braue *Renaldo*, *Grinuiles* puissance bought, *Angelica* from France had neuer fled, Nor madded *Rowland* with inconstancie, But rather slayne him wanting victorie.

Before a storme flewe neuer Doues so fast,
As *Spanyards* from the furie of his fist,
The stout *Reuenge*, about whose forlorne wast,
Whilome so many in their moods persist,
Now all alone, none but the scourge imbrast,
Her foes from handie combats cleane desist;
  Yet still incirkling her within their powers,
  From farre sent shot, as thick as winters showers.

Anger, and Enuie, enemies to *Life*,
Strong smouldering *Heate* and noisom stink of *Smoke*,
With over-labouring *Toyle*, *Deaths* ouglie wife,
These all accord with *Grinuiles* wounded stroke,
To end his liues date by their ciuell strife,
And him vnto a blessed state inyoke,
  But he repelld them whilst repell he might,
  Till feinting power, was tane from power to fight

Then downe he sat, and beat his manlie brest,
Not mourning death, but want of meanes to die;
Those which suruiu'd coragiouslie be blest,
Making them gods for god-like victorie;
Not full twice twentie soules aliue did rest,
Of which the most were mangled cruellie,
  Yet still, whilst words could speake, or signes could show,
  From death he maks eternall life to grow.

The Maister-gunner, which beheld his eyes
Dart fier gainst death triumphant in his face,
Came to sustaine him, and with courage cryes,
How fares my Knight? worlds glory, martiall grace?
Thine honour, former honours ouer-flyes,
And vnto *Heauen* and *Vertue* bids the bace;
  Cheere then thy soule, and if deaths wounding pain it,
  Abram's faire bosome lyes to entertaine it.

Maister, he sayes, euen heers the opned dore,
Through which my spirit bridgroome like must ride,
(And then he bar'd his wounded brest all gore)
To court the blessed virgine Lambe his bride,
Whose innocence the worlds afflictions bore,
Streaming diuine blood from his sliced side,
  And to that heauen my soule with courage flyes,
  Because vnconquered, conquering it dyes.

But yet, replyed the Maister once againe,
Great vertue of our vertues, strive with fate,
Yeeld not a minute vnto death, retaine
Life like thy glory, made to wonder at.
This wounds recouerie well may entertaine
A double triumph to thy conquering state,
  And make thee liue immortall Angell blest,
  Pleaseth thee suffer it be searcht and drest.

Descend then gentle *Grinvile* downe below,
Into my Cabin for a breathing space,
In thee there let thy Surgion stanch our woe,
Giuing recuer to thee, our wounded case,
Our breaths, from thy breaths fountaine gently flow,
If it be dried, our currents loose their grace:
  Then both for vs, and thee, and for the best,
  Descend, to haue thy wound bound vp and drest.

Maister, reply'd the Knight, since last the sunne
Lookt from the hiest period of the sky,
Giuing a signall of the dayes mid noone,
Vnto this hower of midnight, valiantly,
From off this vpper deck I haue not runne,
But fought, and freed, and welcomd victorie,
  Then now to giue new couert to mine head,
  Were to reuiue our foes halfe conquered.

Thus with contrarie arguments they warre,
Diuers in their opinions and their speech,
One seeking means, th' other a will to darre;
Yet both one end, and one desire reach:
Both to keepe honour liuing, plyant are,
Hee by his fame, and he by skilfull leach,
  At length, the Maister winnes, and hath procurd
  The Knight discend, to have his woundings curd.

Downe when he was, and had display'd the port
Through which his life was martching vp to heauen,
Albe the mortall taint all cuers retort,
Yet was his Surgion not of hope bereuen,
But giues him valiant speech of lifes resort,
Saues, longer dayes his longer fame shall euen,
  And for the meanes of his recouerie,
  He finds both arte and possibilitie.

Misfortune hearing this presage of life,
(For what but chimes within immortall eares)
Within her selfe kindles a home-bred strife,
And for those words the Surgions doomes day swears.
With that, her charg'd peece (*Atropos* keene knife,)
Againe she takes, and leueld with dispairs,
  Sent a shrill bullet through the Surgions head,
  Which thence, through *Grinuils* temples like was led.

Downe fell the Surgion, hope and helpe was reft,
His death gaue manumition to his soule,
Misfortune smyld, and euen then shee left
The mournfull Ocean, mourner for this dole;
Away shee flyes, for all was now bereft,
Both hopes and helpe, for life to win deaths gole;
  Yet *Grinuile* vnamaz'd with constant faith,
  Laughing dispisd the second stroke of death.

What foole (saith he) ads to the Sea a drop,
Lends *Etna* sparks, or angry stormes his wind?
Who burnes the root when lightning fiers the top?
Who vnto hell, can worse then hell combind?
Pale hungry Death, thy greedy longings stop,
Hope of long life is banefull to my mind:
  Yet hate not life, but loath captiuitie,
  Where rests no trust to purchase victorie.

Then vp he came with feeble pace againe,
Strength from his blood, blood from his wounds descending,
Saies, here I liu'd, and here wil I sustaine,
The worst of Deaths worst, by my fame defending,
And then he fell to warre with might and maine,
Valure on death most valiantly depending,
  And thus continued aye coragiously,
  Vntil the day chast shadowes from the sky.

But when the mornings dewie locks drunk vp
A mistie moysture from the Oceans face,
Then might he see the source of sorrowes cup,
Plainly prefigured in that hatefull place;
And all the miseries that mortals sup
From their great Grandsire *Adams* band, disgrace;
  For all that did incircle him, was his foe,
  And that incircled, modell of true woe.

His masts were broken, and his tackle torne,
His vpper worke hew'd downe into the Sea,
Naught of his ship aboue the sourge was borne,
But euen leueld with the Ocean lay,
Onely the ships foundation (yet that worne)
Remaind a trophey in that mighty fray;
  Nothing at all aboue the head remained,
  Either for couert, or that force maintained.

Powder for shot, was spent and wasted cleane,
Scarce seene a corne to charge a peece withall,
All her pykes broken, halfe of his best men slaine,
The rest sore wounded, on Deaths Agents call,
On th'other side, her foe in ranks remains,
Displaying multitudes, and store of all
  What euer might auaile for victorie,
  Had they not wanted harts true valiancie.

When *Grinuile* saw his desperate drierie case,
Meerely dispoyled of all success-full thought,
Hee calls before him all within the place,
The Maister, Maister-gunner, and them taught
Rules of true hardiment to purchase grace;
Showes them the end their trauailes toile had bought,
  How sweet it is, swift *Fame* to ouer-goe,
  How vile to diue in captiue ouerthrow.

Gallants (he saith) since three a clock last noone,
Vntill this morning, fifteene howers by course,
We haue maintaind stoute warre, and still vndoone
Our foes assaults, and driue them to the worse,
Fifteene *Armados* boardings haue not wonne
Content or ease, but beene repeld by force,
  Eight hundred Cannon shot against her side,
  Haue not our harts in coward colours died.

Not fifteene thousand men araungd in fight,
And fifteene howers lent them to atchiue,
With fifty three great ships of boundlesse might,
Haue had or meanes or prowesse to contriue
The fall of one, which mayden vertue dight,
Kept in despight of *Spanish* force aliue.
  Then list to mee you imps of memorie,
  Borne to assume to immortalitie.

Sith loosing, we vnlost keepe strong our praise,
And make our glories, gaynours by our ends,
Let not the hope of howers (for tedious dayes
Vnto our lines no longer circuite lends)
Confound our wondred actions and assayes,
Whereon the sweete of mortal eares depends,
  But as we liue by wills victorious,
  So let vs die victours of them and vs.

Wee that haue mercilesse cut Mercies wings,
And muffeld pittie in deaths mistie vale,
Let vs implore no mercie; pittyings,
But from our God, deere fauour to exhale
Our soules to heauen, where all the Angells rings
Renowne of vs, and our deepe tragick tale;
  Let us that cannot liue, yet liue to dye,
  Vnthrald by men, fit tropheys for the skye.

And thus resolu'd since other meane is reft,
Sweet Maister-gunner, split our keele in twaine,
We cannot liue, whom hope of life hath left,
Dying, our deaths more glorious liues retain,
Let not our ship, of shame and foile bereft,
Vnto our foe-men for a prize remaine;
  Sinke her, and sinking with the *Greeke* wee'le cry,
  Best not to be, or beeing soone to dye.

Scarce had his words tane wings from his deere tong,
But the stout Maister-gunner, euer rich
In heauenlie valure and repulsing wrong,
Proud that his hands by action might inritch
His name and nation with a worthie song,
Tow'rd his hart higher then Eagles pitch,
  And instantlie indeuours to effect
  Grinuils desier, by ending Deaths defect.

But th' other Maister, and the other Mat's,
Disented from the honour of their minds,
And humbly praid the Knight to rue their stat's,
Whom miserie to no such mischiefe binds;
To him th' aleadge great reasons, and dilat's
Their foes amazements, whom their valures blinds,
  And maks more eager t'entertaine a truce,
  Then they to offer words for warres excuse.

They show him diuers gallant men of might,
Whose wounds not mortall, hope gaue of recuer,
For their saks sue they to diuorce this night
Of desperate chaunce, calld vnto Deaths black lure,
Their lengthened liues, their countries care might right,
And to their Prince they might good hopes assure.
  Then quod the Captaine, (deare Knight) do not spill,
  The liues whom gods and Fat's seeke not to kill.

And where thou sayst the *Spanyards* shall not braue
T' haue tane one ship due to our virgin Queene,
O knowe, that they, nor all the world can saue,
This wounded Barke, whose like no age hath seene,
Sixe foote shee leaks in hold, three shot beneath the waue,
All whose repaire so insufficient beene,
  That when the Sea shall angrie worke begin,
  She cannot chuse but sinke and dye therein.

Besides, the wounds and brusings which she beares,
Are such, so manie, so incurable,
As to remoue her from this place of feares.
No force, no wit, no meane, nor man is able;
Then since that peace prostrate to vs repaires,
Vnlesse our selues, our selues make miserable,
  Herculeen Knight, for pittie, pittie lend,
  No fame consists in wilfull desperat end.

These words with emphasis and action spent,
Mou'd not Sir *Richard*, but inrag'd him more,
To bow or yeeld, his heart would neare relent,
He still impugns all thought of lifes restore;
The Maister-gunner euer doth consent
To act his wish, swearing, in beds of gore
  Death is most louelie, sweete and amiable,
  But captiu'd life for foulenes admirable.

The Captayne, seeing words could take no place,
Turnes backe from them vnto the liuing few,
Expounds what pittie is, what victors grace;
Bids them them selues, them selues in kindnes rew,
Peace if they please, will kindlie them imbrace,
And they may liue, from whom warres glory grew;
  But if they will to desperate end consent,
  Their guilty soules too late shall mourne repent.

The sillie men, who sought but liuing ioyes,
Cryes to the Captaine for an honord truce,
Life they desire, yet no life that destroyes
Their wonne renownes, but such as might excuse
Their woes, their wounds, and al what els anoyes
Beautie of laude, for other they refuse;
  All which the Captaine swears they shal obtaine,
  Because their foes, in doubtfull states remaine.

O when Sir *Richard* saw them start aside,
More chaynd to life then to a glorius graue,
And those whom hee so oft in dangers tryde,
Now trembling seeke their hatefull liues to saue.
Sorrow and rage, shame, and his honors pride,
Choking his soule, madly compeld him raue,
  Vntil his rage with vigor did confound
  His heauie hart; and left him in a swound.

The Maister-gunner, likewise seeing Fate
Bridle his fortune, and his will to die,
With his sharpe sword sought to set ope the gate,
By which his soule might from his bodie flie,
Had not his freends perforce preseru'd his state,
And lockt him in his Cabbin safe to lie,
  Whilst others swarm'd where haplesse *Grinuile* lay,
  By cryes recalling life, late runne away.

In this too restlesse turmoile of vnrest,
The poore *Reuenges* Maister stole awaye,
And to the *Spanish* Admirall adrest
The dolefull tidings of this mournfull day,
(The *Spanish* Admirall who then oprest,
Houering with doubt, not daring t'end the fray,)
  And pleads for truce, with souldier-like submission
  Anexing to his words a straight condition.

Alfonso, willing to giue end to armes,
For well he knew *Grinuile* would neuer yeild,
Able his power stoode like vnnumbred swarmes,
Yet daring not on stricter tearmes to build,
He offers all what may alay their harmes
Safetie of liues, nor any thrall to weild,
  Free from the Gallie, prisonment, or paine,
  And safe returne vnto their soyle againe

To this he yeelds, as well for his own sake,
Whom desperate hazard might indamage sore,
As for desier the famous Knight to take,
Whom in his hart he seemed to deplore,
And for his valure halfe a God did make,
Extolling him all other men before,
  Admiring with an honourable hart,
  His valure, wisdome, and his Souldiours Art.

With peacefull newes the Maister backe returns,
And rings it in the liuing remnants eares,
They all reioyce, but *Grinuile* deadly mourns,
He frets, he sighs, he sorrowes and despaires,
Hee cryes, this truce, their fame and blisse adiourns,
He rents his locks, and all his garments teares,
  He vowes his hands shall rent the ship in twaine
  Rather then he will *Spanish* yoke sustaine.

The few reseru'd, that life esteem'd too well,
Knowing his words were warrants for his deede,
Vnkindly left him in that monstrous hell,
And fled vnto *Alfonso* with greate speede,
To him their Chieftaines mightines they tell,
And how much valure on his soule doth feede,
  That if preuention, not his actions dim,
  Twill be too late to saue the shyp or him.

Bassan made proude, vnconquering t'ouer-come,
Swore the brave Knight nor ship he would not lose,
Should all the world in a petition come:
And therefore of his gallants, fortie chose
To board Sir *Richard*, charging them be dombe
From threatning words, from anger, and from bloes,
  But with all kindnes, honor, and admire
  To bring him thence, to further *Fames* desire.

Sooner they boarded not the crazed Barke,
But they beheld where speechlesse *Grinuile* lay,
All smeard in blood, and clouded in the darke,
Contagious curtaine of Deaths tragick day;
They wept for pittie, and yet silent marke
Whether his lungs sent liuing breath away,
  Which when they sawe in ayrie blasts to flie,
  They striu'd who first should stanch his misery.

Anon came life, and lift his eye-lids vp,
Whilst they with teares denounce their Generals wil,
Whose honord mind sought to retort the cup
Of deaths sad poyson, well instruckt to kill;
Tells him what fame and grace his eyes might sup
From *Bassans* kindnes, and his Surgions skill,
  Both how he lou'd him, and admir'd his fame,
  To which he sought to lend a liuing flame.

Aye mee (quoth *Grinuile*) simple men, I know
My bodie to your Generall is a pray,
Take it, and as you please my lyms bestow,
For I respect it not, tis earth and clay:
But for my minde that mightier much doth grow,
To heauen it shall, despight of *Spanish* sway.
  He swounded, and did neuer speake againe.
  This said, orecome with anguish and with paine,

They took him vp, and to theyr Generall brought
His mangled carkasse, but vnmaimed minde,
Three dayes hee breath'd, yet neuer spake he ought,
Albe his foes were humble, sad, and kinde;
The fourth came downe the Lambe that all souls bot,
And his pure part, from worser parts refind,
  Bearing his spirite vp to the loftie skyes,
  Leauing his body, wonder to wonders eyes.

When *Bassan* saw the Angell-spirite fled,
Which lent a mortall frame immortall thought,
With pittie, griefe, and admiration led,
He mournfully complaind what Fat's had wrought.
Woe me (he cryes) but now aliue, now dead,
But now inuincible, now captiue brought:
In this, vniust are Fat's, and Death declared,
That mighty ones, no more than meane are spared.
You powers of heauen, rayne honour on his hearse,
And tune the Cherubins to sing his fame,
Let Infants in the last age him rehearse,
And let no more, honour be Honor's name:
Let him that will obtaine immortall vearse,
Conquer the stile of *Grinuile* to the same,
For till that fire shall all the world consume,
Shall neuer name, with *Grinuile* name presume.
Rest then deere soule, in thine all-resting peace,
And take my teares for tropheys to thy tombe,
Let thy lost blood, thy vnlost fame increase,
Make kingly eares thy praises second wombe:
That when all tongues to all reports surcease,
Yet shall thy deeds, out-liue the day of doome,
  For even Angels, in the heasens shall sing,
  Grinuile vnconquered died, still conquering.
                    O ælinam.

Footnotes:

1: Choristers.

2: Hangings, so called from having first been made at Arras.

3: Constellations.

4: Entangled.

5: Blown by being hunted.
    "But being then *imbost*, the stately deer

When he hath gotten ground," &c.
—*Drayton's Polyolbian*, xiii, p. 917.

* * * * *

A true report of a worthy fight, performed in the voyage from Turkie, by fiue ships of London, against 11. Gallies, and two frigats of the King of Spaines, at Pantalarea within the Streights. Anno, 1586. Written by Philip Iones.

The Marchants of London, being of the incorporation of the Turkey trade, hauing receiued intelligencies, and aduertisements, from time to time, that the King of Spaine grudging at the prosperitie of this kingdome, had not onely of late arrested al English ships, bodies, and goods in Spaine, but also maligning the quiet trafique which they vsed to and in the dominions, and prouinces, vnder the obedience of the Great Turke, had giuen order to the Captaines of his gallies in the Leuant, to hinder the passage of all English ships, and to endeuour by their best meanes, to intercept, take, and spoile them, their persons, and goods: they hereupon thought it their best course to set out their flete for Turkie, in such strength and abilitie for their defence, that the purpose of their Spanish enemie might the better be preuented, and the voyage accomplished with greater securitie to the men and shippes. For which cause, fiue tall, and stoute shippes, appertaining to London, and intending onely a Marchants voyage, were prouided and furnished with all things belonging to the Seas; the names whereof were these:

1. The Marchant Royal, a very braue and good shippe, and of great report.

2. The Tobie.

3. The Edward Bonauenture.

4. The William and Iohn.

5. The Susan.

These fiue departing from the coast of England, in the moneth of Nouember 1585. kept together as one fleete, til they came as high as the Isle of Sicilie, within the Leuant. And there, according to the order and direction of the voyage, each shippe began to take leaue of the rest, and to separate himselfe, setting his course for the particular port, whereunto hee was bounde: one for Tripolie in Syria, another for Constantinople, the chiefe Citie of the Turkes Empire, situated vpon the coast of Romania, called of olde, Thracia, and the rest to those places, whereunto they were priuatly appointed. But before they diuided themselues, they altogether consulted, of and about a certaine and speciall place for their meeting againe after the lading of their goods at their seuerall portes. And in conclusion, the generall agreement was to meet at Zante, an Island neere to the maine continent of the West part of Morea, well knowen of all the Pilots, and thought to be the fittest place of their Rendeuous. Concerning which meeting, it was also couenanted on eche side, and promised, that whatsoeuer ship of these 5. should first arriue at Zante, should there stay and expect the comming of the rest of the fleete, for the space of twentie dayes. This being done, ech man made his best hast according as winde and wether woulde serue him to fiulfill his course, and to dispatch his businesse: and no neede was there to admonish or incourage any man, seeing no time was ill spent, nor opportunitie omitted on any side, in the performance of ech mans duetie, according to his place.

It fell out that the Tobie which was bound for Constantinople had made such good speede, and gotten such good weather, that she first of al the rest came back to the appointed place of Zante, and not forgetting the former conclusion, did there cast ancre, attending the arriuall of the rest of the fleete, which accordingly (their busines first performed) failed not to keepe their promise. The first next after the Tobie was the Royal Marchant, which together with the William and Iohn came from Tripolie in Syria, and arriued at Zante within the compasse of the foresaide time limitted. These ships in token of the ioy on all parts concerned for their happy meeting, spared not the discharging af their Ordinance, the sounding of drums and trumpets, the spreading of Ensignes with other warlike and ioyfull behauiours, expressing by these outward signes, the inward gladnesse of their mindes, being all as ready to ioyne together in mutuall consent to resist the cruel enemie, as now in sporting maner they made myrth and pastyme among themselues. These three had not bene long in the hauen, but the Edward Bonauenture also, together with the Susan her consort, were come from Venice with their lading, the sight of whom increased the ioy of the rest, and they no lesse glad of the presence of the others, saluted them in most friendly and kinde sort, according to the maner of the Seas: and whereas some of these ships stoode at that instant in some want of victuals, they were all content to stay in the port, till the necessities of ech shippe were supplied, and nothing wanted to set out for their returne.

In this port of Zante, the newes was fresh and currant, of two seuerall armies and fleetes prouided by the king of Spaine, and lying in waite to intercept them: the one consisting of 30. strong Gallies, so well appointed in all respects for the warre, that no necessary thing wanted: and this fleete houered about the Streights of Gibraltar. The other armie had in it 20. Gailies, whereof some were of Sicilie, and some of the island of Malta, vnder the charge and gouernment of Iohn Andrea Dorea, a Captaine of name seruing the king of Spaine. These two diuers and strong fleetes waited and attended in the Seas for none, but the English shippes, and no doubt made their accompt and sure reckoning that not a shippe should escape their furie. And the opinion, also of the inhabitants of the Isle of Zante was, that in respect of the number of Gallies in both these armies, hauing receiued such straight commandement from the king, our ships and men being but few, and little in comparison of them, it was a thing in humane reason impossible, that wee should passe either without spoiling, if we resisted, or without composition at the least, and acknowledgement of duetie to the Spanish king.

But it was neither the report of the attendance of these armies, nor the opinions of the people, nor any thing else, that could daunt or dismay the courages of our men, who grounding themselues vpon the goodnesse of their cause, and the promise of God, to bee deliuered from such as without reason sought their destruction, carried resolute mindes, notwithstanding all impediments to aduenture through the Seas, and to finish their Nauigations, maugre the beards of the Spanish souldiers. But least they should seeme too carelesse, and too secure of their estate, and by laying the whole and entire burden of their safetie vpon Gods prouidence, should foolishly presume altogether of his helpe, and neglect the meanes which was put into their handes, they failed not to enter into counsell among themselues, and to deliberate aduisedly for their best defence. And in the end with generall consent, the Marchant Royall was appointed Admirall of the fleete, and the Tobie Viceadmiral, by whose orders the rest promised to be directed, and ech shippe vowed not to breake from another, whatsoeuer extremitie should fall out, but to stand to it to the death, for the honour of their Countrey, and the frustrating of the hope of the ambitious and proud enemie.

Thus in good order they left Zante and the Castle of Græcia, and committed themselues againe to the Seas, and proceeded in their course and voyage in quietnes, without sight of any enemie, till they came neere to Pantalarea, an Island so called, betwixt Sicilie, and the coast of Africke: into sight wherof they came the 13. day of Iuly 1586. And the same day in the morning about 7. of the clocke they descried 13. sailes in number, which were of the Gallies, lying in waite of purpose for them, in and about that place. As soone as the English ships had spied them, they by and by according to a common order, made themselues ready for a fight, layd out their Ordinance, scoured, charged, and primed them, displayed their ensignes, and left nothing vndone to arme themselues throughly. In the meane time, the Gallies more and more approched the ships, and in their banners there appeared the armes of the Isles of Sicilia, and Malta, being all as then in the seruice and pay of the Spaniard. Immediatly, both the Admirals of the Gallies sent from ech of them a frigate, to the Admiral of our English ships, which being come neere them, the Sicilian frigat first hailed them, and demanded of them whence they were? They answered that they were of England, the armes whereof appeared in their colours. Whereupon the saide frigat expostulated with them, and asked why they delayed to sende or come with their Captaines and pursers to Don Pedro de Leiua their Geuerall, to acknowledge their duty and obedience to him in the name of the Spanish king, Lord of those seas? Our men replied and said, that they owed no such duetie nor obedience to him, and therefore would acknowledge none, but commanded the frigat to depart with that answere, and not to stay longer a brabling, vpon her perill. With that away she went, and vp comes towards them the other frigat of Malta, and shee in like sort hailed the Admiral, and would needs know whence they were, and where they had bene. Our Englishmen in the Admirall, not disdaining an answere, tolde them that they were of England, Marchants of London, had bene at Turkie, and were now returning home: and to be requited in this case, they also demaunded of the frigat whence she and the rest of the gallies were: the messenger answered, we are of Malta, and for mine owne part my name is Cauallero. These gallies are in seruice and pay to the king of Spaine, vnder the conduct of Don Pedro de Leiua a noble man of Spaine, who hath bene commanded hither by the King with this present force and armie, of purpose to intercept you. You shall therefore (quoth he) do well to repaire to him to know his pleasure, he is a noble man of good behauiour and courtesie, and meanes you no ill. The Captaine of the English Admiral, whose name was M. Edward Wilkinson, replied and said. We purpose not at this time to make triall of Don Pedro his courtesie, whereof we are suspitious and doubtful, and not without good cause: vsing withall good words to the messenger, and willing him to come aboord him, promising securitie and good vsage, that thereby he might the better knowe the Spaniards minde: whereupon hee in deed left his frigat, and came aboord him, whom hee interteined in friendly sort, and caused a cuppe of wine to be drawne for him, which he tooke and beganne, with his cap in his hand, and with reuerend termes to drinke to the health of the Queene of England, speaking very honourably of her Maiestie, and giuing good speeches of the courteous vsage and interteinement that he himselfe had receiued in London, at the time that the duke of Alenson, brother to the late French king was last in England: and after he had well drunke, hee tooke his leaue, speaking well of the sufficiencie and goodnesse of our shippes, and especially of the Marchant Royal, which he confessed to haue seene before, riding in the Thames neere London. He was no sooner come to Don Pedro de Leiua the Spanish general, but he was sent off againe, and returned to the English Admirall, saying that the pleasure of the Generall was this, that either their Captaines, Masters and Pursers should come to him with speed, or else hee would set vpon them, and either take them or sinke them. The reply was made by M. Wilkinson aforesaid, that not a man should come to him; and for the bragge and threat of Don Pedro, it was not that Spanish brauado that should make them yeeld a iot to their hinderance, but they were as ready to make resistance, as he to offer an iniurie. Whereupon Cauallero the messenger left bragging, and began to persuade them in quiet sort and with many wordes, but all his labour was to no purpose, and as his threat did nothing terrifie them, so his perswasion did nothing mooue them to doe that which hee required. At the last he intreated to haue the Marchant of the Admirall caried by him as a messenger to the Generall, so that he might be satisfied, and assured of their mindes by one of their owne company. But M. Wilkinson would agree to no such thing, although Richard Rowit the marchant himselfe seemed willing to bee imployed in that message, and laboured by reasonable perswasions to induce M. Wilkinson to graunt it, as hoping to be an occasion by his presence and discreet answeres to satisfie the Generall, and thereby to saue the effusion of Christian blood, if it should grow to a battel. And he seemed so much the more willing to be sent, by how much deeper the othes and protestations of this Cauallero were, that he would (as hee was a true knight and a souldier) deliuer him backe againe in safetie to his company. Albeit, M. Wilkinson, which by his long experience had receiued sufficient triall of Spanish inconsistencie and periurie, wished him in no case to put his life and libertie in hazard vpon a Spaniards othe. But at last, vpon much intreatie, he yeelded to let him go to the General, thinking in deed, that good speeches and answeres of reason would haue contented him, whereas otherwise refusall to do so, might peraduenture haue prouoked the more discontentment.

M. Rowit therefore passing to the Spanish Generall, the rest of the Gallies hauing espied him, thought in deed that the English were rather determined to yeelde, then to fight, and therefore came flocking about the frigat, euery man crying out, Que nueuas, que nueuas, Haue these Englishmen yeelded? the frigate answered, Not so, they neither haue nor purpose to yeeld, onely they haue sent a man of their company to speake with our Generall: and being come to the Gallie wherein he was, he shewed himselfe to M. Rowit in his armour, his guard of souldiers attending vpon him in armour also, and began to speake very proudly in this sort: Thou Englishman, from whence is your fleete, why stand ye aloofe off, knowe ye not your duetie to the Catholique King, whose person I here represent? Where are your billes of lading, your letters, pasports, and the chiefe of your men? Thinke ye my attendance in these seas to be in vaine, or my person to no purpose? Let al these things be done out of hand as I command, vpon paine of my further displeasure and the spoyle of you all: These wordes of the Spanish Generall were not so outragiously pronounced as they were mildly answered by M. Rowit, who tolde him that they were al Merchantmen, vsing trafique in honest sort, and seeking to passe quietly, if they were not vrged further then reason. As for the king of Spaine, he thought (for his part) that there was amitie betwixt him and his Souereigne the Queene of England, so that neither he nor his officers should goe about to offer any such injurie to English Marchants, who as they were farre from giuing offence to any man, so they would be loath to take an abuse at the handes of any, or sit downe to their losse, where their abilitie was able to make defence. And as, touching his commandement aforesaide, for the acknowledging of duetie, in such particular sort, he told him, that were there was no duetie owing, there none should be performed, assuring him that the whole company and shippes in generall stood resolutely vpon the negatiue, and would not yeeld to any such vnreasonable demaund, joyned with such imperious and absolute maner of commanding. Why then, said he, if they wil neither come to yeeld, nor shew obedience to me in the name of any king, I wil either sinke them or bring them to harbor, and so tell them from me. With that the frigat came away with M. Rowit, and brought him aboord the English Admiral againe according to promise: who was no sooner entred in, but by and by defiance was sounded on both sides: the Spaniards hewed off the noses of the Gallies, that nothing might hinder the leuell of the shot, and the English on the other side courageously prepared themselues to the combat, euery man according to his roome, bent to performe his office with alacritie and diligence. In the meane time a Cannon was discharged from the Admirall of the gallies, which being the onset of the fight, was presently answered by the English Admirall with a Culuering; so the skirmish began, and grew hot and terrible, there was no powder nor shot spared: ech English ship matched it selfe in good order against two Spanish Gallies, besides the inequalitie of the frigats on the Spaniards side: and although our men performed their parts with singular valure according to their strength, insomuch that the enemie as amased therewith would oftentimes pause and stay, and consult what was best to be done, yet they ceased not in the midst of their businesse to make prayer to Almighty God the reuenger of al euils, and the giuer of victories, that it would please him to assist them in that good quarell of theirs, in defending themselues against so proud a tyrant, to teach their handes to warre, and their fingers to fight, that the glory of the victory might redound to his Name, and to the honor of true Religion which the insolent enemie sought so much to ouerthrowe. Contrarily, the foolish Spaniardes cried out according to their maner, not to God, but to our Lady (as they terme the virgin Mary) saying O Lady helpe, O blessed Lady giue vs the victory, and the honour thereof shalbe thine. Thus with blowes and prayers on both sides the fight continued furious and sharpe, and doubtfull a long time to which part the victorie would incline: til at the last the Admiral of the Gallies of Sicilie began to warpe from the fight, and to holde vp her side for feare of sinking, and after her went also two others in like case, whom al the sort of them inclosed, labouring by all their meanes to keep them aboue water, being ready by the force of English shot which they had receiued to perish in the seas: and what slaughter was done among the Spaniards themselues, the English were vncertaine, but by a probable coniecture apparant afar off, they supposed their losse was so great that they wanted men to continue the charging of their pieces: [Sidenote: A fight of fiue houres.] whereupon with shame and dishonor, after 5. houres spent in the battell, they withdrew themselues: and the English contented in respect of their deepe lading, rather to continue their voyage then to follow the chase, ceased from further blowes: with the losse onely of two men slaine amongst them all, and another hurt in his arme, whom M. Wilkinson with his good words and friendly promises did so comfort, that he nothing esteemed the smart of his wound in respect of the honour of the victory, and the shameful repulse of the enemy.

Thus with duetiful thankes to the mercy of God for his gracious assistance in that danger, the English ships proceeded in their Nauigation, and comming as high as Alger, a port towne vpon the coast of Barbary, they fell with it, of purpose to refresh themselues after their wearinesse, and to take in such supply of fresh water and victuals, as they needed: they were no sooner entred into the port, but immediatly the king thereof sent a messenger to the ships to knowe what they were, with which messenger the chiefe master of ech shippe repaired to the king, and acquainted him not onely with the state of their ships in respect of marchandize, but with the late fight which they had passed with the Spanish Gallies, reporting euery particular circumstance in word as it fell out in action: whereof the said king shewed himselfe marueilous glad, interteining them in the best sort, and promising abundant reliefe of all their wants, making generall proclamation in the city vpon paine of death, that no man of what degree or state soeuer he were, should presume either to hinder them in their affaires, or to offer them any maner of inurie in body or goods. By vertue whereof they dispatched al things in excellent good sort, with al fauor and peaceablenesse: only such prisoners and captiues of the Spaniards as were in the Citie, seeing the good vsage which they receiued, and hearing also what seruice they had performed against the foresaide Gallies, grudged exceedingly against them, and sought as much as they could to practise some mischiefe against them: and one amongst the rest seeing an Englishman alone in a certaine lane of the Citie, came vpon him suddenly, and with his knife thrust him in the side, yet made no such great wound, but that it was easily recouered. The English company hearing of it, acquainted the king with the fact, who immediatly sent both for the party that had receiued the wound and the offender also, and caused an executioner in the presence of himselfe and the English, to chastise the slaue euen to death, which was performed to the ende that no man should presume to commit the like part, or to doe any thing in contempt of his royal commandement.

The English hauing receiued this good justice at the kings hands, and al other things that they wanted, or could craue for the furnishing of their shippes; tooke their leaue of him, and of the rest of their friends, that were resident in Alger, and put out to Sea, looking to meete with the second army of the Spanish king, which waited for them about the month of the Straights of Gibraltar, which they were of necessitie to passe. But comming neere to the said Straight, it pleased God to raise at that instant a very darke and mistie fogge, so that one ship could not discerne another, if it were 40. paces off: by meanes whereof; together with the notable faire Easterne winds that then blewe most fit for their course, they passed with great speed through the Straight, and might haue passed with that good gale, had there bene 500. Gallies to withstand them, and the aire neuer so cleare for euery ship to be seene. [Sidenote: The second Spanish fleete lying in watie for the English.] But yet the Spanish Gallies had a sight of them when they, were come within 3. English miles of the towne, and made after them in all Pøssible haste, and although they saw that they were farre out of their reach, yet in a vaine fury and foolish pride, they shot off their Ordinance, and made a stirre in the Sea as if they had bene in the midst of them, which vanitie of theirs ministred to our men notable matter of pleasure and mirth, seeing men to fight with shadowes, and to take so great paines to so small purpose.

But thus it pleased God to deride, and delude all the forces of that proud Spanish king, which, he had prouided of purpose to distressethe English, who notwithstanding passed through both his Armies, in the one, little hurt; and in the other nothing touched, to the glory of his immortall Name, the honour of our Prince and Countrey, and the just commendation of ech mans seruice performed in that voyage.

END OF VOL. VII.

INDICES TO VOLS. V., VI., & VII.

INDICES.

Where the same Document is given in Latin and English, the reference is to the English Version.

N.B.—The large print indicates that the *whole* section refers to the subject mentioned.

Milton Keynes UK
Ingram Content Group UK Ltd.
UKHW030623061024
449204UK00004B/368